Big Pictures on the Small Screen

Big Pictures on the Small Screen

Made-for-TV Movies and Anthology Dramas

Alvin H. Marill

Foreword by Paul Bogart

The Praeger Television Collection
David Bianculli, Series Editor

Westport, Connecticut
London

Library of Congress Cataloging-in-Publication Data

Marill, Alvin H.
 Big pictures on the small screen: made-for-TV movies and anthology dramas/
Alvin H. Marill; foreword by Paul Bogart.
     p. cm. — (The Praeger television collection, ISSN 1549-2257)
 Includes index.
 ISBN-13: 978-0-275-99283-5 (alk. paper)
1. Television broadcasting of films—United States.
2. Made-for-TV movies—United States. I. Title.
PN1992.8.F5M335 2007
791.45'3—dc22   2007026763

British Library Cataloguing in Publication Data is available.

Library of Congress Catalog Card Number: 2007026763
ISBN-13: 978-0-275-99283-5
ISSN: 1549-2257

First published in 2007

Praeger Publishers, 88 Post Road West, Westport, CT 06881
An imprint of Greenwood Publishing Group, Inc.
www.praeger.com

Printed in the United States of America

The paper used in this book complies with the
Permanent Paper Standard issued by the National
Information Standards Organization (Z39.48–1984).

10 9 8 7 6 5 4 3 2 1

For John Frankenheimer

Contents

Foreword

In early 1950, I was a green assistant stage manager on *Your Show of Shows*, the Saturday evening live 90-minute variety program. One night, I had to cue an elderly stagehand to lower a huge bunch of bananas just as the dancers lifted Imogene Coca to reach it. When the moment came, I poked the stagehand and said, "Now." He stared at me. I jabbed his arm and hissed, "Now! *Now!*" He came to and lowered the bananas, but the dance had moved on; Coca, banana-less, was gone, and the moment was gone, the comic intent of the dance gone. I was mortified. After the show, I dreaded seeing producer Max Liebman approach. He gave me an evil look and muttered, "Terrific!" I wanted to die.

Some months later, I directed my first show on *One Man's Family*. At a postrehearsal note session, I ventured a suggestion to Bert Lytell, an actor with a distinguished theatrical career: "Mr. Lytell, don't you think . . . ?" He fixed me with that same look and boomed *NO* in a voice aimed at the second balcony. I blushed all over and took so long to recover that the cast began to shift in their seats. I wanted to die.

There were other learning moments. When I asked Paul Scofield what a certain T. S. Eliot passage meant—"the rock batrachian, the bare branch ophidian"—he thought for a second and said, "I don't know, old boy, but isn't it lovely?"

Live TV was a string of such moments, from on-the-air disasters like cameras that expired or actors who went straight up, to inspired one-time-only moments as they happened. I learned the job: how to improvise my way off the air in a catastrophe and to love the gift of those exciting moments and never to ask, Don't you think? of anybody who does not like you.

And there was a lot to be learned. After my first few shows, I asked Ethel Winant (David Susskind's majordomo) to tell me to whom we were submitting proposed cast lists before we could hire anybody. She smiled grimly and told me about clearing actors who might be blacklisted. I could not believe her. She rolled her eyes and said, "Oh, for God's sake, Paul, *you* wouldn't be here if you hadn't been cleared. Wake up!" We began a sad game: placing the names of unapproved actors on our lists again and again, hoping a slipup would happen and somebody would be granted the right to work. Sometimes it happened.

Then there were the network watchdogs. They were called Continuity Acceptance or Standards and Practices (read *censors*). Taking their cue from the movies, you could rarely say *pregnant*, much less see it. Married people slept in separate beds. All heck broke loose when Lloyd Bridges ad-libbed *Damn!* in an on-the-air moment of passion. Cleavages were routinely stuffed with flowers. Kisses were monitored for length and intensity and tongue visibility. Production companies had their say, too: the Theatre Guild's Armina Marshall complained that when George Grizzard and Geraldine Brooks kissed, it was "not natural, not the way people kiss." I think she meant that it looked really sexy.

Then there were the agency representatives, who often covered the same territory, though their primary function was to protect the interests of their clients, the sponsors. That meant that on the series *Justice*, sponsored by Herbert Tareyton cigarettes, host William Prince held a lighted Tareyton whenever he spoke to the camera, even if he did not have a chance to smoke it. Actors playing good guys were encouraged to smoke Tareytons, but bad guys were forbidden to. The reps came to the first table reading, sitting apart quietly. They voiced their fears: Was that a dirty line? Would the actresses' bosoms be modest? Were the actors' gestures or readings to be suggestive? Can you change *damn* to *darn*, or maybe *gosh*?

Sometimes they screwed up, to our great glee. After dress rehearsal one night for a *United States Steel Hour* show, the rep suddenly realized what he had somehow missed: that the play was about a poor young wife who tells her husband—in carefully worded language—that she not only is pregnant, but also wants to terminate it. The rep flew into a panic and demanded that the play be changed. "Too late," I said. He demanded that I persuade the actress/wife to change her intent. "She's not gonna do it," I said. "I know her, and she won't." He demanded that I speak to her. He did not realize that the actress in question was the indomitable Piper Laurie, a lady of talent and conviction who had probably accepted the script because she liked exactly what he did not. She had only recently been through her own Hollywood wars. I told her his demands. She studied her makeup in her dressing room mirror, worked a powder puff on her neck, and said in a low voice, "Tell him that when I'm finished with this show, he can cut it into pieces, length-wise if he likes, but I won't change a word." The rep retired to the bar across the street.

But then, there were all those stalwart actors faced with emergencies. On that same show, Donald Moffat, playing the young husband, stood in silent mourning at the foot of his just-expired mother's bed when the corpse (Florence Reed) had a massive coughing fit. Walls shook, bedsprings squeaked. Donald stood, head bowed, taking no note. Resurrection was not in the script. My admiration for his control was, and is, unbounded. (This was one of the intermediate shows, live on tape for later broadcast, so I replaced it with the dress rehearsal death scene.) On the other hand, on a *Kraft Theatre*, solid, dependable George C. Scott forgot his lines one night and, in a moment of panic, ground out his cigarette in Angela Thornton's lap.

During these disasters, control room demeanor swung from crushing embarrassment to uncontrolled hilarity. Sometimes nothing was funnier than the wardrobe person caught full on camera, arms loaded with costumes, trying to hide behind a thin fake tree, or the leading man who does not know his fly is open, or the ingenue whose dress is caught in her butt.

I am aware that these anecdotes illustrate only the madness of live television. In the midst of this madness, a phalanx of new and important writers blossomed, the Paddy Chayefskys and Sumner Locke Elliotts and Reginald Roses, who managed to write good plays and to say what they wanted, despite the restrictions under which they labored. Their work has lasted, not only in aged kinescopes, but beyond, and is probably the most significant contribution that television has made to the American arts landscape.

When tape arrived, it was a temperamental two inches wide, editable only with some difficulty. A crease, a fold, a crinkle expressed itself in an unsightly glitch on the screen. Audio and video were a few inches apart, so editing required an L-shaped cut at each end of the splice. The picture went crazy on playback. Terrified editors feared the inevitable finality of the cutting blade, sometimes making successive edits, first wide of the mark, then closer and closer until they were near enough. if not *on* the mark, and they could breathe again.

In live television, production elements like sets and wardrobe were expensive, so the heaviest lifting fell to the writers, the actors, the directors, and the production staff. I found myself working with sleep-deprived authors who staggered in waving the precious rewrites; with the best of Broadway, who could make me laugh or cry, who could sing or dance or do nothing beautifully, and were usually good to look at, too; with set designers like Ben Edwards, who wrung handsome sets (built of old flats and carpet cores) from his tight budgets; and with cameramen who made their instruments do impossible maneuvers.

Most of all, live television was a great medium for actors. In film and tape, there are great moments, but to me none are as thrilling as watching a waiting monitor as Jason Robards or Geraldine Page prepare for the action to reach them or seeing Robert Duvall or Maureen Stapleton rise to transfixing heights, all of it in close-up, in black and white or living color, and that one time only, or feeling the collective control room breath suspend as George Grizzard improvises and takes command of a scene away from an actor who has frozen into gibberish. Sometimes I felt those moments were private performances, just for me and the unseen, unheard audience. Live television was exciting and joyful and frustrating and gratifying and dangerous, and it was great while it lasted.

—Paul Bogart

Note: In a television career spanning 50 years, Paul Bogart directed more than 100 programs during the golden age of the great dramatic shows, from *Goodyear Theatre, Armstrong Circle Theatre, Omnibus, Playhouse 90, The United States Steel Hour, Kraft Television Theatre, The DuPont Show of the Week,* and *CBS Playhouse,* to series such as *The Defenders, All in the Family, Get Smart,* and *The Adams Chronicles* as well as many made-for-TV movies and feature films. He is a five-time Emmy winner as best director and the recipient of a number of Christopher Awards, two DGA Awards, and the prestigious EuroFIPA d'honneur from the French government (Cannes, 1991).

Preface

A talent for drama is not a talent for writing, but is an ability to articulate human relationships.

—*Gore Vidal*

A writer wakes up with his mouth full of pity.

—*Ernest Hemingway*

It started with rabbit ears.

NBC's David Sarnoff, often referred to as the father of American television, predicted in the late 1940s, at the dawn of commercial television, that TV would be cultural diversity in the living room. This was echoed by Sarnoff's counterpart across town, CBS's William S. Paley. These two significant visionaries predicted that television would be more than simply radio with pictures, but a careful pastiche of serious and light drama, news, comedy series (later to known familiarly as sitcoms), variety entertainments, and quiz shows. Drama was to include Shakespeare, opera (the great classics as well as newly commissioned musical works), television restagings of Broadway drama and musical evergreens, and original material by a host of writers, many of whom would be igniting major careers. (At the beginning of 1947, it has been estimated that there were about 5,000 TV sets in use. Not a big audience.)

In his biography *David Sarnoff* (Harper & Row, 1966), author/journalist Eugene Lyon wrote, "His paramount task in the postwar period, Sarnoff knew, would be the unfinished business of overcoming hostility to the introduction of full-scale telecasting. More than any other of his company's enterprises, television had become identified with his name and his personal responsibility." Several years later (September 1948), a summary in *Fortune* put it this way: "In a sense he bullwhipped his RCA organization into making good on it. So television is a personal (and cosmic) mission with this determined man."

In those early days, though, it was not just Sarnoff and Paley. There were a couple other players in the game. And a couple other networks. There might have been NBC and CBS, but there also were DuMont and ABC.

The man who was the face of the one that might have been under other circumstances was inventor Allen B. DuMont, who, in the late 1920s, had worked closely with Lee de Forest on expanding radio. He then started exploring television, but despite his electronic inventions, he had little success with it commercially—even though the fledgling network beat the eventual big boys on the air, premiering as a commercial entity in 1946. Prime-time programming became a major problem for DuMont. It could not pay for expensive shows and thus could not attract significant sponsors. DuMont was forced to settle on fare like the weekly variety show *Cavalcade of Stars*—until the star, Jackie Gleason, departed—on *Captain Video*, the *Arthur Murray Dance Party*, and *Rocky King, Detective*; on wrestling and other sporting events virtually every night; and on *Life Is Worth Living* with Bishop Fulton J. Sheen—even with Uncle Miltie in direct competition on Tuesday nights.

The 2002 cable movie *The Big Time*, a sprightly comedy-drama set in the heady early days of television (circa 1948) and involving a bunch of people—idealists all—who are determined to make a go of a fictional network when everything was live, seemed to have been inspired by the history of DuMont—which in a sense predated both NBC and CBS as a full-scale commercial TV entity.

It was on DuMont, on Christmas day 1947, at the very dawn of commercial network television, when probably the first TV staging of Dickens's *A Christmas Carol* aired, live from New York.

There were a few drama anthologies on DuMont: *Cosmopolitan Theatre* (13 filmed entries featuring New York talent in hour-long adaptations of stories from *Cosmopolitan* magazine) on Tuesday nights in 1951–1952; *Joseph Schildkraut Presents*, which the distinguished Austrian actor hosted and occasionally performed in, on Wednesdays in 1953–1954; and one or two others. But there simply was not enough of an audience to keep going, and the network shut down in 1955, leaving the Big Three to cut up the audience pie for the next 20 odd years.

ABC was in the process of becoming a major player in TV after merging with United Paramount—after Paramount Pictures, like the other major Hollywood movie studios, had to divest themselves of their theatrical distribution arms. Leonard Goldenson, while not as well known as Sarnoff and Paley, had been a top executive at Paramount for many years and was installed as the head of ABC. Its official merger with Paramount was in May 1951. After *Actors Studio*, which it soon lost to the much more powerful CBS following its first season, ABC's first significant anthology show was *Pulitzer Prize Playhouse*, debuting on October 6, 1950. Despite winning an Emmy during its first year, the show lasted just two seasons. It brought to viewers, as the show title indicated, hour-long adaptations of Pulitzer-winning plays every Friday night, by such writers as Maxwell Anderson, George S. Kaufman, Moss Hart, Robert E. Sherwood, Booth Tarkington, Thornton Wilder, and Sinclair Lewis. Among the show's adapters was Budd Schulberg, author of *What Makes Sammy Run?* (1941), who would go on to write *On the Waterfront* and *A Face in the Crowd* for the big screen not many years later.

While not a producer of drama, Leslie Midgely, for several decades the esteemed *CBS News* executive, had an insightful comment that easily can be representative of all the medium: "Television has, in the last 40 years," he wrote in his 1989 autobiography, "opened wide magic windows through which the entire citizenry, down to the youngest, the most impoverished and the least educated, can watch—and hopefully in some degree understand—what is going on."

Among the leading creative forces in TV's early years were Worthington Miner (writer/producer/executive, first at CBS, then at NBC, and one of those responsible for *Studio One*, just one of many of the pioneering entertainments), Herbert Brodkin (*ABC Album* and *Motorola Television Hour* on ABC, then *The Alcoa Hour/Goodyear Playhouse* [alternating], NBC, and the later *Studio One* and *Playhouse 90*, CBS, plus assorted weekly drama series—primarily *The Defenders* and *The Nurses*—that have become classics); Fred Coe (*Philco/Goodyear*, *Producers' Showcase*, and *Playwrights '56*, among others); George Schaefer (with a long and distinguished association with *Hallmark Hall of Fame* on NBC), and peripatetic David Susskind through his Talent Associates Ltd. Their names were stamped on quality drama.

On the occasion, in 1980, of the repeat showing in a package for public television of kinescopes of dramatic shows not seen for many years, Richard Shepard of the *New York Times* observed, "Golden ages rarely seem golden during their time, and that [TV] golden age was no exception. It was rich in dross and minimally generous in its estimation of the common denominator. But there was so much that was memorable, too, and it is the memorable segments that gild the drama series of *Philco* and *Goodyear, Kraft Theatre, Studio One,* and *Playhouse 90.* They often came a cropper, heaven knows, but they gave us the Serlings, the Chayefskys, the Reginald Roses, even Gore Vidal, and the directors and performers who helped make New York the creative capital of the young medium, even as it drew from the city's theater with a rich lode of talent and technique."

At least for the first decade, most of the drama that made up what came to be known as the golden age would be telecast live, seven nights a week (plus, in many cases, on Sunday afternoons—*Omnibus* and *Hallmark Hall of Fame* were two of the prestigious anthologies—and, for a number of years, an impressive daily, initially live drama in color on *NBC Matinee Theatre,* produced by Albert McCleery, ran for 671 shows, including occasional repeats). Movie stars past their acting prime, such as Robert Montgomery, Dick Powell, Ida Lupino, Charles Boyer, Loretta Young, Irene Dunne, Douglas Fairbanks Jr., Barbara Stanwyck, Jane Wyman, Boris Karloff, and Ronald Reagan, and later, Shirley Temple, became prominent TV names as producers, directors, or hosts of weekly TV drama anthologies. And naturally, there was Alfred Hitchcock himself: producing, occasionally directing, and hosting.

Then there were to come kinescoped, filmed, and so-called live-on-tape weekly dramatic series, Westerns, and cop shows. There were even Sunday morning religious-oriented dramas (and comedies) such as *Lamp Unto My Feet,* which ran from 1948 to 1979 (John Frankenheimer was one of the myriad directors), *Look Up and Live,* and *Insight.* These anthologies explored religious and inspirational themes in a remarkably entertaining, non-heavy-handed way.

And decades later, there were nonscripted reality programs following an era of movies made for television and miniseries as well as NBC's umbrella *Novels for Television.* Also, there was the syndicated Operation Prime Time on an ersatz network set up by Paramount Television.

Novels for Television, basically part of the ongoing genre known as movies made for television, were stellar, multipart adaptations of works by contemporary best-selling American writers: Irwin Shaw's *Rich Man, Poor Man* (and its sequel), Taylor Caldwell's *Captain and the Kings,* Anton Myrer's *Once an Eagle,* Arthur Hailey's *The Moneychangers,* Robert Ludlum's *The Rhinemann Exchange,* Arthur Hailey's *Wheels,* and Sara Davidson's *Loose Change,* among others, ran periodically on NBC between 1976 and 1978. Other important miniseries (described as those running at least three or more parts, as opposed to networks' descriptions of anything in more than one part as a miniseries) included the giants of the genre, by virtue of scope and cast. Among them were James Michener's *Centennial*, which encompassed more than 200 years of American history (fictionally) and ran on NBC periodically in two- and three-hour segments over a five-month span, covering 26½ hours (later, it was rebroadcast on HBO on consecutive nights, condensed a bit since the commercials were removed); and some years later, on ABC, both Herman Wouk's *The Winds of War* and its sequel *War and Remembrance*, spanning nearly 30 hours combined. Another Michener book, *Space*, dealing with America's space program, also was made into a miniseries.

All of this follows the evolution of anthology drama on TV, which found its niche in the early days between daily test patterns and nightly flag warnings and the national anthem.

Acknowledgments

Many thanks to the directors, writers, and actors from TV's golden age who shared their thoughts and remembrances in lengthy interviews for this book. Among them are Paul Bogart, Ernest Kinoy, Sidney Lumet, Loring Mandel, Abby Mann, Delbert Mann, Tad Mosel, Robert Mulligan, Arthur Penn, David Shaw, Eva Marie Saint, and Jac Venza.

Also, a nod to Ron Simon, curator of the Museum of Television and Radio (now the Paley Center for Media), and to George Schweitzer, President, CBS Marketing Group.

And not to forget John Adams (WNET/13), John Behrens (CBS), John Cocchi (JCArchives), Jeff DeRome (NBC), Jane Klain (MTR), Howard Mandelbaum (Photofest), and Steve Marill, Joe Messerli, and Vincent Terrace.

It could not be done without you.

Beginnings

In the mid-1930s, NBC began experimenting with television (in the next decade or two, it jokingly was referred to as radio with pictures). David Sarnoff more or less introduced it to the public at the 1939 World's Fair in New York. One of the early efforts starred Eddie Albert and partner Grace Brandt. (Albert was a Broadway performer at the time and was not well known outside New York, where he starred in three George Abbott hit shows in a row before getting into film.) Much of the experimentation, though, would be put on the back burner with America's entry into the war.

By September 1944, a full TV schedule began to take effect, at least in New York—then, as now, the broadcast capital. TV, still local for all practical purposes, aired nightly for about three hours to just a handful of viewers.

Sarnoff and DuMont then raced to see how quickly they could commercialize television. Generally, much of the day would be devoted to a test pattern on a seven-inch screen, and at night, in the case of NBC, in fall 1946, *Gillette Cavalcade of Sports* was broadcast on Mondays and Fridays, while DuMont aired a Western movie every Sunday evening from eight to nine o'clock (the rest of the evening had a blank schedule). On other nights, there were some live game shows. All of this was basically local to the New York area viewer. (CBS did not put out a schedule until fall 1948—most notably the drama anthology *Studio One* at 7:30 on Sunday nights and Ed Sullivan's *Toast of the Town* at nine o'clock.)

To be sure, there were some West Coast players in the young game: KTLA in Los Angeles, for one. That station went on the air on January 22, 1947, with Paramount star Bob Hope as host. KTLA was the first commercial station west of the Mississippi and broadcast its signal to all of the 300 television sets in Los Angeles. Ultimately, in the 1960s, Gene Autry bought the station from Paramount Pictures.

In the late 1940s and early 1950s, NBC and CBS as well as the infant ABC, created out of the old NBC Blue (radio) Network during World War II, relied, at least until the new decade, on local programming (old films, bowling shows, cooking programs, etc.) and on the soon-to-be-defunct DuMont Network. In commercial television, virtually everything originated from New York, and the actors were mainly from the New York stage or, if photogenic, from radio. The movie industry, increasingly concerned with this new competition, almost universally refused to allow its actors to appear on television (most were under contract and were not free to explore other performing gigs). Until the coaxial cable allowed the West Coast to telecast shows simultaneously with the East Coast circa 1952, New York–based shows had to be kinescoped (filmed from images on the picture tube) and sent across the country for later repeat airing.

Even after being connected by cable coast to coast, television's live programming frequently had to be staged twice to coordinate the three-hour time difference, and even in recent years, when programs were staged live for stunt telecasting, there were an initial presentation for the East Coast and a live restaging three hours later for the West Coast. Sixty years ago it began with a test pattern and a set of rabbit ears.

THE KRAFTING OF TELEVISION

Kraft Television Theatre (NBC, premiering May 4, 1947) was one of the first important live television anthology dramas. It was produced by the J. Walter Thompson advertising agency in conjunction with its client Kraft. Initially, novice TV writers adapted stage successes (greater and lesser) to a 60-minute format—with commercials for Kraft food products, described enticingly for most of the series's run by genial Ed Herlihy—over 11 seasons (plus 17 more productions as the newly titled *Kraft Mystery Theatre* in 1958). The premiere drama, an original by Elizabeth McFadden, was called *Double Door* and starred John Baragrey, soon to be one of the acting mainstays on live television. The next week, there was an adaptation of *Merton of the Movies*. Among the memorable productions through the years were *All the King's Men* in two parts, directed by Sidney Lumet; Rod Serling's boardroom backbiting *Patterns*, directed by Fielder Cook, who then took it to the big screen; and JFK's *A Profile in Courage*, with Kennedy (then a 38-year-old senator) himself introducing the program. Director George Roy Hill's seminal production of *A Night to Remember,* from Walter Lord's definitive account of the sinking of the *Titanic,* was staged live in late March 1956 (kinescoped to the West Coast) and, because of enthusiastic critical and audience response, was restaged (not rerun) five weeks later with newly built sets. The show was narrated by Claude Rains, who also headed a cast of 107 speaking actors.

Since much of TV drama was live up to the mid-1950s, very few complete episodes of *Kraft Television Theatre* and others that followed in the early years exist. They are the equivalent of the so-called lost films of the silent movie era. During its 11 ½ years, based on its own published history, *Kraft Theatre,* generally (though not quite accurately) considered television's first commercial program, had presented 650 plays chosen from 18,845 scripts, starred or featured 3,955 actors and actresses in 6,750 roles, and rehearsed 26,000 hours on 5,236 sets. Costs rose from $3,000 for the debut production in 1947 to $165,000 in 1958.

Prolific television director Paul Bogart worked on *Kraft Theatre* during the middle years. A recipient through the years of Emmys, Christopher Awards, Golden Globes, DGA Awards, and a French honor for his TV and film work, Bogart recalls the early days of the golden age. He began his career in 1946 with the Berkeley Marionettes as a puppeteer and actor and then started out at NBC, figuratively on the ground floor as floor manager on *Broadway Open House* and then as one of two stage managers for *Your Show of Shows,* arranging props and scenery and giving Sid Caesar his cue to get onto the set. After that, he moved on to become assistant director on *One Man's Family:*

Carlton E. Morse was a crusty old guy who was the man behind *One Man's,* mailing in the scripts both on radio and then TV. Bert Lytell was equally crotchety, and he'd come down on you if you dared trying to correct his performance in rehearsals or offer him constructive criticism. He came down hard on me at one point, and it was dear Eva Marie Saint, who played his daughter Claudia, who ran interference and was the set's great calmer downer.

I directed *OMF* about every fourth week. I would take a leave from my NBC staff floor manager/[assistant director] job—different network job description—to do so, but I didn't quit.

Later, I found myself working as [assistant director] in the summer of 1954 on Hume Cronyn and Jessica Tandy's NBC show *The Marriage*—Jessie and Hume were lovely people. The network was testing its new color technology on this series. Until then, color had been used on the news and some experimental ventures that generally required only a fixed camera. Somewhere along the way, NBC was having trouble with the show's director, and Hume went through several and, perhaps in desperation, turned to me. I was told, "You do it," and then I was directing. We eventually became good friends—not on a big star/lowly [assistant director] basis—and besides, I had a hopeless crush on Jessie and didn't mind being around her.

Like everyone else behind the camera, I was making it up as we went along, trying to avoid disaster. In those days, with a half-hour show, we had the luxury of rehearsing for four days, then blocking on the fifth, doing a run through with camera, taking a bit of time off for lunch, coming back for fixes, then doing dress [rehearsal], and going on live. A kinescope was provided for the West Coast three hours or three days later. Real heady days, flying, as they say, by the seat of your pants.

Troubles? Glitches? I remember doing an *Armstrong Circle Theatre* show when we lost one camera (we generally worked with three). It literally blew up on us on the air. It was gone in a sudden puff of smoke in a little mushroom cloud. Suddenly, we—the actors, the crew—had to improvise because we were live. Two cameras . . . we had to dolly past walls and hope that there weren't naughty words written on the sides or backs of them. Audiences of those days probably never knew there was a problem.

Despite this, I was still on the network payroll as an assistant director, and eventually, NBC got tired of my absences in that slot and suggested that I get off the pot. For the next 40 some years—until I retired—I worked freelance.

Bogart, for one, was a prodigious director who worked in a variety of genres both in television and feature films from the mid-1950s onward. In *The American Vein* (E. P. Dutton, 1979), by Christopher Wicking and Tise Vahimagi, a view of directors in television, Bogart is placed among the "aristocrats of American TV." They judged that "Bogart has continuously been in the vanguard of TV quality, taking over from the Schaffners, Pollacks, and Roy Hills those assignments which most resemble 'Art' on TV."

He became associated initially with David Susskind (who also had been his first agent) and then producer Herbert Brodkin—writer Reginald Rose put them together—and did multiple episodes of *The Defenders*. In sitcoms, Bogart was one of the directing mainstays on *All in the Family* (92 episodes beginning with the sixth season) and *The Golden Girls*. Later, he directed several of the early episodes of PBS's historical miniseries *The Adams Chronicles*. There also were his frequent Jason Robards collaborations: a series of periodic holiday-themed dramas on CBS—*The House without a Christmas Tree* (1972), *The Holiday Treasure* (1973), *The Easter Promise* (1975)—and even the *Hallmark Hall of Fame* adaptation of Clifford Odets's nonholiday *The Country Girl*. And Bogart's work with James Garner included the cult turn-of-the-century *Nichols* series in 1971 and both *Marlowe* (as in Philip) and *Skin Game* for the big screen.

Bogart also directed TV musicals such as *Hansel and Gretel* with Barbara Cook and Red Buttons, *Pinocchio* with Mickey Rooney and Walter Slezak (both productions were live), *Kiss Me Kate* with Robert Goulet and Carol Lawrence, and *Carousel*, again with Goulet, as well as Stephen Sondheim's early, hour-long, now classic *Evening Primrose*. Additionally, he directed Arthur Miller's adaptation of *An Enemy of the People* in 1966, Miller's *A Memory of Two Mondays* in 1977, Harvey Fierstein's *Torch Song Trilogy* in 1988, Neil Simon's *Broadway Bound* in 1992, and Wendy Wasserstein's *The Heidi Chronicles* three years later. And that was just for TV.

Broadway Television Theatre (1952–1954) was a syndicated anthology that offered film adaptations of 74 plays from the Great White Way—evergreens with an assortment of East Coast talent—among them *Three Men on a Horse, The Jazz Singer, Angel Street, Burlesque, Night Must Fall,* and *The Twentieth Century,* all with the likes of Orson Bean, Lola Montez, Virginia Gilmore, Buddy Ebsen, Edward Everett Horton, and Victor Jory in a stock company of sorts. Warren Wade was the producer of this series.

CHAPTER 2

Author, Author; Actor, Actor

One of the premier drama writers of the twentieth century, Horton Foote, became a significant name in television as far back as *Kraft Television Theatre* in January 1948. He already was a noted author and playwright by the time his *Only the Heart* became one of the early *Kraft* dramas (based on Foote's 1944 play, his first) and several years later was restaged by *Kraft* with a different cast. Set in Harrison, Texas, *Only the Heart* centered on a domineering mother in a loveless marriage and the teenage daughter she pushed into marriage with a family employee. By the 1952–1953 season, Foote's name was familiar to viewers, with nearly a dozen dramas on *Philco/Goodyear* and one on *Hallmark Hall of Fame*.

"Those were exciting years to be involved in television," Foote noted in a published interview just prior to his 90th birthday. "There was little money to be made. When I wrote the teleplay for *The Trip to Bountiful* I made less than $5,000, but actors, writers and producers had a lot of freedom.

"In those early days of television shows were produced much like the theatre," he recalled. "Many shows were live, and they were produced in a small studio. We could take chances and experiment. Lillian Gish—my Carrie Watts on TV and Broadway—told me early television was like the early days of film," when the technology to edit film came along and television moved to the West Coast.

Foote writes quiet plays about everyday small-town life, exploring his characters' emotions and relationships deftly and with a deep compassion for the minute details that shape a lifetime, with themes of belonging and longing for home. Actress Kim Stanley, who was to be the leading Foote interpreter of the time, had one of her early TV roles as Wilma Thompson in his *A Young Lady of Property* (*Philco*, 1953), a teen from the Texas gulf coast striving to make sense of her mother's death and her father's imminent remarriage, remembering that, on her deathbed, her mother had instructed that the family home be given to Wilma when she reached maturity. In the *New York Times*, TV critic Jack Gould wrote that her performance in the Foote drama "was outstanding regardless of the medium in which it is seen." Later, Stanley played another teenager forced to run off to San Antonio with her first love, rather than confirm her family's fear that she had married a no-good, in Foote's *Flight* (*Playwrights* '56); portrayed Georgette Thomas, repeating her praised Broadway performance as the deserted mother and housewife in *The Traveling Lady* (*Studio One*, 1957); and costarred in Foote's adaptation of Faulkner's *Tomorrow* (*Playhouse 90*, 1960) with Richard Boone. Stanley later was the offscreen narrator of *To Kill a Mockingbird*, for which Foote wrote the screenplay. She also toured in the road company of his *The Trip to Bountiful* opposite Lillian Gish, who starred in the well-remembered *Philco Playhouse* version in 1953 and the Broadway production that followed.

Lillian's sister Dorothy was the star of several of the *Philco/Goodyear* Foote dramas, as were veteran performer E. G. Marshall, possibly the hardest working actor during the golden age, and an up-and-coming Joanne Woodward, and Helen Hayes starred with Burgess Meredith in 1956 in a tale Horton Foote wrote for *Omnibus* called *Drugstore: Sunday Noon*.

The now nonagenarian literary treasure's trademark are his small-town Texas stories dating back to listening to his haberdasher father's compassionate accounts of his customers' lives in Wharton, about 50 miles from Houston. Foote himself still lives there. As his biographer, Charles Watson, notes, "He is not a social protester like Arthur Miller, a constant experimenter with dramatic techniques like Eugene O'Neill, or a psychological investigator like Tennessee Williams. Rather it is his sensitivity to the troubled men and women who live in Southeast Texas that gives his work unity." However, Foote's leisurely stories are deceptively simple in that his accounts of people's lives also run commentary on the changes in American culture and the need to come to terms with them.

Among Foote's other television plays are the original adaptation on *Playhouse 90* (for producer Fred Coe) of William Faulkner's *Old Man*, directed by John Frankenheimer, about a farm woman (Geraldine Page) and a convict (Sterling Hayden) trying to survive a flood on the Mississippi, and an original play about the last 30 years of Mark Twain's life, *The Shape of the River*—the penultimate *Playhouse 90* offering. After that, he wrote the very last show in the equally heralded anthology series *The DuPont Show of the Month*, titled *The Night of the Storm* and produced by David Susskind, directed by Daniel Petrie, and starring Julie Harris and E. G. Marshall. Then Foote left TV for films and authored adaptations like Brando's *The Chase* and Michael Caine and Jane Fonda's *Hurry Sundown*; originals like Robert Duvall's *Tender Mercies* and Geraldine Page's *The Trip to Bountiful*, and returned many years later with offerings on PBS (his own and Faulkner adaptations) and TV movies in the 1990s based on some of his plays.

In addition to the National Medal for the Arts, Foote won the Pulitzer Prize for his 1995 play *The Young Man from Atlanta* and two Oscars for his adaptation of Harper Lee's *To Kill a Mockingbird* and for his *Tender Mercies* original; he also won an Emmy for the mid-1990s *Hallmark Hall of Fame* version of his adaptation of Faulkner's *Old Man*. Oddly, he never won a Tony for his works on the stage.

By 1948, TV drama really began to establish itself. *Actors Studio* bowed on ABC on September 26 of that year with Hume Cronyn directing wife Jessica Tandy in Tennessee Williams's *Portrait of a Madonna* (this was the basis for his 1959 Broadway one-actor also starring Hume and Jessie). Others like Julie Harris, Cloris Leachman, John Forsythe, Eva Marie Saint, E. G. Marshall, Kim Hunter, David Wayne, and a young Grace Kelly would star over the weeks in assorted, mainly original dramas. Marlon Brando would make his TV acting debut in *I'm No Hero* (January 9, 1949). *Variety,* in an early television review, judged that "as the medico forced at gunpoint to perform an operation on a wounded yegg, Brando was competent but imparted no special edge to the role." The young actor, of course, had already done some Broadway and was hot off *A Streetcar Named Desire*, but he was virtually unknown outside of the Big Apple (and perhaps his home-town of Omaha). At the time, he had not appeared on the big screen. Brando was not seen by many as becoming the most exciting actor of his age. Not long afterward, he played a young boxer in a live drama, *Come Out Fighting*, on NBC (spring 1950). He would act on television only one other time, three decades later, winning an Emmy for his supporting role as neo-Nazi George Lincoln Rockwell in *Roots: The Next Generations*. Donald Davis was series producer on *Actors Studio* and got the works of such authors as James Thurber, Ring Lardner, Budd Schulberg, William Saroyan, John Galsworthy, Ben Hecht, and others on the small tube, many adapted by young writing talents like David Shaw and Alvin Sapinsley, in this prestige program with some of Broadway's bright lights.

When *Actors Studio* switched over to CBS during the second season, Marc Connelly, the actor/playwright, came aboard as series host: CBS house director Yul Brynner became a mainstay in the control booth. Halfway through the second season, the series morphed into *The Play's the Thing*. One of the last offerings (in 1950) was a version of Molnar's *The Swan*, with Grace Kelly as Princess Alexandra. Six years later, now a major film star, Kelly made her acting swan song in MGM's film of the Molnar play.

A week after *Actors Studio* had its premiere, the hour-long *Philco Television Playhouse*, one of early TV's crown jewels, debuted on NBC (October 3, 1948) with Edna Ferber and George S. Kaufman's stellar *Dinner at Eight*, produced and directed by Fred Coe. As either producer or director, Coe was one of the most influential creative figures in the early days of television. He was involved in virtually every drama anthology produced at NBC well into the 1950s. He had been around in commercial TV since its infancy, producing shows, even before getting to NBC, like the long-forgotten 1946 series *Laughter in Paris* and a TV version of radio's *Mr. and Mrs. North*, which developed into a series several years later. NBC programming chief Sylvester "Pat" Weaver brought Coe to the network, initially as production manager, and offered him a directing assignment: working with stage star Gertrude Lawrence in her TV acting debut on an NBC production of Shaw's *Great Catherine* in 1948. Coe then was installed as producer on *Lights Out*, the mystery/supernatural/back-from-the-dead series that NBC had brought over from radio, where it had been a staple since 1934.

He also was producer of the not-well-remembered 1949–1952 NBC murder/suspense series *The Clock*, also from radio. The show was built around a clock (sort of an antecedent of the current generation's *24*), and each story had time playing a vital role. Eva Marie Saint recalled acting in several of *The Clock*'s half-hour dramas as well as working with Fred Coe on *Lights Out* (in the second episode of that series): "Fred was one of those indispensable producing geniuses of television in its first couple of decades. I loved him. Everybody did. I also did a *Studio One* production of the Ring Lardner/George S. Kaufman play *June Moon* around the same time [1949], along with another man I positively loved, Jack Lemmon." But the man she *really* loved was young actor-turned-TV-director Jeffrey Hayden. They wed in October 1951 and are still working on the marriage 56 years later.

It was at NBC where Fred Coe created *Philco*, and then *Goodyear Theatre*, which alternated with it, producing the show and directing many of the early offerings such as Budd Schulberg's *What Makes Sammy Run?* in spring 1949 and F. Scott Fitzgerald's *The Last Tycoon* in the fall. After establishing himself in anthology drama on the network, Coe also created one of the most popular sitcoms of the day, *Mr. Peepers*. Additionally, he was to become the driving force behind *Playwrights '56* and *Producers' Showcase*, among other series. Prolific Mr. Coe brought Chayefsky's *Marty* and Horton Foote's *The Trip to Bountiful* to television as well as the famed production of *Peter Pan* with Mary Martin and, conservatively, hundreds of other notable (and less so) shows. Later, he departed NBC and became one of the guiding talents behind *Playhouse 90* at CBS, while also working in theater and film. The highlights of Coe's later career included producing and directing a number of segments of PBS's monumental *The Adams Chronicles*. Having produced *The Miracle Worker* originally in the 1950s, then both the stage and screen versions, he returned to the famed William Gibson play in a new made-for-TV version with Patty Duke (now playing Annie Sullivan, rather than Helen Keller), shortly before his death in spring 1979.

For *Philco*, his *Dinner at Eight* was followed seven nights later by Daphne du Maurier's *Rebecca* and then Dumas's *Camille*. Arguably the most important of the live drama anthologies of the still infant medium, *Philco* initially would concentrate on quality adaptations of stage hits. Later, it would introduce fresh young writing talents like JP Miller, Tad Mosel, Reginald Rose, N. Richard Nash, Sumner Locke Elliott, David Shaw, Abby Mann, and Gore Vidal, in addition to Chayefsky and Foote.

On the debut of *Philco Television Playhouse*, *Daily Variety*'s critic wrote, on November 26, 1948, "Broadway is a long way off to most of the nation's populace and only a small percentage ever see a successful stage play. . . . Now that television is on the market and set volume is moving into seven figures, Broadway is being brought into the home. Premiering the movement is *Philco*, which Coast-premiered its *Television Playhouse* Sunday night on KFI-TV. . . . That it was as big time as the original must have been the general consensus. There were a few flaws to be detected by the critical eye, but the overall picture was easily acceptable. . . . It's not Broadway, but it's the next big thing to it—and it's free. (Kinescoped from the live New York presentation by NBC for showing in other stations around the country.)"

In 1951, the weekly *Philco Playhouse* would begin alternating with *Goodyear Theatre* and then *The Alcoa Hour*. There was a small coterie of directors, with Coe (who directed as well as produced most of the entries during the first season), Gordon Duff, Delbert Mann, Vincent J. Donehue, and Arthur Penn sharing helming responsibilities on a rotating basis. Their technique was to work three weeks ahead, with one show in preparation, one in rehearsal, and one on the studio floor for telecasting on Sunday at 9:00 P.M. This series (live well into the 1950s) would span nine seasons and 447 productions, with other up-and-coming directors like Robert Mulligan, Jeffrey Hayden, Sidney Lumet, Robert Altman, Ralph Nelson, and Martin Ritt honing their craft.

About those early, live days of TV drama, Delbert Mann reminisced in the *New York Times* in December 1982 that "it's both opening night and closing night at the same time. There's no chance to repeat, to add or delete footage. But the apprehension and panic at the thought of making any mistakes being visible instantly to millions of viewers also provides the adrenaline to do something extraordinary." Mann, who had directed both the TV version of *Marty* and the film of it several years later, found himself calling the shots on rare live drama on the occasional *NBC Live Theatre* in the early 1980s: new television stagings in front of college audiences of Tad Mosel's adaptation of James Agee's *All the Way Home* with Sally Field and William Hurt and Carson McCullers's *The Member of the Wedding* with Pearl Bailey. (NBC publicized its 1980 production of *The Oldest Living Graduate* with Henry Fonda as the first live drama on television since 1962.)

In a 2006 interview with this author, Mann, often described by those who remember "Mr. *Philco Playhouse*," admitted, "In the days of the golden age—when live television was the only television—rehearsal time was more than a week to 10 days, and the sweating was indeed profuse. But it was a wonderful period of experimentation, and some very good things came out of it." Mann said that "at the time, it was just a job to get on with. The production values were terrible—the sets, the lighting, all the technical aspects wouldn't stand up by today's standards."

The person Mann credits with his success was Fred Coe, "a most remarkable man. He was the best damn teacher and television's best producer." They had met at Nashville Community College in the mid-1930s, when Mann was in his teens and Coe was a couple of years older, and formed a lifelong friendship. "He'd always be with me or behind me in the control room and throughout the show would challenge me, in the best sense of the word. 'You really like that shot?' he demanded, and I'd say, 'Goddamn right,' and he'd say, 'Good, go with it.' All the while I'm trying to run the camera live and be sure the actors were on their mark." In Mann's autobiography, *Looking Back . . . At Live Television & Other Matters*, he writes, "Without him I would have had no career. I owe it all to Fred Coe." Delbert Mann joined *Philco* in its second season with the Coe production of Fitzgerald's *The Last Tycoon*, starring John Baragrey. (Mann received the billing "Staged by.") Mann and Coe were, in effect, the Edward R. Murrow and Fred Friendly of dramatic television.

Scoffing at the idea that he specialized in social issues for his TV projects, Mann insisted that they should not be thought of in those terms, but were stories about people. "They were just awfully good drama." He liked to work with just one camera, he admitted—and Fred Coe both complained about that and then turned around and encouraged him.

Challenged to pick out one of his works as the best, the most satisfying, Mann skipped over *Marty*, *The Bachelor Party*, the others he had done with Paddy Chayefsky (Mann also did the film versions of both), and the productions he had directed in London, such as *David Copperfield*, *Kidnapped*, and *Jane Eyre*. The director zeroed in on his 1979 TV movie remake of *All Quiet on the Western Front*, with Richard Thomas and Ernest Borgnine. "Difficult as the filming was, I got everything I wanted. It's a wonderful story—back when it was first filmed and it held up all those years later." Another of which he is particularly proud is *The Day Lincoln Was Shot*, with Raymond Massey, Lillian Gish, Jack Lemmon (as John Wilkes Booth), and Charles Laughton narrating (*Ford Star Jubilee*, 1956). "I got a chance to do a bunch of difficult montages—live—and Fred slapped me on the back in appreciation, after telling me to scrap the damn things." And then there was that TV adaptation directed by Mann of Thornton Wilder's *Our Town*, musicalized with a miniscore by Sammy Cahn and James Van Heusen. Paul Newman and Eva Marie Saint were the young lovers and Frank Sinatra the stage manager, singing "Love and Marriage."

Mann jokes that he was involved with the infamous *Heidi* in 1968, "but at least I'd done my job and was gone, and it was the NBC guy who threw the switch that cut off the football game that ran overtime." (This, of course, was the notable New York Jets–Oakland Raiders contest with 50 seconds to go, and after the quick switch to the beginning of *Heidi*, the game went into overtime and the outcome changed—to the dismay of sports fans as well as network executives.) Mann worked in television, movies, and the stage (he even did a production of *Othello* with Walter Matthau as Iago) until the mid-1990s, when, for all practical purposes, he hung up his megaphone.

Veteran actress Eva Marie Saint figures that she worked with Delbert Mann most frequently during her so-called first television career, which spanned eight years—with time out for her initial movie, *On the Waterfront*, and a baby two nights after winning the Oscar as best supporting actress in her film debut. In an interview with the author, she reminisced, "With Del, I did several *Goodyears* and Paddy Chayefsky's May/December romance *Middle of the Night* with E. G. Marshall—I just loved that one—on *Philco*, and *Our Town*, the musical, and a live, black-and-white production of *Yellow Jack* with a wonderful all-star cast that included E. G. and Rod Steiger and Wally Cox and Jackie Cooper and Raymond Massey. Both of those were for *Producers' Showcase* in 1955. I was pregnant at the time of *Yellow Jack* and showing and asked Del Mann what to do. He told me, 'Well, you're playing a nurse, so we'll have you walk around with a big clipboard or a medical chart or something and no one will know.'"

Getting into television, literally on the ground floor, in 1947, mere months after graduating from Bowling Green College (where there now is a campus theater with her name on it), Eva Marie Saint costarred as young Ebenezer Scrooge's flame in one of TV's earliest versions of *A Christmas Carol*, with John Carradine as the older Scrooge. She became a sought-after young actress, appearing on *Kraft, The Clock, Lights Out*, and *Studio One* and the other live drama shows during the early years. Talking to the author in a 2006 interview about her days as a young actress, she recalled:

> On *One Man's Family*, I originally was not Claudia Barbour, but Claudia's best friend. Then, over a weekend, they decided to make me Claudia, and they didn't get a single letter. Nancy Franklin, who was Claudia originally, was short and dark haired, and I was a little taller and blonde. Nancy came back the following year in another role. Tony Randall was in it with me, and every day, we'd just hang together, and we'd be making the casting rounds together.
>
> Actually, the first thing I did after college was try out for *Mister Roberts* in New York, and I understudied Jocelyn Brando, Marlon's sister. And then I became involved in live television. I think my first job was as an applauder—applauding offstage at several variety shows of the time—sort of sweetening up the audience reaction. I got a big 10 dollars applauding offstage, and I told my mom I'm on television—but not quite. And I did some of the live commercials, so I guess *A Christmas Carol* was the very first, and by then I felt very confident.

And from there, it was dozens and dozens of credits. She costarred in *Dodsworth* on *Prudential Family Playhouse* and *The Old Maid* on *Kraft*, and particularly in Horton Foote's *The Trip to Bountiful*, Sumner Locke Elliott's *Wish on the Moon*, and Paddy Chayesky's *Middle of the Night*. "It was a very creative time, the late 1940s to early 1950s. And Fred Coe was there, the father of us all. And we almost had a repertory company going with actors, directors—my husband was one of them—and of course, Del Mann. I recall doing an *Omnibus* episode with my husband as director. But *Omnibus* was something out of the ordinary, with its potpourri of genres—something educational perhaps, a short drama, or maybe one taking up the entire 90 minutes, maybe a musical or dance segment—each in its own milieu."

What was it like working in the live atmosphere of early television?

> When we were going through it, you didn't think about 'Wow, this was great. This is a dream.' It was very much like doing theater because we had those seven to ten days of rehearsal, and then you just needed an audience. *Middle of the Night* was a particular joy, working with Del Mann and E. G. [Marshall].

I remember—it was an older man and a younger woman—Freddy March and Kim Novak did it in the movies later. I went to Macy's a couple of days after it aired back in 1954, and a young woman came up to me and asked, 'How did it [the relationship] work out?' And I said I'm only an actress. I only did the show. But people really believed in the story. These were stories about the human condition, about relationships. These were stories without violence, without crudities, without sexual overtones.

In those days, during TV's first real decade, we had writers like Paddy and Sumner Locke Elliott and Tad Mosel and David Shaw, who used the Arthur Millers and the Tennessee Williamses and the Eugene O'Neills and the Scotty Fitzgeralds as classic writing models. And you had the writer right there on the set or in the control room in case the director or the actor saw that something wasn't working and needed a hasty bit of rewriting. Today, you have a generation of writers who don't go back far enough to learn how real character writing is done. Today's decade is relying on the previous decade's people. And today, you never even meet the writers—and with reality shows, there aren't even writers.

Eva Marie Saint, curiously, did Broadway only twice: in the stage version of *The Trip to Bountiful*, playing, as she did on television some months earlier, opposite Lillian Gish. *Bountiful,* now considered a classic piece of work, lasted, strangely, only a month on the New York stage. Two decades later, Saint returned to Broadway as Mary Todd to Fred Gwynne's Abraham Lincoln in *The Lincoln Mask,* which folded after just eight performances. Otherwise, her stage work has been in regional theater, generally touring, sometimes with her husband, in vehicles like *The Rainmaker, Love Letters,* and *On Golden Pond.*

In the mid-1950s, she started doing movies and was away from TV generally for the next 20 years. She returned in a series of made-for-TV movies and dressed them up just by being in them: *The Macahans,* a frontier drama based on the movie *How the West Was Won* (she then repeated her role in the series that followed); the brave military wife in *When Hell Was in Session,* about naval commander Jeremiah Denton, who spent seven and a half years as a Vietnam prisoner of war (Hal Holbrook played the role, and they acted together again a few years later in *I'll Be Home for Christmas*); Melissa Gilbert's concerned mom in the TV version of William Inge's *Splendor in the Grass;* and with Jason Robards in *A Christmas to Remember, Breaking Home Ties,* and *My Antonia.* And after three earlier nominations, she won the Emmy as outstanding supporting actress in the 1990 TV movie *People Like Us,* from Dominick Dunne's book. She is also remembered by *Moonlighting* fans as Cybill Shepherd's mom during the 1987–1988 season. Most recently, Eva

Marie Saint played Clark Kent's adoptive mother Martha back in Smallville in the multi-million-dollar *Superman Returns* on the big screen.

Recalling the *Philco/Goodyear* days, writer Tad Mosel also harbors fond memories. In a long interview with this author in the spring of 2006, he told how Fred Coe was "the man" to all TV's creative talent at the time. "I worked with Fred and Del [Mann] and Gordon [Duff] and actors like dear Eileen Heckart, who acted in a number of my scripts—she was just wonderful—on a regular basis on *Philco* and *Goodyear*. Like my colleagues in the writing community, I had to turn in a script of about 48 minutes and keep it relatively simple. There'd be little time for costume changes and big gaps in time. One of my scripts, which took place in Greenwich Village, played out in real time. Forty-eight minutes on a Sunday night between 9 and 10—just like *Philco*. Fred Coe loved that. No wardrobe changes or other interruptions aside from the commercials." Mosel pointed out the fact that Fred Coe always wanted his people to be an active part of the creative process in the studio, right up to air time, always, for the writer, not simply dropping off the script 10 days in advance and then moving on to the next project. Mosel: "It was like a little community. We all knew each other—the producers, the directors, the talent—and we all had a say in how the production would be put together, despite having only about a bit more than a week to pull it together. It was such a wonderful, enervating time."

One of Mosel's earliest TV credits was a play called *Jinxed*, which he had written sometime before and which was staged on the *Chevrolet Tele-Theatre* in January 1949. His original material started flowing onto the small, 10-inch screen in 1953—a story called *Ernie Barger Is Fifty*—on *Goodyear Playhouse* for Coe. Gordon Duff directed it, and Ed Begley starred. He went on to say,

> Then came *Other People's Houses*, with Heckart and Rod Steiger. Rod was all over the place in this one, and Eileen was the steady hand, making certain we got on and off in time—with commercials. She and E. G. Marshall did my play *The Out-of-Towners* on *Studio One* in 1957, and we suddenly noticed in run up to air time that after blocking and condensing and fidgeting around with it, there was only 33 minutes of play instead of 48 or so, and it was Eileen who somehow managed to play it out for another 15 minutes completely in character. It was Geraldine Page who had the role when Del Mann made it into a big-screen movie called *Dear Heart* seven or so years later.
>
> And there was working with Henry Fonda [in an adaptation of Sinclair Lewis's *Arrowsmith* on *Medallion Theatre* and in an adaptation of Robert Sherwood's *The Petrified Forest* with Bogart and Bacall on *Producers' Showcase*] and Paul Newman and Kim Stanley and Patricia Neal. Doing a musical on

Goodyear with Jerry Herman—it was called *Madame Aphrodite*—was an experience that I really should have avoided. Jerry came along with nearly a dozen songs and presented them to me to incorporate into a script. You'll notice that there are no other musicals in my writing résumé. [Actually, he and André and Dory Previn worked on a musical version of Dickens's *Great Expectations* in the mid-1960s, but it remains unproduced.]

Mosel also did some short plays for *Omnibus* (adaptations of Thurber) and a handful of *Playhouse 90* scripts, just as live television was fading away. And later, with producer Fred Coe, he did the play *All the Way Home*, which he adapted from James Agee's *A Death in the Family* and which earned him the Pulitzer Prize for drama in 1961. Coe also produced the movie of it in 1963 and produced and directed the *Hallmark Hall of Fame* production of it in 1971. Mosel and Coe worked together for the last time as writer and producer/director on a couple of episodes of PBS's miniseries *The Adams Chronicles* in the late 1970s, shortly before Coe's death.

To veteran director Arthur Penn,

The golden era was very important. A lot of the guys were veterans, and we were in such a dangerous medium—that is, untried—so that when you went on the air, you were *on* the air . . . you were flying a plane, and it took nerves of steel in those control rooms. Was there a pecking order among the young directors of that time? It wasn't a pecking order, it was just . . . it was a tough business and a question of how much control room experience you possessed.

I started as a floor manager, then I became an [assistant director] on the *Colgate Comedy Hour*. There was this director who also used to do *Lights Out* and now *Colgate*, Kingman Moore, and he, during a show, became violently ill, and he had to be taken out of the control room, and I moved into the chair. There was a lot of pressure—a *lot* of pressure.

Fred Coe was there in the control room during the blocking, but for air, he was elsewhere in the building, and I'd see him at the end of the show. Fred and I went on to do so much—on television and on the stage. He produced that Gore Vidal–written Western *The Left-Handed Gun* with Newman, and from there I brought him to *Two for the Seesaw* with Annie Bancroft—that was her Broadway debut, you know—and he produced that and then *The Miracle Worker*, also with Annie, and then *All the Way Home* on Broadway, and we did *Wait Until Dark*, with Lee Remick and Bob Duvall.

Penn directed the original *Playhouse 90* production of *The Miracle Worker*, starring Teresa Wright and Patty McCormack, *Invitation to a Gunfighter*, which later became a movie with Yul Brynner, and a handful of other dramas for that seminal 90-minute series, before gravitating to films (*Bonnie and Clyde, Mickey One, The Chase, Alice's Restaurant,* etc.) and the Broadway stage until the 1990s:

> With *Seesaw*—Shirley MacLaine and Robert Mitchum, and Robert Wise direct-ing—in those days, they could start the film even though the play was still running, not with Annie at the time but Lee Grant as Gittel. And Wise started rehearsing the film, and Ray Stark [actually it was Walter Mirisch] was the producer, and got very nervous because they couldn't find any laughs. They could tell because there was nothing funny around the table, and Mitchum wasn't what you call a comic actor and Shirley didn't get the flavor. So the producer called and said he and Wise would like to come into New York. "We'll pay for the performance—and photograph the play as it is now for where the laughs are."

CHAPTER 3

A Ford in Television's Future

CBS first got into drama anthology in October 1948 with *Ford Theatre* coming over from radio, where it, like *Studio One*, was created by producer Fletcher Markle. It was the network's first sponsored series, an hour-long Friday night show that aired on alternating weeks. The live CBS series, with Marc Daniels as primary director, used New York–based actors, primarily those working on Broadway. Fredric March, for instance, starred as Oscar Jaffe opposite Lilli Palmer's Lily Garland in an adaptation of Ben Hecht and Charles MacArthur's *Twentieth Century*, and Peggy Ann Garner starred as Beth March in a production of *Little Women*, alongside Kim Hunter, June Lockhart, and Karl Malden. (Hunter and Malden had been starring on Broadway together in *A Streetcar Named Desire*.) In other live drama adaptations, Fay Bainter, Mildred Dunnock, and a young Cloris Leachman acted together in Emlyn Williams's *Night Must Fall*, and Edward Everett Horton played Sheridan Whiteside in *The Man Who Came to Dinner* (Zero Mostel, Vicki Cummings, and Kevin McCarthy were in the cast). In *Ford*'s production of *Arsenic and Old Lace*, Boris Karloff recreated his fabled Broadway performance of earlier in the decade.

In its television life spanning nine years, *Ford Theatre* would be produced on all three networks: on NBC (1952–1956) and ABC (1956–1957) after moving on from CBS in a 30-minute filmed version from Hollywood. There, such film personalities as Robert Young, Shelley Winters, Ernest Borgnine, Claudette Colbert, Thomas Mitchell, and others made early (if not debut) TV performances, and Ronald Reagan and Nancy Davis acted together for the first time in a playlet called *The First Born*.

Westinghouse Presents Studio One made its distinguished bow on CBS one month after *Ford Theatre* (November 7, 1948) with a mystery called *The Storm*, costarring Margaret Sullavan and Dean Jagger, and a couple weeks after that, it offered a staging of Gian-Carlo Menotti's 1947 opera *The Medium* and a play, *Flowers from a Stranger*, with Felicia Montealegre (who would be one of the acting divas from the days of live television and the wife of composer Leonard Bernstein) and Yul Brynner.

Brynner, in fact, would become one of the directors of *Studio One* during its second season and then of CBS's *Danger* (he had been a fledgling house director for the network in New York since the late 1940s, overseeing primarily United Nations sessions to occupy afternoon airtime, a la television's much later C-Span). Rodgers and Hammerstein then, at the suggestion of Mary Martin—who had starred with Brynner on Broadway in *Lute Song* in 1946—enlisted him to be (reluctantly, according to Brynner) the king of Siam—although he had hoped to keep his day job. When then hirsute Brynner departed for another career, directing chores at CBS fell mainly to a young Sidney Lumet.

It was the estimable Worthington Miner who translated *Studio One* to television. It had begun as a CBS radio drama anthology show in 1947. He brought both quality adaptations of Shakespeare (the 1948 modern-dress *Julius Caesar*, with William Post Jr. in the title role and Robert Keith as Brutus, was restaged live just six weeks after initially premiering) and Brontë (the 1949 *Jane Eyre*, with a young Charlton Heston and Mary Sinclair) and a remarkable innovation in those early days: *Battleship Bismark*, starring Paul Lukas, used three-camera live editing within a confined, waterlogged set measuring 65 by 45 feet.

Mary Poppins came to television for the first time in 1949, with Mary Wickes in the lead (many years before Julie Andrews floated down for Disney holding her airborne umbrella). In spring 1950, Burgess Meredith starred as eccentric artist Gulley Jimson in a version of British actress Joyce Carey's *The Horse's Mouth*—the role Alec Guinness years later would play in the film version.

And under Miner, who shortly had a falling out with CBS and, in spring 1952, went over to NBC, there was more Shakespeare (Charlton Heston starred as Macbeth) and Pirandello and Henry James and Robert Louis Stevenson, along with lighter fare. The *New York Times* said about *Studio One*'s *Julius Caesar* that "its presentation in modern dress was one of the most stimulating and exciting theatrical experiences of the year, regardless of media, and the first work worthy of a place in television's permanent repertoire." And it was on *Studio One* where Westinghouse spokeswoman

Betty Furness famously battled live with an obstinate refrigerator that refused to open during one of the commercials.

More than 110 *Studio One* dramas between 1949 and 1956 were directed by Franklin J. Schaffner before he moved on to other shows like *Ford Theatre, Kaiser Aluminum Hour, The DuPont Show of the Week,* and *Playhouse 90,* and then to the big screen (*Planet of the Apes, Patton, Papillon, The Boys from Brazil*). He also was Edward R. Murrow's director on *Person to Person* from 1953 to 1959 and directed TV tours of the White House for Jack and Jacqueline Kennedy.

In 1949, at the second annual Emmy Awards (West Coast based), *Studio One* was nominated for best kinescope show as the only dramatic program among the group; the next year, it was nominated as best dramatic show (opposite *Fireside Theatre, I Remember Mama, Philco Television Playhouse,* and the winning *Pulitzer Prize Playhouse* on ABC). It won as best dramatic show in 1951 and was Emmy nominated in that category for the next four consecutive years. *Studio One* had the distinction of running year-round (*Studio One Summer Theatre* from June through September) and ended up with 432 productions in nine and a half seasons. In 1958, the show relocated from New York to the West Coast and was renamed *Studio One in Hollywood* for its final season; then, it appeared on film.

On *Studio One,* there was a rarity in what was seemingly the all-male club of directors during the first decade or so of network television. With a drama titled *The Blonde Comes First,* Lela Swift was installed by Worthington Miner as a regular director in November 1950 and called the shots from the control booth on alternate shows through much of that season. Swift had begun her career as a gofer at CBS in the mid-1940s, when television was still in its experimental stage, and eventually was recruited by Miner as an assistant director on *Studio One.* At the time, Franklin Schaffner and Paul Nickell were the chief directors on the series, and when Schaffner moved on, Swift got her shot. She later went on to direct episodes of *Suspense, The Web,* Dan Curtis's *Dark Shadows,* and ultimately, the long-running soap *Ryan's Hope.* It was difficult to find another female director on a live network dramatic program (to say nothing, regrettably, about women writers). The only other major one until probably the 1970s was former actress Ida Lupino, who, about 1953, began helming some episodes on *Four Star Playhouse* (where she had become one of the four producing principals) and then *Alfred Hitchcock Presents,* and went on from there to a significant directing career on television. But then, as was pointed out, she worked exclusively on *filmed* television.

The Talented Mr. Ripley, based on Patricia Highsmith's novel, was produced for *Studio One* in 1956, a decade before it was made into Alain Delon's French movie *Purple Noon* and into Matt Damon's movie under the original name decades after that. The *Studio One* version was directed by Franklin Schaffner, and Keefe Brasselle starred.

It was during the middle years of *Studio One* when the man once called by the *New York Times* "the jack-of-all-writing," Gore Vidal, did his first TV work. Vidal, author of two dozen novels between 1946 and the new millennium, and a critic, a playwright, and, in later years, a literary lion, a liberal political thinker, and even a one-time presidential candidate, made his TV writing debut with a play called *Dark Possession*, which aired on *Studio One* in February 1954. This drama about a widow (Geraldine Fitzgerald, starring with Leslie Nielsen) who begins receiving anonymous letters accusing her of having killed her husband was later staged two different times on *NBC Matinee Theatre* and again on *Chevy Mystery Show* in 1960.

Within a year of his first TV script, Vidal had adapted Henry James's *The Turn of the Screw* (with Geraldine Page) for *Omnibus*, *Stage Door* for *The Best of Broadway*, and both *Dr. Jekyll and Mr. Hyde* and *A Farewell to Arms* for *Climax!* He wrote originals like *The Death of Billy the Kid* (with Paul Newman) and *A Sense of Justice* for *Philco*, *Visit to a Small Planet* for *Goodyear*, and *A Man and Two Gods* and *Summer Pavilion* for *Studio One*. Vidal told the *New York Times* in 1956, "Until 1954, I had watched only one television drama to get the general hang of the thing. . . . I picked writers such as Horton Foote, Reginald Rose, and Chayefsky, whom I admire and who represent different ideas in TV writing." *Visit to a Small Planet* became a Broadway play and then a movie—with, to Vidal's reported dismay, Jerry Lewis in the lead, with the role enacted on TV and on the stage by debonair Cyril Ritchard.

Vidal also went on to write the screenplay for *Suddenly, Last Summer, The Best Man* (from his hit Broadway drama), *Is Paris Burning?*, *Myra Breckinridge* (from his satirical Hollywood novel), and the bawdy *Caligula*. And in the 1980s, for television, he revisited the William Bonney story in *Gore Vidal's Billy the Kid*, and his 1984 historical fiction *Lincoln* was adapted by longtime colleague from his golden age days Ernest Kinoy. Vidal, having conveniently been born (in 1925) at West Point, also did the television adaptation of Lucian Truscott's West Point drama *Dress Gray*. Vidal is one of the rare off-camera television talents to get a full biographical portrait on television (PBS's *American Masters*).

FROM THE AIRWAVES

Two truly great half-hour radio mystery and suspense anthologies came over to television, where they were equally as successful: *Autolite Presents Suspense* premiered on CBS on March 1, 1949, and *Lights Out*, sponsored by

Admiral and hosted with the proper amount of creepiness first by Jack La Rue and later by Frank Gallop, premiered on NBC on July 19, 1949. A number of the dramas on *Suspense*—which ran for six seasons, a 30-minute Tuesday night staple—were TV versions of radio presentations, most notably the chilling *Dead Ernest* (which Hitchcock later also adapted to TV). Additionally, there were *The Money's Paw*, adapted from the W. W. Jacobs classic, with Boris Karloff menacing Mildred Natwick; Edgar Allan Poe's *The Cask of Amontillado*, with Bela Lugosi; Robert Louis Stevenson's *The Suicide Club* and *Dr. Jekyll and Mr. Hyde*, the latter starring Basil Rathbone; Kipling's *The Man Who Would Be King*; Maugham's *The Letter*; and Dickens's *The Mystery of Edwin Drood*.

Lights Out, the popular ghost story series created for radio in the 1930s by Wyllis Cooper and popularized by Arch Oboler, had a tryout in commercial TV's infancy in 1946 with a handful of episodes (locally in New York) produced and directed by Fred Coe. NBC brought the series back on the network in the summer of 1949 and it ran for 148 half-hour episodes over three TV seasons. It had been a radio staple from 1936 to 1948. In addition to original short stories (by Ray Bradbury, among others), basically of the supernatural, there were adaptations of Hawthorne's *Dr. Heidegger's Experiment* and *Rappaccini's Daughter*. Lesser known New York actors found work on *Lights Out*, but there were more familiar faces such as Veronica Lake, William Bendix, Anthony Quinn, Jack Palance, Eva Marie Saint, Burgess Meredith, Anne Francis, Arlene Francis, and, naturally, Boris Karloff.

Together with Martin Manulis, Fred Coe, and Worthington Miner, and possibly David Susskind, Herbert Brodkin was a creative visionary producing for early television. A scenic designer for the stage, including the New York City Opera, in his formative days, Brodkin moved into TV circa 1950, producing and designing a show for CBS called *Charlie Wild, Private Detective* (later, it went to NBC and then to DuMont). Through the years, he flourished in the medium with some of its best-remembered early series, written by the likes of Ernest Kinoy, Sumner Locke Elliott, Robert Alan Aurthur, Tad Mosel, Reginald Rose, N. Richard Nash, David Swift, David Shaw, Rod Serling, and Abby Mann. In a 1985 Museum of Broadcasting live seminar—basically a conversation between Kinoy and him—Brodkin observed, "There is no question that we were beginning, during what became known as the golden era, to develop a new medium, that we were finding a way of doing shows live that was unlike any other medium."

"Some of the shows on which I had a producer credit," Brodkin told this writer in the early 1980s for an article in *Films in Review*, "helped Len Goldenson put the fledgling ABC on the TV map, with several dramatic anthologies that aired between 1952 and 1955 such as *ABC Album*—you might find it in TV historical compilations as *The Plymouth Theatre*—then *Motorola TV Hour*, then *Center Stage*, then *The Elgin Hour*. On *Motorola*, where I was series producer, we did what might have been TV's first live Western drama—with horses on a TV set! It was called *Outlaw's Releasing* and starred, I think, Eddie Albert and Jane Wyatt and Lee Marvin—playing the bad varmint, as usual in those days."

We [some great early directors, including Ralph Nelson, Don Richardson, Dan Petrie, and Sidney Lumet] did what I think are top-drawer productions—*live*—including the very first American TV staging of Dickens's *A Tale of Two Cities*. That was a two-part dramatization starring Wendell Corey.

It was up to me to give the go ahead for Reggie Rose's at the time controversial urban drama *Crime in the Streets*. Lumet, who directed it with up-and-coming John Cassavetes and fellow future director Mark Rydell and Sal Mineo as angry teen dropouts who plan a murder. And Leonard Rosenman did the music—maybe his first TV work. Look at the talent involved in that major drama. It premiered on the *Elgin Hour* in early 1955. John, Mark, and Sal went on to do the movie version of it a year or so later, for director Don Siegel. Because of poor distribution, the movie, unfortunately, hasn't been seen much [until a revival of Siegel's work at the Film Forum in New York in spring 2006].

Then I got a call from NBC, who induced me to come over to work on *The Alcoa Hour* and *Goodyear Theatre*, which was doing splendid, groundbreaking dramatic work in those days. And I was lucky to become part of that. Sidney and Dan worked quite often with me on that alternating series during the 1955–1956 season, along with Bob Mulligan and Paul Bogart, and the cream of television actors of the day: E. G. Marshall, Kim Stanley, Cassavetes, Tony Randall, Bob Preston (he had also been in *Crime in the Streets*), Ralph Bellamy, and dear Hume Cronyn and Jessie Tandy. And everything they—we—were doing was *live*. There might be a few existing kinescopes lying around someplace.

I was back at CBS for *Studio One*, where I oversaw a wonderful lawyer drama by Reggie Rose called *The Defender*. It was directed, in two parts, by Bob Mulligan and starred Ralph Bellamy and William Shatner as a father-son team of lawyers. And a young, intense Steve McQueen also was in it as a murder suspect. That would be the pilot to the series we later did—we added an *s* to the title—which won wide acceptance with TV viewers and ran for several seasons in the early 1960s, with E. G. Marshall and Robert Reed stepping in for Ralph and Bill. It also was called by critics kind of provocative and somewhat controversial in its time, and I had a number of battles with CBS to keep the vision of the great writers who turned in thoughtful scripts. One was on blacklisting, which was written by Ernest Kinoy and starred Jack Klugman. Each won an Emmy for the show [*Blacklist*] that year. We also won Emmys for *The Defenders* as outstanding drama program during the 1961–1962, 1962–1963, and 1963–1964 seasons. In the show's last season, director Paul Bogart and writer David Karp won Emmys for the two-part episode called *The 700 Year Old Gang*, which starred Jack Gilford.

Brodkin, unfortunately, was not around to see *The Defenders* revived in a series of Showtime TV movies, with E. G. Marshall and Beau Bridges, at the end of the 1990s. (It was Marshall's last work, and he died before making the third in the new series.)

And after *The Defender* on *Studio One*, I did Abby Mann's story *A Child Is Waiting*, with Vincent Donehue directing. One of my acting students, John Cassavetes, ended up directing Judy Garland, his wife, Gena Rowlands, and Burt Lancaster in the film version of it some years afterward. The *Studio One* stint led to *Playhouse 90* at CBS, and I had the great opportunity to bring Rod Serling's *The Velvet Alley* with Art Carney, Reggie Rose's *A Quiet Game of Cards* with E. G. Marshall and Franchot Tone and others, Loring Mandel's *The Raider*, Abby Mann's *Judgment at Nuremberg*, and Horton Foote's adaptation of Faulkner's *Tomorrow* to discerning golden age audiences.

We—Buzz Berger and I—put together our Titus Productions company for *The Defenders* and other series like *Brenner*, with Edward Binns and James Broderick, *The Nurses* (and then *The Doctors and the Nurses*)—all for CBS—and *Shane* (from the movie) for NBC. David Carradine starred. Then there was the show that might have been ahead of its time, *Coronet Blue*, which I did with Angela Lansbury's producing brother Edgar. Eventually, all of this led to what a lot of TV historians have come to call a truly great TV movie, *Holocaust*—I humbly thank them for that—with a young Meryl Streep. And to Ernie Kinoy's *Skokie*, with Danny Kaye in his only dramatic role on television, and to several semifictional, speculative movies about Scotty Fitzgerald and Zelda.

Brodkin's last producing credits included writer David Rintels's gritty, award-winning *Sakharov* (about the famed Soviet dissident) for HBO and the TV movie *Johnny Bull*, a drama by first-time writer Kathleen Betsko Yale, under the auspices of the National Playwright Conference of the Eugene O'Neill Memorial Theater Center. Jason Robards starred in the former with Glenda Jackson and in the latter with Colleen Dewhurst. Brodkin was also executive producer in the late 1980s for the other movie about Edward R. Murrow, with Daniel J. Travanti as the famed broadcaster, the TV movie *Mandela* with Danny Glover, and several of the popular detective films about New York City cop Frank Janek (from the William Bayer books), with Richard Crenna. And with *Sakharov, Murrow,* and *Mandela*, the Brodkin era on TV ended on a satisfyingly high note.

Among the major television directors whose dozens of credits spanned his career in live television drama was Robert Mulligan, who did multiple episodes of *Suspense* (his first work) and *Studio One* beginning in that show's ninth season.

In a conversation with fellow directors Arthur Penn and John Frankenheimer before an audience at then Museum of Broadcasting in New York in the mid-1990s, Robert Mulligan recalled, "My memories of television was that small box that existed in our apartment in the Bronx. My brother Dick [late actor Richard Mulligan of *Soap* and *Empty Nest*] and I decided then and there we wanted to get into TV. I made it to the mailroom of CBS after getting out of Fordham [he'd also been in the Marine Corps in World War II and then worked in the editorial department of the *New York Times*]. Then I moved up to production assistant for the producer of *Suspense*, and then to assistant director to director to taking it over completely for the last two years it was on."

Mulligan ultimately went over to NBC circa 1954 and was put into the director rotation on the *Philco/Goodyear Playhouse* by producer Fred Coe, calling the shots for about 30 episodes, including *A Man Is Ten Feet Tall* with Sidney Poitier, Gore Vidal's *The Death of Billy the Kid* with Paul Newman, and Paddy Chayefsky's *The Catered Affair* with Thelma Ritter. "We really had to fight the top brass to get Poitier. Here was a dramatic hour on the most prestigious show on television with a black actor in the lead for the first time. But because of the blacklisting and the publication *Red Channels*, put out by conservative zealots—which had the unfortunate power to alert sponsors to those people they might want not want to employ because of their political leanings—Poitier's name came up."

Now that was not because of Poitier's background of the time but because he had worked in a film several years before with the wonderful Canada Lee, who's past *was* in question. Poitier became so enraged at being called in and grilled by NBC's top executives about this after the fact—and having to admit that to work in that film being shot in South Africa, he and Lee had to sign on as indentured servants to the producer—he threatened to walk, and it was up to me and Fred Coe, writer Robert Alan Aurthur, and a number of other courageous men that we marched into the front office en masse and forced the issue. We wanted Poitier or the show doesn't go on, and the brass backed down. This was really a terrible and shameful guilt-by-association time in broadcasting and the arts, although it never really touched Broadway.

A Man Is Ten Feet Tall was the powerful story of two blue-collar buddies, one black, the other white (played by Don Murray), dockworkers on the

Brooklyn waterfront. Sidney Poitier later did the film version of it as *Edge of the City* opposite John Cassavetes. Mulligan's TV colleague Martin Ritt made his film directing debut with it. And when the movie version of Gore Vidal's Billy the Kid tale that Mulligan helmed came to the big screen as *The Left-Handed Gun*, with right-handed Paul Newman (as was the real William Bonney a.k.a. Billy the Kid) repeating his role, another Mulligan TV cohort, Arthur Penn, made *his* feature directing debut.

Back at CBS, Mulligan worked on such memorable *Studio One* presentations as Reginald Rose's lawyer drama *The Defender* (one of the early live two-part dramas, each episode a week apart), Sumner Locke Elliott's *Love at Fourth Sight*, and Horton Foote's *A Member of the Family*, with Hume Cronyn, and *The Traveling Lady*, with Kim Stanley. (In this case, when *The Traveling Lady* came to the screen years later as *Baby the Rain Must Fall*, with Lee Remick and Steve McQueen, Mulligan finally got the chance to direct one of the projects he originated on TV.)

On *The DuPont Show of the Month*, his directing credits included Carson McCullers's *The Member of the Wedding* and Thornton Wilder's *The Bridge of San Luis Rey* in 1958 and Herman Melville's *Billy Budd* in 1959. On *Playhouse 90*, Mulligan directed David Shaw's original *The Mystery of Thirteen* in 1957 with Jack Lemmon (the plot: an English physician steals from the patients, has an affair with the ward of his professor, and is hung, for ultimately was said to have killed 13 people) and, in 1960, Horton Foote's adaptation of Faulkner's short story *Tomorrow*, with Kim Stanley.

Mulligan directed the *Hallmark Hall of Fame*'s critically praised 1959 production of O'Neill's *Ah Wilderness*, and he received the Emmy as outstanding director for Maugham's *The Moon and Sixpence*, which marked Laurence Olivier's American TV debut in 1959. After *Tomorrow*, Mulligan left television for the big screen, never to return. Mulligan in fact worked—between TV and the movies—with everyone from Olivier to Sandra Dee.

Said Mulligan, "My whole theatrical training all took place in television—before I went off to do movies . . . as a p.a. [production assistant], then as an [assistant director]. Sometimes all of the panic, all the noise that we [directors] shared and remembered so well, became second nature to me. Everything I learned was from good writers, good actors, good producers. You literally never stopped working. You did 52 shows a year. And working with Marty Manulis and Fred Coe. . . . Fred was the single best producer in live TV at the time. He invented what live TV became. It was much like the early days of flight—a lot of fly, crash, burn. When they talk about the golden age of TV, they don't count in the number of daily, weekly crashes and burns we all went through."

Robert Mulligan and his production partner Alan Pakula (they had joined forces a few years earlier, in 1957, for Mulligan's film debut, directing *Fear Strikes Out*, with Anthony Perkins as baseball star Jimmy Piersall) made a series of acclaimed movies. Among them, of course, were *To Kill a Mockingbird*, for which Mulligan won the Academy Award, *Inside Daisy Clover*, *Up the Down Staircase*, *Summer of '42*, and *The Other*.

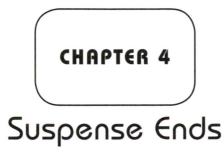

CHAPTER 4

Suspense Ends

The final *Suspense*, the 260th, airing on August 17, 1954, was an adaptation of William Faulkner's *Barn Burning*, with E. G. Marshall (he had also done another Faulkner tale, *Smoke*, not long before). Marshall played embittered antebellum Southern arsonist Abner Snopes. Decades later, on *PBS American Short Story*, Tommy Lee Jones played Abner in Horton Foote's adaptation of Faulkner's 1939 story.

Jack Lemmon went back to the early TV days in a role in *The Gray Helmet* in late December 1949 on *Suspense* (and before that, radio soap operas). In a question and answer session at a 1985 seminar at what was then the Museum of Broadcasting in New York, Lemmon waxed nostalgic: "Live television was incredibly exciting. It really was a middle ground between theater and film because it was live, and the curtain went up and you were on, giving a sustained performance even if the camera went to black and came up again and you jumped to another set at another time." He pressed the point: "Since everybody was experimenting during those early days, you might try anything and actors were not typecast. I might be playing John Wilkes Booth one week and doing *Charley's Aunt* in a dress the week after. It was a terrific opportunity to grow and learn. It was fun, with no economic or professional pressures."

I can remember doing a show down in Grand Central Station, where a lot of the shows were done, and while I was rehearsing, every time I'd take a break, I'd go outside into the hall and I'd see this young girl pacing up and down, working on some other show there. She called herself Anne Marno, then changed it to Bancroft and did pretty well. Chuck Heston, Rod Steiger, and Walter Matthau are just a few whom I worked with. The writers include JP Miller, Tad Mosel, Rod Serling, Paddy Chayefsky, and oh so many others. There was incredible talent that was developing. You were getting a lot of pap, as we do today, but you'd also get some terrific stuff. We didn't know that it was terrific. In retrospect, it was.

Both *Suspense* and *Lights Out*, being televised from the East Coast, were cast primarily with New York actors and lesser Broadway names. The latter show began in summer 1949 as four creepy specials under the supervision of Fred Coe and encouraged NBC to bring it back—on what appeared to be a bigger budget—in the fall, and it ran for the next four seasons on Monday nights at nine o'clock. Talent on the level of Boris Karloff, Eddie Albert, Burgess Meredith, Basil Rathbone, and Raymond Massey acted on this series, as did a couple of bright young actresses, Eva Marie Saint and Grace Kelly. (Jack Palance, for one, had one of his earliest TV roles on *Lights Out* in a 1950 episode titled *The Man Who Couldn't Remember.*) Original dramas were the weekly norm, although mixed in were adaptations of Poe, Hawthorne, and others.

Also coming over from radio at around the same time were the supernatural and the superbly eerie series *Escape* (CBS, 1950) and the prestigious *DuPont Cavalcade of America*, dramas about great events and figures from this country's history in the first three of its five television seasons on NBC (beginning in 1952). *Cavalcade* could be thought of as weekly dollops of history on the air, with its filmed dramas celebrating the acts of individual initiative and achievement. *Poor Richard*, the series's debut program, told of the wit and inventiveness of Ben Franklin, portrayed by Cecil Kellaway. Later stories had Richard Denning playing Eli Whitney, Sean McClory playing Andrew Jackson, and Raymond Greenleaf playing Thomas Jefferson. The sponsor's familiar "Better things for better living" motto became a household phrase of the time, just as Hallmark's "When you care enough to send the very best" remains to this day. By mid-decade, more contemporary story subjects were introduced to freshen things up and expand the historical venue that was the darling of the politically conservative DuPont Company, which had been around since the beginning of the nineteenth century. DuPont ultimately phased out the historical past and returned to television in September 1967 with its *The DuPont Show of the Month*, a series of classy 90-minute color dramas and spectaculars.

Fireside Theatre, hosted by, among others, show producer Frank Wisbar, former screen star Gene Raymond, and then Jane Wyman, premiered on NBC in the spring of 1949 and was a Tuesday night staple through the end of the 1956–1957 television season. (It then moved to a new night for one more year.) *Fireside Theatre* was among the earliest filmed drama anthologies and was popular enough to rank second behind *Texaco Star Theatre* with Milton Berle (and ahead of *Philco Television Playhouse*) during its second season. Early on, it provided a mixture of dramas, comedies, musicals (an adaptation of Leonard Sillman's *New Faces*), and other programming ideas for network consideration. Yul Brynner and then wife Virginia Gilmore starred in the premiere, a comedy called *Friend of the Family*. Between September 1949 and the following spring, *Fireside Theatre* experimented with doubling up its dramas, each running approximately 15 minutes, and concentrated exclusively on filmed dramas with a wide range of name and lesser actors. It returned to half-hour dramas after that and for the remainder of its long run. During Jane Wyman's tenure (1955–1958) as host and frequent performer on the anthology, it became familiarly known as *The Jane Wyman Show.*

Robert Montgomery Presents Your Lucky Strike Theatre (NBC, premiering January 30, 1950) aired its first show with onetime romantic leading man Montgomery hosting his production of Maugham's *The Letter* with Madeleine Carroll. The hour-long biweekly dramatic series (alternating with *Somerset Maugham Theatre* for a while) spent the first two seasons with adaptations of popular movies, including *Ride the Pink Horse,* in which Montgomery recreated his screen role. This chase thriller later would be remade by director Don Siegel as one of the earliest made-for-TV movies in the mid-1960s under NBC's Project 120 banner. Montgomery also later starred most notably on his series in TV versions of *The Great Gatsby* and *The Lost Weekend* (in the latter, early Walter Matthau played the bartender). Peter Falk made what might have been his first TV appearance (May 1957) in a Montgomery production of Milton Gelman's *Return Visit.* In a season-end assessment of television in 1951, the *New York Times*'s television critic felt that "Robert Montgomery's hour of drama is probably most representative of the application of moviemaking technique in TV drama."

Robert Montgomery Presents, during the summers, featured a stock company of young players performing in repertory of sorts. One of the actors was Elizabeth Montgomery, the noted producer's daughter, soon to be noted herself.

Elizabeth actually made her TV debut acting opposite her dad in a December 1951 production by writer Thomas W. Phipps titled *Top Secret,* which also happened to be the first time a story was written directly for the Montgomery series. (Practically all of the previous ones were stage, literature, or film adaptations.) Shortly after this production was another first for the live anthology series: a documentary-style drama, *Class of '67,* telecast live on New Year's Eve 1951 on location from a New York City hospital. Montgomery's landmark series—which also presented two-part adaptations of *Great Expectations, David Copperfield,* and *The Hunchback of Notre Dame*—aired year-round for 321 dramas (and comedies). The distinguished movie actor turned World War II hero turned film director turned star/host then left acting and moved to another profession: into politics and as close communications advisor to Dwight D. Eisenhower.

Cameo Theatre (NBC, May 1950 through April 1952, and then again during the summer of 1955 in various time slots), produced by Albert McCleery, was a distinctive 30-minute occasional drama anthology with a twist: it was staged arena-style, in the round with a black background, had a bare minimum of props, and, to focus on the characterizations of the individual actors, cast mainly players from New York (among them, June Havoc, Alfred Drake, Tod Andrews, Ernest Truex, Clare Luce, and Ed Begley). McCleery utilized close-ups and other innovative (of the day) camera techniques. The anthology series premiered with a lesser-known Arthur Miller piece, *It Takes a Thief* (it had been published in *Collier's* in 1947) and later staged the Shirley Jackson short story "The Lottery," Roald Dahl's *The Man from the South,* G. B. Shaw's Graustarkian tale *The Inca of Perusalem,* Durrenmatt's *The Visit,* and an admirable three-part adaptation of Ibsen's *Peer Gynt* as well. William Saroyan's first original drama for television, *A Daughter to Think About,* was also part of the lineup in 1950.

The *New York Times*'s Jack Gould judged that "the arena staging as executed by Albert McCleery, in practice proved to be thirty minutes of close-ups. Unfortunately such shots quickly lose their impact upon excessive repetition and the movement on the screen often seemed self-conscious and contrived." In a year-end TV roundup, he described NBC's series: "*Cameo Theatre* has followed a commendably experimental turn, but has been more concerned with being arty than being good."

It was on *Cameo Theatre* where, in 1952, Abby Mann had his first television script produced, *The Gathering Twilight,* which costarred Sylvia Sidney and Douglass Montgomery. Mann, in a 2005 interview with the author, recalled: "Around the same time I had another of my scripts done on NBC's *Gulf Playhouse.* It was about my friend Tony Bennett, who had just made a big splash as a recording artist. *Gulf* was one of those live shows produced by the terrific Albert McCleery, who also created *Matinee Theatre* for NBC, and he produced a couple of my scripts there, too. The *Gulf* show was *Scream of the Crowd,* and Robert Sterling did the Bennett character, opposite the wonderful Felicia Montealegre. Her husband, Leonard Bernstein, sort of snuck into the studio to watch her work, I recall." *The Gulf Playhouse* staged just 13 shows in late 1952.

Abby Mann noted that in addition to writing about Tony Bennett, he did a script for *Robert Montgomery Presents* several years later (1955), a thinly disguised drama about actor John Garfield called *The World to Nothing*. "Eddie Albert was in it, but for some reason his performance was all wrong. To compound that, Jack Gould, in the *New York Times*, talked about the show and kept referring to me as Miss Mann. [The *Times* corrected it a couple days later.] Just goes to show how well known I was at that time.

"I also did an adaptation of a Joseph Conrad short story for Montgomery. The drama was called *The End of the Tether* from his turn-of-the-last-century seafaring novel. That wonderful British actor Barry Jones starred as the ship's captain." At a later time, after *A Child Is Waiting* ("The show dealt with developmentally challenged children," Mann remembered, "and I was shot down by the network when I wanted to fill the kids' roles with real-life challenged ones.") and after *Judgment at Nuremberg*, with its censorship problems ("Even the government, I think, tried the show quashed—it was the Eisenhower era, at the height of the Cold War—because they did not want to risk offending the Germans, now our allies."), both of those major shows later were filmed, and both, coincidentally, had Burt Lancaster and Judy Garland in the cast.

Mann left television for more than 15 years. He came back with a number of projects dealing with social injustice: *The Marcus-Nelson Murders* (which evolved into the Telly Savalas *Kojak* series); *King*, a much-admired two-part biography about Martin Luther King Jr. with a strong performance by Paul Winfield (Mann not only wrote it, but directed it as well); and *The Atlanta Child Murders*, about a black man convicted of the killings of a number of black schoolchildren over the years but, Mann felt, was never adequately tried and proven the killer. And there was *Indictment: The McMartin Trial*, an Emmy-winning TV film about California's real-life McMartin preschool trial of the 1980s, one of the longest, most expensive trials in U.S. history (seven years) and one of the most explosive, dealing with countless allegations of child molestation. The much-hailed movie also earned Emmy nominations for James Woods as the slimy McMartin defense lawyer and for both Shirley Knight and Sada Thompson as well as for Abby Mann and his wife, Myra (they cowrote it).

Nash Airflyte Theatre (CBS, 1950–1951), with William Gaxton hosting, was a not especially memorable New York–based live half-hour anthology show, airing Thursday nights at 10:30, that mixed music like Gilbert and Sullivan to Steinbeck and O. Henry and back to opera stars such as Marguerite Piazza in an original musical comedy. Among those starring in straight dramatic works were Fredric March and David Niven, each in possibly his earliest TV acting gig; Joan Bennett; Joan Blondell; and Grace

Kelly. The leading director on the show was Marc Daniels, who next went on to be the primary director of *I Love Lucy* and amassed an impressive TV directing résumé, right up to his death in 1989. As for the show's sponsor, Nash was a popular post–World War II car of the day, and Airflyte was one of its models.

Hollywood Theater Time (ABC, 1950–1955) was one of the first dramatic anthology series to originate from the West Coast, seen in the East via kinescopes. The half-hour series mixed dramatic presentations with variety shows, situation comedies, and scenes from notable plays. Originally, this was called *Hollywood Premiere Theatre.*

Armstrong Circle Theatre (NBC, June 1950–1955 as a weekly live half-hour drama, after that, as hour-long programs) continued the then tradition of having the (sole) sponsor's name in the title. At the time of its premiere in summer 1950, there were more than a dozen other anthology programs already airing regularly, but *Armstrong* became one of the longest running (14 seasons in all). *Armstrong* was created by Talent Associates Ltd., which was formed by David Susskind and Alfred Levy (Talent Associates also would produce the *Kaiser Aluminum Hour* and *The DuPont Show of the Month*). Initially, the series, like the other drama programs, offered formula dramas, although in spring 1953, it premiered the first operetta commissioned for television, *The Parrot,* with a book by Frank Felitta and a music score for two pianos by Darrell Peter. In advance of the production, a notice appeared in the personals of the *New York Times:* "Parrot Wanted. Any color but white . . . for the title role in a comic opera on television. Must be able to scream on cue." Ultimately, the producers (Robert Costello, Jacqueline Babbin, Ralph Nelson, and others) brought in a stable of first-time writers, along with, occasionally, Rod Serling, Jerome Coopersmith, and Irve Tunick.

Armstrong moved out of NBC after the 1956–1957 season (at that point, a shift in format had the show doing fact-based docudramas, with the likes of legendary newscaster John Cameron Swayze as host/narrator, and inspired-by-true-events dramas like the sinking of the *Andrea Doria* and the effect of Hurricane Diane on a small Connecticut town). The show returned on film to CBS in 1957 in an hour-long form (with CBS news anchor Douglas Edwards replacing Swayze) to alternate with *The United States Steel Hour* through 1963. Robert Duvall, Anne Jackson, and Telly Savalas were among those who played their first major dramatic roles in this series. *Armstrong* continued with periodic specials like an adaptation in October 1966 of Lerner and Loewe's musical *Brigadoon,* adapted by Ernest Kinoy and directed by Fielder Cook. Robert Goulet, Sally Ann Howes, and Peter Falk starred (no, Falk did not sing!).

CHAPTER 5

Sterling Serling

Rod Serling, one of the preeminent writers of drama on television, penned well over 200 plays for the medium, starting with *The Storm,* a series produced locally in Cincinnati between 1950 and 1953. Some of his first work seen nationally was in 1952 for the *Lux Video Theatre* (*Mr. Finchley versus the Bomb,* January 7) and *Armstrong Circle Theatre* (*The Sergeant,* April 29). Serling wrote for *Hallmark Hall of Fame* (five programs), *Kraft Television Theatre* (six programs, including the award-winning *Patterns*), *Studio One* (six programs), *Medallion Theatre* (three programs), *Ford Theatre* (two programs), *Playhouse 90* (10 programs), *Climax!* (three programs), *The United States Steel Hour* (three programs), and *Matinee Theatre* (two programs), and he wrote *Carol for Another Christmas,* an adaptation of Dickens, the first of several stellar television movies made for the United Nations by the Xerox people, and dozens more before *The Twilight Zone.* His original scripts also were produced on *Bob Hope Presents the Chrysler Theatre* and on his own 1965–1966 Western drama series *The Loner,* and finally on *Night Gallery.*

In a program brochure for a 1984 exhibition of his work at the Museum of Broadcasting in New York (later the Museum of Television and Radio, and more recently renamed the Paley Center for Media, after founder William S. Paley) nine years after his death, there were Serling reminiscences about writing for, among others, *Kraft Television Theatre.* "They wouldn't permit a writer at rehearsal until the day of the show. His presence at that late hour was probably a guarantee against intrusion. For by then the lines had been changed, the interpretations made, the blocking and camera arranged. The writer could protest, but only as a gesture. The show was a fait accompli before his arrival in the kindred areas of rewriting, casting, music, et al."

Serling also noted, in an introductory essay in *Patterns: Four Television Plays* (Simon and Schuster, 1957), that "the TV writer is never trained to be a TV writer. There are no courses, however specialized and applied, that will catapult him (the writer) into the profession. . . . In my case the decision to become a television writer arose from no professional master plan. I was on the writing staff of a radio station in the Midwest. Staff writing is a particularly dreamless occupation characterized by assembly-line writing almost around the clock."

Of the profession that put him—and a dozen or so talented scribes—on the cultural map, Serling concluded, "The major advance in the television play was a thematic one. The medium began to show a cognizance of its own particular fortés. . . . In my case it happened because of a single show that emanated live out of New York City. This was the *Lux Video Theatre*." (Seven of his early scripts were produced on *Lux* in 18 months.) Serling's first television scripts, he remembered, had been sold in early 1950 to *Stars over Hollywood*, an NBC film series on the West Coast.

Danger (CBS, premiering September 19, 1950), for which Serling had two scripts produced, was a popular 30-minute Tuesday night series that featured dramas dealing with psychological subjects and murder. The primary director on *Danger* at the beginning was Yul Brynner:

I was cutting my teeth on live drama as Yul's assistant on the series," Sidney Lumet later recalled. "When Yul left for the stage and *The King and I*, I was bumped up to lead director, and my assistant was John Frankenheimer, who came to CBS as an apprentice after being an Air Force cameraman in Korea. That's the way it worked in the golden age. There was a pecking order of directors on the network staffs. Chuck Heston, Jimmy Dean [the actor, not the country singer and sausage king], John Cassavetes, Rod Steiger, Grace Kelly, Kim Stanley, and Jack Lemmon were among the young up-and-coming actors who worked on the series [which lasted for five seasons]. We had guitarist Tony Mottola, who created our theme and scored every episode—much as Henry Mancini did many years later with *Peter Gunn* and *Mr. Lucky*.

"And we had that wonderful announcer, Dick Stark, who kept the aura of suspense going even during the commercial break, with a tremble in his voice." Lumet continued, "One of the first shows I did on *Danger* was something called *The Corpse and Tighe O'Kane* with character actor J. Pat O'Malley. A few weeks later, there was a thriller called *Blue Murder* with Anthony Quinn, who had left Hollywood for the New York stage and live television at the time, and then *The Killer Scarf*, with a talented young actress named Anne Marno. Soon she was to become Anne Bancroft. The script to that one was by Walter Bernstein, who was on the verge of being blacklisted."

Prudential Family Playhouse (CBS, 1950–1951) offered 13 hour-long shows on Tuesdays, rotating with *Sure As Fate*, with classy adaptations of Broadway evergreens acted by top stars ranging from Helen Hayes in *The Barretts of Wimpole Street*, Ruth Gordon in *Over 21*, and Bert Lahr in *Burlesque*, to Gertrude Lawrence in *Biography*, Ruth Chatterton in *Dodsworth*, and Grace Kelly in *Berkeley Square*. Two words explain why this top-drawer anthology show failed to make the grade: Milton Berle. CBS unwisely slotted this glittering show, produced and directed by Donald Davis, with the best the American stage had to offer, opposite Uncle Miltie and *The Texaco Star Theater*, the biggest television phenomenon of the day. (In hindsight, *Prudential Family Playhouse* might have had a better shot had it followed Ed Sullivan's *Toast of the Town* on Sundays.)

Lux Video Theatre (CBS, 1950–1955), although another television series that came over from radio, differed somewhat in that for the most part, until its fifth season, it did not offer abbreviated TV adaptations of movies. At that point, the format changed to the one best remembered from radio, James Mason and later Gordon MacRae were brought in to host, and there were hour-long versions of popular films such as *Sunset Boulevard* with Miriam Hopkins; *Shadow of a Doubt*, the Hitchcock movie, here with Frank Lovejoy; *Casablanca*, featuring Paul Douglas, Arlene Dahl, and Hoagy Carmichael; and *A Place in the Sun* with John Derek, Ann Blyth, and Marilyn Erskine (in the Montgomery Clift, Elizabeth Taylor, and Shelley Winters roles) and Raymond Burr repeating his screen part as the prosecutor, along with Ronald Reagan as guest host for this episode. Lux might have condensed the original movies—crammed them into less than an hour—but production values were not skimped. *A Place in the Sun*, for one, directed by Buzz Kulik, used 67 players and 17 sets. *Variety* considered that "a good part of the dramatic wallop was retained in the TV version." Similarly, *The Twentieth Century-Fox Hour*, running periodically through the 1956 season, presented 50-minute vest-pocket adaptations of popular films from that studio's vaults, though mainly under alternate titles. *Laura* became *Portrait for Murder*, *The Late George Apley* became *Back Bay Romance*, and *Miracle on 34th Street* became *Meet Mr. Kringle*. *Pontiac's Playwrights '56*, which alternated with that anthology hour, offered such live fare as writer Arnold Schulman's *Lost*, directed by Arthur Penn; Horton Foote's *Flight* with Kim Stanley; *Keyhole* with Lee Grant, directed by Fred Coe; and Gore Vidal's *Honor* with Ralph Bellamy, also directed by Penn.

Somerset Maugham TV Theatre (CBS, 1950–1951; NBC, 1951) was among the first TV drama programs that had the name of the author of most of the dramas (rather than the corporate sponsor) in its title. Maugham hosted adaptations of his stories and novels, performed live from New York, although Maugham's appearances were filmed at his home on the French Riviera. Martin Ritt produced and sometimes directed this half-hour series (hour-long for the last seven on NBC), along with Yul Brynner, Daniel Petrie, and others. Lee J. Cobb starred in a version of the author/host's *The Moon and Sixpence*, Cloris Leachman in *Of Human Bondage*, Jessica Tandy in *The Man from Glasgow*, and Anthony Quinn in *Partners*. (Brynner directed the Quinn episode; years later, Quinn directed Brynner in the big-screen remake of *The Buccaneer*.) Interestingly, the radio version of *Somerset Maugham Theatre* aired concurrently on Saturday mornings (on CBS and NBC), but with different stories.

The Peabody Award–winning *Celanese Theatre*, ABC's single-season (1951–1952) anthology drama series, specialized in adaptations of works by noted playwrights. "Going to the head of the class this season," wrote critic Jack Gould of the *New York Times*, "has been the *Celanese Theatre* which obtained a corner on a number of works by Eugene O'Neill, Robert E. Sherwood, Maxwell Anderson, Elmer Rice, John Van Druten, and Paul Osborne, among others. Sparing no expense in casting and production, it was been impeccable theatre directed with fluidity by Alex Segal." (Segal was also the series producer.) While not especially well remembered among the seminal drama anthologies of the day, *Celanese Theatre* nevertheless was much admired by the television critics of the time. The show, in particular, found itself at the center of the blacklisting controversy when Rice, one of the major author/playwrights of the era, publicly challenged the publication *Red Channels'* interference with the show's casting. *Celanese Theatre* aired weekly on Wednesdays for an hour during the first months of its run, then was pared down to 30 minutes. June Havoc and a young Richard Burton (in what was probably his American television acting debut) starred in a production of *Anna Christie*, David Niven and Kim Hunter were the stars of *The Petrified Forest*, and Thomas Mitchell and Roddy McDowall acted in *Ah, Wilderness*.

Tales of Tomorrow (ABC, 1951–1953) was one of TV's earliest science fiction, flying saucers, and supernatural tales series, and it predated *The Twilight Zone* and others of that ilk by a good 15 years. Cloris Leachman and Leslie Nielsen, two now veteran stars who go back to the earliest days of commercial television, acted in episodes, as did some of the greats from big-screen horror movies: Lon Chaney, who literally got carried away playing Frankenstein's monster live (smashing up the sets on camera, in an adaptation of Mary Shelley's classic), and Boris Karloff, who did not. There were versions of H. G. Wells and even Jules Verne in a two-part *20,000 Leagues under the Sea* with Nielsen and Thomas Mitchell (as Captain Nemo). And John Newland, later to be creator and star of another classic sci-fi show, *One Step Beyond*, starred in both *Frankenstein* (as Victor) and *The Picture of Dorian Gray* (as Dorian). More contemporary writers included Ray Bradbury and John D. MacDonald. A young Paul Newman made an early TV acting appearance—perhaps his earliest—in *Ice from Space*, and Joanne Woodward made her TV debut on the show several months afterward in *The Bitter Storm*. Rod Steiger had an early role toward the end of the series in spring 1953 as a mad doctor in *The Evil Within*, and in a tiny role as his lab assistant was James Dean. George F. Foley Jr. was the producer of this anthology, and Franklin J. Schaffner, Don Medford, and Charles Dubin were among the series directors.

Competing in the same adult-oriented genre with *Tales of Tomorrow*, at least briefly, was the CBS sci-fi anthology *Out There*. From the end of October 1951 through mid-January 1952, the show occupied Sunday evenings at six o'clock in the East with half-hour adaptations (by TV scribes David Shaw, Reginald Rose, and others) of published tales by prominent sci-fi writers, ranging from Theodore Sturgeon to Ray Bradbury to Robert Heinlein. The initial entry, viewed by TV critics of the time as being similar in plot to the then current feature *The Day the Earth Stood Still*, dealt with a warning to Earth about its atomic weapons, a message brought back to Earth by an Air Force officer (played by Robert Webber) who had been abducted by aliens. A later tale gave up-and-coming Kim Stanley one of her early TV roles in *The Bus to Nowhere*, one of the dramas Rose wrote for the series—quite possibly his first television script. Executive produced by Donald Davis, who also directed along with Byron Paul and Andrew McCullough, *Out There* was one of the first series to mix live action and filmed special effects. The innovative anthology, which did not have a sponsor, was canceled after a dozen episodes.

CHAPTER 6

Cultural Oasis on a Sunday Afternoon

Hallmark Hall of Fame (NBC, premiering December 24, 1951) launched its prestigious run through the decades with an NBC Opera presentation of Gian-Carlo Menotti's *Amahl and the Night Visitors*, which would be restaged by Hallmark four more times in the next four years. *Amahl* remains in the history books as the first opera written especially for television. The *Hall of Fame* then became a Sunday afternoon staple with Sarah Churchill, Sir Winston's actress daughter, hosting and frequently starring in half-hour productions. After 162 presentations, *Hallmark Hall of Fame*, with George Schaefer and Albert McCleery as producers/directors, changed to a series of hour-long and sometimes 90-minute specials, initially hosted by Maurice Evans (the first seven still being telecast on Sunday afternoons).

The good folks at Hallmark, who care to send you the very best, are never loathe to boast of their production of *Hamlet*, starring Evans with Sarah Churchill as Ophelia, on the night of April 26, 1953, the first time the classic play had been staged for television. More people saw it than had seen it in the total of the 350 years since it was written. (*Hamlet*, of course, is not something produced on the tube all that often. The next major production, also by Hallmark, was in 1970 and starred Richard Chamberlain, followed by one for its Hallmark Channel in December 2000. It was directed by and starred Campbell Scott, actor son of George C. Scott and Colleen Dewhurst.) Maurice Evans also brought *Macbeth* to the *Hall of Fame* in 1960 along with Judith Anderson. It won the Emmy as program of the year and one each for the two stars and director George Schaefer. (Interestingly, Dame Judith had also won the Emmy for a previous Hallmark *Macbeth* production six years earlier, with Evans and Schaefer.)

While offering such fare as Shakespeare and Shaw on a fairly regular basis, and a bit of Gilbert and Sullivan (*The Yeomen of the Guard*, for one, with Alfred Drake and Barbara Cook) carefully programmed in, Hallmark also offered more audience-accessible productions such as *Kiss Me Kate*, with Alfred Drake and Patricia Morison recreating their Broadway roles; *Abe Lincoln in Illinois*; and even *The Fantasticks*. Hallmark's cultural oasis on NBC soon had a direct competitor in CBS's more diverse *Omnibus* beginning in 1952. They certainly were not what later FCC Chairman Newton Minow had in mind when he gave his famous "Vast Wasteland" speech in 1961 before the National Association of Broadcasters about how television was culturally devoid: "When television is good, nothing—not the theater, not the magazines or newspapers—nothing is better. But when television is bad, nothing is worse. I invite you to sit down in front of your television set when your station goes on the air and stay there without a book, magazine, newspaper, profit-and-loss sheet, or rating book to distract you—and keep your eyes glued to that set until the station signs off. I can assure you that you will observe a vast wasteland."

Through the years, *Hallmark Hall of Fame*—known by the current generation for its periodic TV movie presentations on CBS generally four to five times a year around assorted holidays to promote the company's greeting cards—has become the only drama show to be telecast under its umbrella banner on all three major networks as well as PBS (minus the commercials) at one time or another. It remains television's longest continuously running series under the same sponsor.

Omnibus would be a Sunday afternoon fixture beginning on CBS on November 9, 1952, but through the years, it also turned up on ABC (for one season) and NBC (for three). This was the first major foray of the Ford Foundation into television and was hosted distinctively by British-born Alistair Cooke for every one of its 164 programs on the three networks. The series presented an amazing potpourri of programming ideas, often in various segments in a single 90 minutes: dramas, musicals, documentaries. The initial show featured excerpts from *The Mikado* by Gilbert and Sullivan, the debut of an original television play by William Saroyan called *The Bad Man* (which happened to feature a walk-on by a little known Sidney Poitier), and several other pieces. The first season included a multipart *Mr. Lincoln*, written by James Agee, with Royal Dano as Abe, together with a new TV actress, Joanne Woodward, as Ann Rutledge, as well as plays by

Tennessee Williams and Maxwell Anderson, adaptations of Sophocles and Chekhov, performances by the Metropolitan Opera Orchestra, Shaw's *Arms and the Man* with Jean-Pierre Aumont, an original Agnes De Mille ballet, Shakespeare's *King Lear* (pared down) with Orson Welles in his dramatic TV debut *HMS Pinafore,* and so on. *Omnibus* even presented the television premiere of William Schuman's American baseball opera *The Mighty Casey* (1955), adapted from Ernest L. Thayer's poem "Casey at the Bat." It was a truly cultural grab bag, top drawer all the way.

Over the succeeding years, Alistair Cooke would introduce original short plays by John Steinbeck, James Thurber, William Inge, Tad Mosel, Sidney Carroll, S. J. Perelman, Horton Foote, and Peter Ustinov as well as Saroyan, Agee, and Anderson. Sidney Lumet would direct a production of *Antigone* and Gower Champion an adaptation of George M. Cohan's 1905 musical *Forty-Five Minutes from Broadway.* One particular *Omnibus* program in January 1957, *Lee at Gettysburg,* directed by Delbert Mann from a script by Alvin Sapinsley, with James Daly as Robert E. Lee, was judged by *Variety* to be "its finest hour-and-a-half."

Under the financing initially of the Ford Foundation, *Omnibus* with its wide-ranging, eclectic programming was what later cultural historians came to observe as the forerunner of public television that would be 15 years into the future. It was designed—under the aegis of Robert Saudek (who was installed by advertising pioneer James Webb Young, then head of the foundation's TV-Radio Workshop)—as entertainment that educated in a weekly TV magazine format.

Alistair Cooke, who, when first engaged as host, was a 44-year-old BBC correspondent (he had already been a permanent resident of the United States for many years), once noted, "Bob Saudek foresaw so many things that we now take for granted. And it wasn't a question of just saying: 'Let's have documentaries, let's have history, let's have opera, let's have original drama, let's have orchestras.' . . . He'd say, 'Well, I tell you what we do. We bring in Sam Sneed and have him show the most beautiful golf swing. . . . We bring in Gene Kelly who'd weave those Kelly motions together and show that 'Dancing Is a Man's Game' [as that show, part of the cornucopia, would be titled]. And he brought in William Saroyan, and Leonard Bernstein, and excerpts from contemporary theatre, and, well you get the idea." Ultimately, the Ford Foundation ended its funding, and an increasing amount of commercial sponsorship signaled an unfortunate dumbing down of sorts. On April 16, 1961, Cooke brought the curtain down on the final program of the season. His invitation to rejoin *Omnibus* the next fall was not to be. The ambitious series, admirable as it was, fell victim to the insatiable network thirst for bigger audiences and higher revenues, despite the series airing in the almost vacuum of Sunday afternoons.

Columbia Television Workshop (CBS, premiering January 13, 1952) aired, as one of its live productions, a version of Cervantes's *Don Quixote*, featuring Boris Karloff in the lead and Grace Kelly as Dulcinea. Sidney Lumet was the director. Another, *Rainy Day in Paradise Junction*, starred a youthful Audrey Hepburn in what might have been her American TV acting debut. Martin Ritt, the director, did a stint as actor in a *Workshop* staging of Ray Bradbury's *Rocket*. The experimental drama series ran on Sunday afternoons for just 14 weeks.

You Are There was a well-remembered 1950s CBS series, coming out of radio, that was an amalgam of news and entertainment, directed primarily by Sidney Lumet, and sometimes by Bernard Girard, and in later years, occasionally, by John Frankenheimer. Walter Cronkite hosted, and a battery of CBS news correspondents and reporters were dispatched to various places in the world at various times in history to cover important stories as they were being reenacted. *The Capture of Jesse James*, with on-the-cusp-of-stardom James Dean, had CBS cameras and microphones on the scene, and Jesse and others were interviewed during the ongoing events. In *The Assassination of Julius Caesar*, Paul Newman portrayed Brutus (wags through the years have questioned how *CBS News* knew that Caesar was about to be done in by disgruntled toga-clad Roman senators and had its correspondents, in early 1950s garb, on site, or, in a program on the sinking of the *Titanic*, how the reporters got on board in mid-ocean and how they got off as the ship was going down), and in *The Boston Tea Party*, E. G. Marshall portrayed Samuel Adams, the patriot instigator. Reporters in modern dress conducted interviews, sometimes breathless, with costumed performers on early Sunday evening between 1953 and 1957 (145 episodes). Fifty years on, Sidney Lumet, now the senior American filmmaker still working, reminisced on the *PBS American Masters* Walter Cronkite profile in 2006 that "it was a rather silly concept . . . yet it worked wonderfully well and was really a wonderful show." "What sort of a day was it?" Cronkite intoned at the close of every show. "It was a day like all other days, filled with those events which alter and illuminate our times—and you were there."

THE CAMERA'S "I"

In the summer of 1953, *First Person Playhouse*, a most unusual NBC dramatic anthology, premiered with a subjective camera technique: the main action was seen through the camera's eye, with actors talking directly to the audience. Also known as *Gulf Playhouse: 1st Person*, it was the brainchild of ever innovative Fred Coe, who brought over several of his up-and-coming directors. One was Arthur Penn, who recalls directing at least 5 of the 10 episodes that aired live each Friday night from eight thirty to nine o'clock.

"If further proof was needed that series drama can be presented with taste and distinction," *Variety* wrote of this greatly admired but short-lived series following its premiere, "then conclusive evidence was offered on NBC's *First Person* in the Fred Coe production of Horton Foote's original teleplay, *Death of the Old Man* [directed by Penn]. The half-hour dramatic series is one of television's best." Among the talents were Wally Cox, Mildred Natwick, Kim Stanley, Leo Penn, and Jessie Royce Landis. Arthur Penn remembers this as probably his first work as a director: "I'd come out of the army along with Gordon Duff, Martin Ritt, and a group of other would-be TV people, and we all gravitated to NBC. Fred Coe took us under his wing there as the top producer during the first decade of TV's golden age under programming chief Pat Weaver. My first job was as stage manager on *Colgate Comedy Hour* on the West Coast, and then assistant director on a couple of other shows. Coe, the pride of Alligator, Mississippi, saw on my rather meager résumé that I had done some writing, and he called me to New York to ask if I could tackle something new and different. And that's what *First Person Playhouse* was." (Film buffs remember the subjective camera from Robert Montgomery's unique use of it in his 1946 Philip Marlowe movie *Lady in the Lake*, in which all the screen action took place through his eyes, and the only time he was seen was when he happened to pass a mirror. A similar technique, though not as sophisticated, was used in DuMont's *The Plainclothesman*, a live, half-hour, 1949 cop series with Kenneth Lynch.)

Penn says that Coe added him to the rotation of directors, including Delbert Mann and Vincent J. Donehue as well as Fred himself and Gordon Duff, on the *Philco/Goodyear Playhouse* in 1953 as the workload increased, and then he put Robert Mulligan into the mix:

My first job in the director's chair on the series, I think, was a drama by the wonderful N. Richard Nash called *The Happy Rest* at the start of the show's sixth season. Julie Harris, E. G. Marshall, and Mildred Natwick were the stars. And not long after that one was writer David Shaw's *The Glorification of Al Toolum*, starring Walter Matthau and Betsy Palmer. And then Sumner Locke Elliott's *The King and Mrs. Candle* featuring Cyril Ritchard and Joan Greenwood.

Funny thing about that one was that 18 months later, Fred Coe had me redo *The King and Mrs. Candle* as a musical, using most of the original cast and crew, on *Producers' Showcase* because NBC, which was just getting into color, wanted something exciting and splashy to make use of the huge cameras that were used at the time in color telecasting.

This was one of the rare musicals that Penn directed. The only other one, in fact, was on Broadway: *Golden Boy,* with Sammy Davis Jr.

Revlon Mirror Theatre began on NBC as a live summer series in 1953 from New York, switching to film when transferring to CBS in the fall from Hollywood. This dramatic anthology series, aimed primarily at women (the sponsor's target audience), was produced by Donald Davis and directed mainly by Daniel Petrie, and was hosted by Robin Chandler. Joan Crawford made her television acting debut on this series, and other performers on the *Mirror Theatre* included Agnes Moorehead, Angela Lansbury, Jack Haley, Charles Bickford, and Jackie Cooper. The initial offering, in June 1953, was *The Little Wife,* with Eddie Albert and Georgann Johnson—a new version of David Shaw's playlet that had been produced several years before on *Actors Studio.*

Chrysler Medallion Theatre (CBS, 1953–1954) was produced by William Spier—one of the foremost radio producers, who created, wrote, and directed *Suspense,* which highlighted the golden age of that medium—and directed initially by Ralph Nelson and Seymour Robbie. Spier also was the initial producer on TV's *Omnibus* series with Robert Saudek. A Saturday night staple, *Medallion Theatre,* at the beginning, offered half-hour live condensations (there would be 39 of them) of Sinclair Lewis's *Arrowsmith* with Henry Fonda, O. Henry's *Jimmy Valentine* with Ronald Reagan, Victor Hugo's *Les Misérables* (here under the title *The Bishop's Candlesticks,* and featuring Victor Jory), and Oscar Wilde's *The Canterville Ghost* with Edward Everett Horton. In addition, there was a series of original dramas over two seasons with the likes of Robert Preston, Jack Lemmon, Janet Gaynor, Charlton Heston, June Havoc, Ben Gazzara, Maria Riva (acting diva of the time and who was Marlene Dietrich's daughter), and Helen Hayes—playing Harriet Beecher Stowe in *Battle Hymn,* by Norman Lessing.

CHAPTER 7

Filmed Drama and the Star Host

Schlitz *Playhouse of Stars* (CBS, premiering October 5, 1951) was a long-running, quality series of original half-hour filmed dramas (nearly 350 of them) spanning the entire decade and running 52 weeks a year. The series was hosted initially by popular former movie star Irene Dunne, who, like elegant big-screen colleagues such as Jane Wyman, Loretta Young, Barbara Stanwyck, and so on, made graceful transitions into television hosting chores in shows that bore their names in the title. The premiere *Playhouse of Stars* presentation was a drama by Thomas W. Phipps titled *Not a Chance*, which costarred Helen Hayes and David Niven and was directed by Frank Telford. Host Irene Dunne acted in probably one out of every three entries in the series through the years.

Four Star Playhouse (CBS, September 25, 1952, through 1965) was a popular half-hour series hosted alternately by David Niven, Charles Boyer, Dick Powell, and Ida Lupino (originally, Rosalind Russell and Joel McCrea were to have been in the mix, but they dropped out). Powell appeared frequently as nightclub owner Willie Dante, a character that he would use as a pilot to the 1960–1961 series *Dante* that would star Lupino's husband, Howard Duff. The show's format wavered between comedy and drama, all originals (initially it alternated with *Amos 'n' Andy* on Thursday nights and then became a weekly show), and featured a roster of Hollywood pals of the four founding *Four Star* actors like Ronald Colman, Joan Fontaine, Merle Oberon, and others in their television acting debuts. Each of the four hosts starred alternately in one show a month. Robert Florey was the most frequent director, along with Roy Kellino; among the others directing on an occasional basis were Robert Aldrich, Blake Edwards (his earliest TV work before going on to create and direct *Peter Gunn* and *Mr. Lucky*), James Neilson, and William Asher.

General Electric Theatre (hosted after the first season by Ronald Reagan, who occasionally acted) was another popular anthology drama series on CBS for 11 seasons beginning in 1953. Basically filmed in Hollywood, it was long a half-hour Sunday night staple, most notable for, among other things, the number of major film stars who made their TV acting debuts, including Bette Davis, Alan Ladd, Jimmy Stewart, Fred MacMurray, Tony Curtis, and Fred Astaire. James Dean costarred with Natalie Wood (young lovers in *Rebel without a Cause*) in a late 1954 adaptation of Sherwood Anderson's play *I Am a Fool*. Lou Costello (post Bud Abbott) was the dramatic star in *Blaze of Glory* in 1958, shortly before his death, and Bud Abbott did his only dramatic acting in a 1961 episode called *The Joke's on Me*. Harpo and Chico Marx starred together in *The Incredible Jewel Robbery*, with Groucho turning up in a cameo. It would be the brothers' last time all together as performers. Veteran director John Ford, in 1955, did a rare bit of TV helming, calling the shots on a sports story by his frequent writing collaborator, Frank Nugent. It was called *Rookie of the Year* and starred not only John Wayne, but also other Ford favorites: Ward Bond, Patrick Wayne, and Vera Miles.

Series host Ronald Reagan, as an occasional performer, acted with wife Nancy in several episodes: in *The Long Way 'Round* (1954); in the ironically titled *A Turkey for the President* (1958), with both playing Native Americans; and in *Money for the Minister* (1961). And on Christmas night 1960, they also hosted, with daughter Patty and son Ronald, the *General Electric* drama *The Other Wise Man*, a Yuletide tale about the fourth Magus, absent from the Nativity. Reagan, in fact, acted in 33 episodes of the anthology series, including a comedy Western takeoff on Tolstoy, *War and Peace on the Range*.

After being the distinctive and genial *General Electric* spokesman on television until 1962 and for the organization itself, Ronald Reagan was recruited by the Borax Company to take over hosting chores in cowboy hat and chaps for (and to occasionally act in) *Death Valley Days*. That series was a decades long anthology Western that had started in radio in 1930 and moved over to television in 1952. When the program began on TV, for Gene Autry's Flying A Productions, approximately two dozen of its shows a year were filmed on location in and around Death Valley, each an entity unto itself with one or more familiar actors. The original host was Stanley Andrews as the Old Ranger. Reagan succeeded him for several years in the 1960s until turning his attention to state and national politics, becoming, of course, governor of California for two terms, and then president for two more. Ex-movie matinee idol Robert Taylor took the Conestoga reins and cowboy hat from Reagan, and then Dale Robertson took over from him, until the series reached the end of the trail in 1972. Only a few other Western dramas on TV were anthologies: Dick Powell's *Zane Grey Theatre*, Rod Serling's *The Loner*, and *Wagon Train* among them (despite having a basic recurring cast headed first by Ward Bond and, when he died, by John McIntire). The last named show, in black and white initially and then in color, represented the apex of Western drama anthologies, a staple on NBC from 1957 to 1962, and then on ABC from 1962 to 1965. There were 284 episodes, each with a name guest star.

The Loretta Young Show (NBC, 1953–1961) found the beautiful former movie star sweeping elegantly clothed and coiffed through a doorway into a living room set every Sunday night at 10 to introduce a new television play (and even starring in roughly one out of every two). Guest starring on her show in assorted dramas were the likes of Eddie Albert, Elizabeth Montgomery, Richard Carlson, Don DeFore, Jean-Pierre Aumont, Charles Bronson, Merle Oberon, Hugh O'Brian, John Newland (her frequent costar and sometimes director of the series), Ricardo Montalban (her brother-in-law), and others. When the series premiered in September 1953, it was titled *Letter to Loretta*, with the star reading a letter supposedly written to her by her multitude of fans from her days on the big screen, which the writers crafted into a 22-minute drama. This device became cumbersome, however, and after the show's second season, the format was changed. On occasion, a guest hostess would come aboard to give Loretta a night off (Rosalind Russell, Irene Dunne, Barbara Stanwyck, and other of her big-screen contemporaries). When her anthology show left the air in 1961, she moved into a single-season CBS sitcom *The New Loretta Young Show* and then went into retirement—letting future generations of comics send up her extravagantly sweeping entrances. She came back to television toward the end of her life in two made-for-TV movies, looking as stunning as she had when making her fabulous opening scene appearances.

The United States Steel Hour, initially under the title *The Theatre Guild on the Air*, began a 10-year biweekly run in 1953, first on ABC on Tuesday nights, then, after its first two years (alternating with the *Motorola Television Hour*), on CBS on Wednesdays at 10:00. There it shared a time slot with *The Twentieth Century-Fox Hour* and *Armstrong Circle Theatre*. It was on *The United States Steel Hour*, a live show originating from New York, and because of its association with the Theatre Guild, that a number of Broadway stars again were brought to television. On the premiere show, writer David Davidson's war story *P.O.W.* was enacted by a stellar cast including Richard Kiley, Gary Merrill, Brian Keith, Phyllis Kirk, and Sally Forrest. Alex Segal, one of the primary directors on the series while on ABC, helmed. Other presentations included Tallulah Bankhead in Ibsen's *Hedda Gabler,* Rex Harrison and Lilli Palmer (then husband and wife) in *The Man in Possession,* Andy Griffith (in his TV debut) in *No Time for Sergeant*—a role he would later repeat on Broadway and then in the 1958 film *The Last Notch,* by writer Frank Gilroy, with Richard Jaeckel (Glenn Ford would later star in the film adaptation, retitled *The Fastest Gun Alive*)—and Rod Serling's Korean War set play *The Rack* (Paul Newman had the lead in the later film version). When the show moved to CBS, it relied less on Broadway performers. On the first CBS production, Wally Cox and Betsy Palmer starred in *The Meanest Man in the World,* directed by Sidney Lumet. Julie Harris later starred (for director Daniel Petrie) in James Costigan's *A Wind from the South,* about an Irish country girl's first love. Lumet also directed *Incident in an Alley,* another Rod Serling drama, starring Farley Granger.

Another memorable *Steel Hour* production was the 1961 drama *The Two Worlds of Charlie Gordon,* directed by Fielder Cook. Cliff Robertson played the pivotal lead as a mentally challenged young man who is given an experimental drug that had been successful on lab rats and soon becomes a genius—only to retrogress as the drugs wear off. Robertson won an Emmy nomination for his performance, and when he later starred in the film version, now titled *Charly,* he won the Academy Award as best actor. Based on Daniel Keyes's 1959 short story *Flowers for Algernon* (the name of the lucky lab rat), about the possibility of increasing human intelligence artificially, it later was adapted as a stage play under that title, then as a musical on London's West End, with Michael Crawford and a score by David Rogers and Charles Strouse. Ultimately, it played on Broadway in 1980 as *Charlie and Algernon* but had a short life (17 performances). The circle was complete when it came back as a movie made for television in 2000, with Matthew Modine in the lead.

Producers' Showcase (NBC, premiering October 18, 1954), a prestigious, live, 90-minute anthology, aired once a month for three seasons and staged lavish adaptations of Broadway dramas and musicals, many produced by Fred Coe. Among the wide array of material were Audrey Hepburn starring in *Mayerling* with husband Mel Ferrer, produced and directed by Anatole Litvak, and a version of Robert Sherwood's *The Petrified Forest,* which marked Humphrey Bogart's only TV acting, opposite Lauren Bacall and Henry Fonda.

Bogart, in effect, became a rarity as a major star, having played the role of Duke Mantee on Broadway, in films, on radio, and on television. The memorable Mary Martin version of *Peter Pan* was staged twice by Jerome Robbins, in 1955 and again about a year later. Also part of the prestigious series were the ballets *Sleeping Beauty* and *Cinderella*, danced by Margot Fonteyn and Michael Soames. A similar monthly show, *The Best of Broadway*, which premiered four weeks earlier on CBS, also restaged Broadway classics with name casts, including Ethel Merman repeating her original role in Cole Porter's *Panama Hattie*, but the series had only nine productions.

The Elgin TV Hour (ABC, 1954–1955) was telecast live from New York, alternating on Tuesday nights with *The United States Steel Hour* and featuring such talent as Gertrude Berg, Ralph Bellamy, Ruth Hussey, Franchot Tone, Polly Bergen, and John Forsythe. John Cassavetes starred as a young hood in arguably the most famous of the dramas on the series, Reginald Rose's *Crime in the Streets*, directed by Sidney Lumet.

A TV ROSE BY ANY NAME

New Yorker Reginald Rose, it has been acknowledged, was one of the outstanding television playwrights to emerge from the golden age. He had been a marine officer during World War II who, returning home, landed a job as an ad agency copywriter. One of his earliest teleplays was *The Bus to Nowhere*, broadcast in 1951 on CBS's sci-fi anthology *Out There*. (Kim Stanley starred in it as one of six disparate people who find themselves stranded in the Nevada desert.) Then he began writing prolifically for *Studio One*, turning out such acclaimed, socially aware dramas as *Thunder on Sycamore Street* (an ex-con, played by Kenneth Utt, moves with his family to an upscale neighborhood to make a new beginning, but when his past is uncovered, the community organizes to drive him away). Rose wrote the family to be black—not necessarily a former convict attempting to go straight—but was pressured by the suits at *Studio One*, fearful of offending programmers in the South, who were edgy about having a black actor in a leading role on the tube (this was not long before Sidney Poitier broke the mold in *A Man Is Ten Feet Tall* on *Philco*). The 1954–1955 season has come to be known in TV lore as the "Reginald Rose season" on *Studio One*, where nine of his television plays were produced.

Rose's most memorable work was arguably his 1954 *Studio One* drama *12 Angry Men*, confining the cast (headed by Robert Cummings) to a claustrophobic jury room on a stifling summer day while deliberating a murder case—with one of them holding out for acquittal and gradually winning the others over. Rose won the Emmy for that script (beating out Paddy Chayefsky and *Marty*). The screen adaptations of Henry Fonda's *12 Angry Men* (Lumet's film directing debut) and *Marty* (Delbert Mann's) marked the breakthrough of the television drama into feature films. Rose's *Crime in the Streets* and *Dino*, each dealing with juvenile delinquency, also were turned into films, both starring Sal Mineo, with John Cassavetes repeating his TV role in the former. Another *Studio One* drama written by Rose was *The Defender*, which aired in 1957 and became the pilot for the later series with the final *s* added. Rose won Emmys in 1962 and 1963 for writing episodes of *The Defenders*.

Among the dramas written by Rose for *Goodyear Playhouse* was 1955's *The Expendable House*, which costarred Cassavetes and his wife, Gena Rowlands. For *The Alcoa Hour* in 1956, he wrote the controversial *Tragedy in a Temporary Town*, which Lumet directed. It dramatized mob violence in a migrant village. Lloyd Bridges and Jack Warden starred. Rose recalled that "Bridges, at one point, came forth with a string of invectives [which may or may not have been written into the script], and the NBC switchboards lit up. It made headlines." The day after *Tragedy* aired, the critic for the *New York Times* referred to it as "one of the more violently melodramatic climaxes in the annals of television drama."

Rose's *Incredible World of Horace Ford*, written for *Studio One* in 1955, later was restaged for Rod Serling's *The Twilight Zone* in 1963. Art Carney, in the original, played a toy designer who spends hours reminiscing about his idyllic childhood but has a bitter taste of reality when he gets a chance to go back to those years.

For *Playhouse 90*, Rose penned three shows in 1959 and 1960, notably *A Quiet Game of Cards*, in which five high-stakes poker players decide to go for even higher stakes. *Black Monday*, a *Play of the Week* drama he did in 1961, focused on three families—two white, one black—on the first day their high school's student body is integrated. It was, he told the *New York Times* at the time, "the most complex subject I ever tried to handle. The thing I've tried to do is explore the points of view of all kinds of people—moderates, racists, and liberals." Ruby Dee gave a moving performance as the mother of the black student, pressured to send him to school. Ivan Dixon, Juano Hernandez, Pat Hingle, Marc Connelly, Nancy Coleman, and Robert Redford were in the cast. An elaborate television production (originally, it was written for the stage), it was *Play of the Week*'s first original drama after all the adaptations since it began airing three years earlier, and it had about 50 players and multiple settings. Ralph Nelson directed, and David Susskind and Worthington Miner were involved as producers. "An original drama on a contemporary theme is so increasingly rare of television," critic Jack Gould wrote after its airing, "that *Play of the Week* is entitled to a suitable palm for keeping the medium's front door ajar."

Just prior to *Black Monday* (for which Rose reportedly received $2,000 plus a percentage), his top-notch 1960 docudrama *The Sacco-Vanzetti Story* aired on NBC's *Sunday Showcase* as a critically acclaimed two-parter directed by Lumet. Martin Balsam and Steven Hill played the two ill-fated immigrants who lacked the command of the English language and were executed during the 1920s following a landmark (some maintain political) trial in Massachusetts for having been participants in a robbery that ended in a death. The drama was Emmy nominated as outstanding program in the 1960–1961 season, and Rose received a nomination for outstanding writing in drama (he lost that year to Serling).

Sometime before his death in 2000, Reginald Rose told this author (a native of the area where eight decades later the Sacco-Vanzetti case remains part of local history): "I became interested in the case as a miscarriage of justice while writing the screenplay to *12 Angry Men*, and the more research I had done into the extensively documented event from so many years back, the more contentious I found it to be. There was a streak of mob violence involved—the kind many television historians seemed to have found in my dramas of the time—but perhaps that is what I found to be profound with me. It's in *Tragedy in a Temporary Town*, it's in *The Cruel Day* that I wrote for *Playhouse 90*, it's in *Thunder on Sycamore Street*, it's in *Black Monday* that I did for David Susskind on *Play of the Week*. And I think it's even in the TV movie *Escape from Sobibor*, where I wrote about one of the great mass Nazi death camp breakouts." (Rose got another Emmy nomination for that teleplay.) Rose and Lumet seemed to be simpatico in their social consciousness. They worked together at least six times, beginning with Rose's *Operation Nightmare* on *Danger* in 1953.

In later years, Reginald Rose adapted James T. Farrell's onetime salacious 1930s novel *Studs Lonigan* to a three-part miniseries in 1979 and created and wrote some episodes of the British-made *The Zoo Gang*. Additionally, he wrote the moving marital dramas *Dear Friends* for *CBS Playhouse* in 1967 (still another Emmy nomination) and *The Rules of Marriage*, a 1982 made-for-TV movie. His last works, for cable television, were the 1997 slightly expanded update of his *12 Angry Men* (a woman judge, played by Mary McDonnell, was added to the original all-male mix) and one of the three new TV movies based on *The Defenders*, also the same year. The original *Studio One* version of *12 Angry Men*, incidentally, was just 52 minutes long, which the movie expanded to 90 minutes. Rose added 10 minutes of character for the new cable TV production of it, which included Jack Lemmon and George C. Scott together with, among others, James Gandolfini, long before morphing into Tony Soprano, on the jury.

The 2002 obituary on Rose in the *Los Angeles Times* had the following to say:

> He began his career writing advertising copy and publicity with little success. But then he encountered the new medium of television when it was attempting to put plays into people's living rooms. "They had all these anthologies and they were desperate for scripts, absolutely desperate. . . . " he told *The Times* in 1982. "I had been trying to sell short stories, novels and God knows what else, and I never was able to sell anything. The first time I wrote a TV script I sold it, and when I sold that first one they said, 'More, more, more!' and I haven't stopped since.
>
> "In those years from 1953 to 1960, the writer was the star of the show. It was never to happen again."

Climax! (CBS, 1954–1958), cohosted by B-list actor William Lundigan and singer Mary Costa, started as live drama show, then switched to film. And being a live show, things happen, some of which became the source of urban legends. One has been verified by the *New York Times* as well as the *Chicago Tribune*, whose TV critics could hardly believe what they were seeing in the very first *Climax!* Dick Powell starred on the premiere as Philip Marlowe in *The Long Goodbye,* and somewhere in the script, character actor Tristram Coffin, playing a dead body with a blanket drawn over him, got up from the floor and walked out of the shot in full camera range. Powell, the cool pro, just kept on doing what he was doing; he and the other actors just continued on as if nothing had happened. These were the boo-boos of television in the glory days, when it was live and things like these were to be cherished. Another misfired incident seen live by TV viewers was recounted by *Variety* in its review of the later, John Frankenheimer–directed episode *Figures in Clay:* "It's unfortunate that live video hasn't solved all of its technical problems, as witness the key story point of this teleplay. A dangerous religious fanatic (Henry Hull) points a pistol at the camera and pulls the trigger, supposedly to gun down Lloyd Bridges. Instead of a terrifying roar, the revolver sputters a couple of times, the sparks ludicrously, effectively killing the point instead of the actor."

Other than Powell playing Raymond Chandler's famed private eye—for the second time: he was Marlowe in the 1944 movie *Murder My Sweet*—there was, on *Climax!,* Barry Nelson portraying Ian Fleming's 007, a decade before the James Bond franchise had been gobbled up for the big screen by Cubby

Broccoli. In a variation of *Casino Royale*, Nelson was not James Bond, suave British agent, but shambling Jimmy Bond of the CIA. The villain of the piece was played by Peter Lorre. *Climax!* was to offer productions of *Sorry Wrong Number* with Shelley Winters; *Dr. Jekyll and Mr. Hyde*, with an adaptation of Robert Louis Stevenson by writer Gore Vidal, and starring Michael Rennie in the lead(s); and Rory Calhoun (in Kirk Douglas's screen role) in *Champion*, which Rod Serling adapted from Ring Lardner's short story. Comedian Red Skelton had a more or less serious acting role in *Public Pigeon #1*; Guy Madison and Diana Lynn starred in Hemingway's *A Farewell to Arms* (another Gore Vidal adaptation), and Tab Hunter portrayed troubled 1950s Red Sox star Jimmy Piersall in *Fear Strikes Out*. *Climax!* shared a Thursday night time slot with the once-a-month *Shower of Stars*, and many of the dramas were directed by John Frankenheimer.

Front Row Center (CBS summer series 1955), produced and directed by Fletcher Markle, offered live one-hour adaptations of Broadway plays and notable literary works, from *Dinner at Eight* and *The Barretts of Wimpole Street* to *Dark Victory* and *Tender Is the Night*. It continued during the 1955–1956 season with original works such as Ernest Kinoy's *Strange Suspicion* with James Daly and Betsy Palmer. A summer replacement for *The United States Steel Hour*, this show was not to be confused with an earlier one on DuMont with the same title: a musical variety series during the 1949–1950 season.

Also during the 1955–1956 season was NBC's dramatic anthology *Playwrights '56*, focusing on works by such writers as Hemingway and Faulkner and original dramas by Sumner Locke Elliott, Gore Vidal, Horton Foote, J. P. Miller, Tad Mosel, and David Swift. Paul Newman played the lead in A. E. Hotchner's adaptation of Hemingway's short story "The Battler" and later reprised the character on the big screen and on stage. Edmond O'Brien starred in Arnold Schulman's *The Heart's a Forgotten Hotel*, which later was reworked as the short-lived Broadway play with Paul Douglas and the Sinatra movie *A Hole in the Head*.

Ford Star Jubilee (CBS) offered as one of its acclaimed, periodic, 90-minute productions *The Caine Mutiny Court-Martial*, adapted for television by author Herman Wouk from his own Pulitzer Prize novel and produced by Charles Laughton and Paul Gregory and directed by Franklin Schaffner. Another was *The Twentieth Century*, adapted from the 1932 Ben Hecht/Charles MacArthur play, costarring Orson Welles and Betty Grable. Others featured musical revues and variety specials. A highlight of these was a filmed musical version of Maxwell Anderson's *High Tor* with Bing Crosby and, in her TV debut, 20-year-old Julie Andrews. There were 15 entries between October 1955 (including a 90-minute Judy Garland special in color, produced by her husband, Sid Luft) and a Sonja Henie ice-skating special just before Christmas 1956.

The Alcoa Hour (NBC, 1955–1957) alternated with *Philco Television Playhouse* and then *Goodyear Theatre* as the first of several drama series sponsored by the aluminum company. It aired on generally every other or every third Sunday night from New York, mostly with dramas and stars of the Broadway community like Joanne Woodward and Walter Matthau. It was assumed that Broadway actors were generally available and eager to perform since Sunday nights are dark in theaters on the Great White Way and the talent was at liberty. There would be an occasional original musical on the series, most notably a version of *A Christmas Carol* (here called *The Stingiest Man in Town*) with a singing Basil Rathbone and Vic Damone. Kirk Browning also staged a new production of *Amahl and the Night Visitors*. An adaptation of the Maxwell Anderson play and Bogart/Bacall movie *Key Largo* was directed by Alex Segal and starred Broadwayites Alfred Drake and Anne Bancroft. Other directors on *Alcoa* included Robert Mulligan, Sidney Lumet, Martin Ritt, and Daniel Petrie.

CHAPTER 8

Television Gets Hitch'd

Alfred Hitchcock Presents premiered on CBS in 1955 and ran for five seasons in a half-hour format before switching over to NBC for two, and then returning to CBS for two more as an hour-long show, rechristened The Alfred Hitchcock Hour. Having been directing films on the big screen for three decades, Hitchcock brought a known style, quantity, and quality to television in a very recognizable form: himself. Introducing each of his shows beginning with the Hitchcock silhouette, he offered a few sardonic comments at the opening and end. Just by being Hitchcock, he was able to bring name actors to his series, and a number of the shows he directed himself. Ron Simon, curator of the Museum of Television and Radio (MTR) in New York, makes the case that "anthology drama certainly changed when Hitchcock created his own series, and he obviously gave it a Hollywood feel, bringing in his own brand name to the series and began to put the live programs onto film. He decided he was going to do a 30-minute show in three days; he was able to do that and create a whole production line. You could make the argument that it was Hitchcock that really also helped kill the idea of live television."

Among others, Hitchcock directed two of the most famous episodes of the series. One of these was Breakdown, with one of his 1940s' leading men, Joseph Cotten. (The tale had been dramatized earlier as Dead Ernest on Suspense and was popularized on the radio version of that series years before. It was with Breakdown that Hitchcock made his TV directing debut, although it was not shown until about a dozen episodes into the series.) A cold businessman, critically injured in an auto accident, is paralyzed—except for his pinkie finger, which happens to be under him when he is discovered and taken to the morgue, thought to be dead. He tries to shout out from his inner being that he is alive and finally is able to breathe on the morgue attendant's glasses as he is about to be autopsied, and then sheds a tear. And there was the classic *Lamb to the Slaughter*, a Roald Dahl tale in which Barbara Bel Geddes beats her overbearing husband to death in their kitchen with a frozen leg of lamb and cooks it into a meal and feeds the evidence to the investigating detective.

Hitch, though, was not the only director on the series; he helmed 20 of the 358 half-hour and later hour-long episodes in the program bearing his imprint and produced by his Shamus Productions. Many tales were directed by his associate Robert Stevens, and others by James Neilson, former actors Paul Henreid and Ida Lupino, et al. Among the performers making appearances were Hitchcock favorite Vera Miles, Steve McQueen, Art Carney, Robert Alda, Ralph Meeker, Jessica Tandy, Vincent Price, William Shatner, and Claude Rains.

Aside from Dahl, noted writers whose works turned up on *Alfred Hitchcock Presents* and *The Alfred Hitchcock Hour* were Cornell Woolrich, H. G. Wells, Ray Bradbury, "Ellery Queen," Francis Cockrell, Stirling Silliphant, and others. And among the superior teleplays was a three-parter (on three consecutive weeks) titled *I Killed the Count*, in which there was an overabundance of suspects (Hitchcock favorite John Williams starred—the very proper British actor, not the American composer/conductor or the classical guitarist, both also having made careers with the same name.) Alfred Hitchcock also was induced to direct one episode each on two other drama series: *Suspicion* in 1957 and *Ford Startime* in 1960.

MTR curator Ron Simon observed, in an interview for this book,

It was only after the first years of anthology drama that the whole idea of original dramas came in. I've seen letters that said we've been using all of the novels, we've seen all of Shakespeare; we've got to come up with new ways to create drama. That allowed people like Paddy Chayefsky and Gore Vidal to get to write original teleplays. That created the original golden age of television, these original dramas for TV. In many ways, the Hitchcock series certainly defined the possibility of television drama. He created a mood, he created an environment, and people knew what to expect.

Unlike the *Kraft Television Theatre* or *Studio One*, where the dramas were very different in different moods, different genres each and every week, it was not predictable, with Hitchcock you knew it would be predictable because you knew there was going to be some type of twist, there was going to be suspense, it would be Hitchcockian in a way. He sort of changed that direction, leading to Serling's *Twilight Zone*. In many ways, *[Twilight Zone]* became the model of what the anthology drama would be, mystery, suspense, or science fiction, a dark side. It became the dominant trend in anthology drama. That and Boris Karloff's *Thriller* sort of restricted the anthology drama. Instead of being about anything else, it had to be in that genre each week. . . .

In talking "Hitch" with the author, Simon mused:

In many ways, the Hitchcock series certainly redefined the possibility of television drama (after the initial rush of the live anthology dramas from New York).

Obviously, there are other anthology dramas throughout the 1950s. Loretta Young kind of defined the woman's picture for the anthology drama. But the only type that lingered on over the decades is this Hitchcock/Rod Serling-type mystery-suspense format.

The experimental *CBS Television Workshop* (1960), also sort of ran irregularly, broadcast at noon on Sundays on the East Coast, with New York stars such as Maureen Stapleton, Uta Hagen, Ben Piazza. *Workshop* was brash enough to present an episode entitled *Afterthought,* described as "a play without actors or dialogue." [This show was not to be confused with an earlier series of the same title from the previous decade.] Even in 1967–1968, NBC had a show called *Experiment in Television*—it wasn't prime time—and ABC had their *Stage '67,* which had some dramas, especially Truman Capote's wonderful *A Christmas Memory,* which he narrated, and starring Geraldine Page, both winning Emmys, but also had some music, like Stephen Sondheim's original, now classic *Evening Primrose,* with Anthony Perkins, written for television by James Goldman and directed by Paul Bogart.

Basically, now anthologies go against the grain of every television mandate because with them you don't know what's on next. The only type of anthology are these male genres of mystery and suspense—the HBO series *Tales from the Crypt* and *The Hitchhiker,* everything based on Stephen King or Ray Bradbury, again suspense writers in *The Twilight Zone* tradition.

Many years later, the long-departed Hitchcock was morphed electronically into, first, a made-for-TV movie in 1985 that redid four of his best-remembered stories, and then a returning version of the popular series on NBC during the 1985–1986 season. Again, in 1987–1988, it was resurrected with new episodes (and old, colorized Hitchcock introductions) on the USA Network on cable.

Lesser remembered drama anthologies of the 1950s included *Douglas Fairbanks Jr. Presents the Rheingold Theatre* (1952–1957), a syndicated series filmed in England with lesser known, basically British actors. The debonair host acted in several episodes, and Buster Keaton made one of his first dramatic appearances in a teleplay called *The Awakening*, while Christopher Lee made one of his earliest ones for the American viewer in *Destination Milan*. Abby Mann and Lawrence Marcus, among others, wrote for this series, which had 119 entries.

Ben Hecht's Tales of the City (CBS, 1953) was a summer replacement for *Four Star Playhouse* on Thursday nights, a half-hour filmed anthology drama series with writer Hecht (though not seen on screen, just a narration of introduction and afterword) hosting a batch of short stories written by him and directed by Robert Stevens. Officially, it was called *Willys Theatre Presenting Ben Hecht's Tales of the City*, Willys being a popular, low-priced automobile of the time.

Damon Runyon Theatre was a weekly half-hour filmed anthology based on Runyon short stories of 1920s–1930s New York. Hosted by Donald Woods, it aired on CBS on Saturday nights at 10:30 during the 1955–1958 seasons, and *The O. Henry Playhouse* (syndicated in 1957, with 18 episodes) featured Thomas Mitchell hosting in the guise of O. Henry (nom de plume of William Sidney Porter, who had died back in 1910). Ernest Borgnine starred as an Old West sheriff in the show's premiere episode, a half-hour adaptation of O. Henry's *The Reformation of Calliope*. Other fading movie stars hosted brief half-hour drama series with their names in the title: *George Sanders Mystery Theatre* (NBC, summer 1957) and, filmed in Europe, *Errol Flynn Theatre* (syndicated in 1957, with Flynn acting in some of the playlets).

Suspicion (NBC, 1957–1958) was a one-season (40-episode) filmed mystery/suspense anthology show, inspired, of course, by the success of *Alfred Hitchcock Presents*, which kicked off with an episode called *Four O'Clock*, directed by Hitchcock and starring E. G. Marshall and Nancy Kelly. Initially, the series was hosted by former movie star Dennis O'Keefe, and then by veteran actor Walter Abel. Among the directors on *Suspicion*, which came from Hitchcock's production company, were Arthur Hiller, John Brahm, Ray Milland, and veteran Lewis Milestone.

Among the sponsors whose faith in quality drama in television continued strong was the Aluminum Company of America: Alcoa. They put their corporate name into the titles of several series, beginning with the live anthology *The Alcoa Hour*, which alternated on Sunday nights with *Goodyear Theatre* from 1955 to 1957. With a switch in October 1958 to Monday nights on NBC in a half-hour filmed format, it became *Alcoa Theatre*, continuing to alternate with *Goodyear*. (Sometimes this combination drama series was called *A Turn of Fate*.) For a while, it featured stars/hosts David Niven, Robert Ryan, Jane Powell, Jack Lemmon, and Charles Boyer. Niven and Boyer had been part of the rotating group of hosts/players in

Four Star Playhouse (*Four Star* actually produced *Alcoa Theatre*). That format was dropped after the first of three seasons. Many of the *Alcoa* productions would be in the dramatic vein mixed in with occasional light comedies, directed by such talent as Arthur Hiller, Ray Milland, Paul Henreid, Robert Ellis Miller, Boris Sagal, David Greene, and Don Taylor.

Author Arthur Hailey's taut, white-knuckles *Flight into Danger,* an hour-long story of peril in the air, was reviewed by the *New York Times*'s Jack Gould as "a superb thriller, one of the finest ever done on live television." It later was made into the feature film *Zero Hour!* with Dana Andrews.

One of the many top-drawer writers on *The Alcoa Hour* was Ernest Kinoy, who has had a distinguished career in the medium, journeying over from radio, where he began his craft after coming out of World War II. Kinoy wrote for *The Goldbergs,* on radio and early television, and scripts for *Schlitz Playhouse of Stars* and others. For *Alcoa* in 1956, he wrote *The Confidence Man* for his friends Hume Cronyn and Jessica Tandy. He had been a writer on their sitcom, *The Marriage,* both on radio and television. Later, he drew on his own experience, a somewhat traumatic one, for a lighthearted play called *Weekend in Vermont.* It told how he was invited to his future wife's parents' New England home: "I remember, I went to see Phil Barry [show producer Philip Barry Jr., son of the noted playwright of the 1920s and 1930s] with this idea about something autobiographical. Tony Randall played me and Patricia Barry [Phil's wife] played my fiancée. The in-laws were that wonderful stage couple Howard Lindsay and Dorothy Stickney. Anyway, I put in some bits from my life as I remembered them, and in one scene, there was a recipe being described, and later, when my mother-in-law saw the show, she told me I got the whole thing wrong. Not the show, but the recipe."

Kinoy also recalled another equally traumatic play, this one much darker: "I used an event in my life earlier on a *Studio One* some months before the one on *Alcoa*—something based on my life experiences—called *Walk Down the Hill.* As you know, I was a GI in World War II, and I became a German POW. This one told about a Jewish soldier (me, played by actor William Smithers) who questions his heritage when he finds himself in a German prison camp. As I remember it, the Germans tried to separate the Jewish prisoners from the others, and just before that, as I was about to be captured, I had thrown away my dog tags that had a J for *Jewish* on them. I registered as a Protestant. But I agonized about the decision and finally turned myself in as a Jew and walked down the hill toward where the special barracks where the Jews were."

About his views of writing for TV, he related, "How it worked, you went in to see the producer with a story pitch. 'I'm thinking of a show like this,' and then you give them a spiel and they told me to get them an outline. You got a contract, you wrote an outline, and they decided whether to go forward. You did the first draft and you did the second one, and then—at least during the live days—you sat with it during the production. A lot of those filmed shows you weren't there all the time, unless you developed a relationship with the director." What Kinoy gave them, apparently, made him one of the major talents from the golden age of television, and he wrote dozens of notable scripts, mainly for producer Herb Brodkin, for *Studio One, Philco/Goodyear, The United States Steel Hour, Suspicion, Playhouse 90*, and *Bob Hope Presents the Chrysler Theatre*. Many dealt with social issues, primarily the famous episode of *The Defenders* called "Blacklist," which starred Jack Klugman and won an Emmy for both of them—for acting and writing. (Klugman portrayed a blacklisted actor making his living in a shoe store, and E. G. Marshall and Robert Reed take up his cause.)

Brodkin always has been known for his association with socially conscious themes. Kinoy comments,

> Now Herb Brodkin, a fascinating guy, in reality was not particularly a left wing kind of fellow—he was right down the middle. . . . But when it came to the issues of his writers and producers who knew what the hell he wanted to do, he took no nonsense from anybody. He was absolutely firm, and he argued constantly with the networks and almost always won. I know once or twice I heard of them [the networks] throwing some actors out—because of blacklisting—but I seem to know he cast the same actors that he really wanted in show after show. He was very tough. On *The Defenders*, I discussed the story I was writing with Herb and his producing partner Buzz Berger. We did a lot of things on public issues, serious issues, and one of the things about that series was that the issue of the story was much more important than the characters. We decided not to make the story about someone who was a star but who was an ordinary working actor—on the edge—and when he was blacklisted, he was done.
>
> Well, I had suggested someone safe [i.e., not blacklisted] to play on the show and was very miffed when Brodkin informed me that the network said they'd hired someone else—who actually had been blacklisted! Then, when they learned of it, they tried to fire the actor, and Brodkin, in high dudgeon, stormed in and said, "Look, you gave him a contract, you hired him. I'm using him. You'll have to end up paying him, and paying for the show to be done. Then it's up to you to air it or not." He stuck it to them.

Kinoy wrote several other *Defenders* episodes and others for such 1960s series as *The Untouchables, Naked City, Burke's Law, Route 66, The Nurses*, and *For the People*. For *Hallmark Hall of Fame*, he wrote the 1968 version of *Pinocchio* for Peter Noone of Herman's Hermits and Burl Ives. Among his later TV movies were *The Story of Jacob and Joseph* and *The Story of David,* a pair of two-part biblical tales, plus the first two episodes of *Roots* (with William Blinn) and five more for *Roots: The Next Generations,* winning his second Emmy. He also wrote *Victory at Entebbe*—the live-on-tape version that got on the air ahead of the competing *Raid on Entebbe* in 1976, the earlier movie of Edward R. Murrow, beating George Clooney by two decades, the controversial TV film about Chernobyl in 1991. Kinoy also had an interest in Lincoln, with a 1975 *Hallmark Hall of Fame* adaptation of *The Rivalry,* Norman Corwin's play about the 1858 Lincoln–Douglas debates (Arthur Hill and Charles Durning starred); an adaptation of Gore Vidal's *Lincoln;* and another Lincoln movie, *Tad,* six years later. His script to *Skokie* in 1981, which had Danny Kaye in a rare serious role; a PBS adaptation of Isaac Bashevis Singer's *The Cafeteria;* and the segment of the Barbra Streisand–produced *Rescuers: Stories of Courage* in the late 1990s were very close to Kinoy and his Jewish heritage, as were the biblical plays and the Entebbe movie.

Alcoa Presents (ABC, 1959–1961, a.k.a. *One Step Beyond*) offered an intriguing occult half-hour filmed anthology that began midseason. Created, hosted, and directed by urbane actor John Newland, this cult series predated Serling's *The Twilight Zone* by eight months. Newland prepared the viewer in the same way each week: "What you are about to see is a matter of human record. Explain it, we cannot. Disprove it, we cannot. We simply invite you to explore with us the amazing world of the unknown, to take that one step beyond." Its format was composed of allegedly real stories of hauntings, strange creatures, and supernatural phenomena and the mystical, with dramatic recreations of them for each new episode. It was quite economical in its storytelling on a seemingly minuscule budget, but it attracted such acting talent over its three original seasons (96 episodes) as, on the American side, Elizabeth Montgomery, Robert Blake, Warren Beatty, Joan Fontaine, and Charles Bronson, and, on the British side, Christopher Lee, Donald Pleasance, Patrick Macnee, and Michael Crawford. Among the more notable shows produced on *One Step Beyond* were *The Peter Hukos Story* (in two parts), starring Albert Salmi as the famed psychic reader; *Night of April 14th,* with Macnee as a man with premonitions of the *Titanic* sinking; and *Earthquake,* featuring David Opatoshu as a turn-of-the-century hotel worker who foresaw the 1906 San Francisco earthquake. In 1978, Newland revived the idea with *The Next Step Beyond,* for USA Cable, but it never recaptured the old (black) magic. Newland, who also directed occasionally for Hitchcock's TV series *The Sixth Sense* and others, died in 2000 almost totally forgotten.

Alcoa Premiere (ABC, 1961–1963) was hosted by Fred Astaire, who also acted in five of its dramas. This hour-long filmed anthology was on a par

with *Playhouse 90* in its perspective and execution from the very first pro-
gram, the Emmy-nominated *People Need People*, a powerful, fact-based drama
about the rehabilitation of a war veteran who is psychologically disturbed.
Lee Marvin (also Emmy nominated as outstanding actor) starred, along with
Arthur Kennedy (as his psychiatrist), Keir Dullea, and Jocelyn Brando, under
Alex Segal's direction (he earned a third Emmy nomination for the drama).
The venerable John Ford made one of his handful of TV directing efforts with
a baseball tale called *Flashing Spikes,* with James Stewart (and John Wayne in
a cameo). Astaire himself starred with Elizabeth Montgomery in *Mr. Lucifer,*
directed by Alan Crosland Jr. He played the devil in assorted disguises.

   Dick Powell's Zane Grey Theatre (CBS, 1956–1962) was the second of
three popular series of Hollywood musical ingenue turned movie tough
guy turned TV movie producer and affable host and sometimes star. This
Western anthology series that ran for a half dozen seasons focused initially
on the works of the prolific American author who died in 1959, but ultimately, Powell and his production company, Four Star, ran through Grey's
library and had to generate new stories of the Old West. Most of the early
episodes had directors Bernard Girard and Felix Feist alternating, and later,
John English. Robert Ryan and Cloris Leachman were the stars of the initial
drama, *You Only Run Once,* and other actors included Claudette Colbert,
James Whitmore, John Forsythe, Barbara Stanwyck, Jack Palance, Ida
Lupino, Lee J. Cobb, Eddie Albert, Jack Lemmon, Edward G. Robinson, Hedy
Lamarr, Sammy Davis Jr., and frequently, Powell himself. Stirling Silliphant,
Christopher Knopf, and Aaron Spelling (who later was to head his own TV-
producing empire) were just three of the writers, and Western specialists
Sam Peckinpah and Budd Boetticher, among others, were directors.

   MTR curator Ron Simon observed,

> The whole beginnings of television and drama starts with the anthology drama
> series based on radio, the one defining radio series being *Lux Radio Theatre,*
> which C. B. DeMille hosted. [Or perhaps earlier, *The Campbell Playhouse,*
> with Orson Welles and his Mercury Players.] Lux signaled the possibilities of
> Hollywood's participation in creating programming for broadcasting. When
> the anthology dramas first began, they represented the New York theater
> spirit. So many of them were done in New York, from *Kraft Television Theatre* to
> *Studio One* and *Danger. Kraft* or *Armstrong Circle Theatre* really used the people
> who were working in the theater—certainly had a feel of live theater.
>
>   There were always anthology dramas that came from Los Angeles. One of
> the most significant series, *Playhouse 90,* came from L.A., and the whole basis
> was to bring Hollywood talent to the anthology drama. So it has always been
> this relationship between theater people and Hollywood people.

CHAPTER 9

Apex

layhouse 90 (CBS, premiering October 4, 1956) might well have represented the acme of serious drama telecast in anthology style, as live television was ending its reign and being almost permanently supplanted by tape and film. Coming basically out of Hollywood (by 1956, much of television production had moved from the East Coast to the West), it arguably was the most ambitious, with more than 100 original plays by television's greatest writers of the time, and its best directors, creating the medium's best-known original works remembered to this day. With Martin Manulis as the series's original producer, the landmark, live, 90-minute weekly show kicked off with Rod Serling's *Forbidden Area*, with a cast headed by Charlton Heston and Vincent Price and directed by John Frankenheimer (the first of 21 *Playhouse 90*s he helmed). The next week, it was Serling's masterful *Requiem for a Heavyweight*, directed by Ralph Nelson and starring Jack Palance (Emmy winner for best single program of the 1956–1957 season and for best actor). There would be the memorable productions of *The Miracle Worker* that later would be staged on Broadway and *Days of Wine and Roses* (Frankenheimer again), with Cliff Robertson and Piper Laurie. Such a wealth of unforgettable, basically original TV drama through the end of the 1950s—with a little dross thrown in—was the last gasp of live television, although videotaped portions were snuck into the live material. Actually, beginning in January 1957, more and more of *Playhouse 90* was on film, shot at Screen Gems, although lovers of golden age television would rather remember the show as being done live right up to the end—in May 1960, with Rod Serling's *In the Presence of Mine Enemies*. Serling's drama about the

Warsaw Ghetto uprising would be resurrected in 1997 as a cable movie on Showtime.

Among the writing talents that kept *Playhouse 90* and other drama programs so great was David Shaw. A veteran who was one of Fred Coe's notable "stable" (Shaw's word) of writers from earlier in the decade, Shaw was prolific and quite important to the medium. He provided nearly three dozen dramas, both originals and some adaptations, for *Philco/Goodyear*, most of them, perhaps by design, directed by Delbert Mann; seven for *Studio One*; a half dozen for *Playhouse 90*; and several for *Producers' Showcase* (Sinclair Lewis's *Dodsworth*, the musical of Thornton Wilder's *Our Town*, Robert E. Sherwood's *Reunion in Vienna*, and Harry Leon Wilson's *Ruggles of Red Gap* among them). Brooklyn-born Shaw, who began writing movie scripts in the years following World War II, did his first TV dramas for *Actors Studio* in 1948. He adapted, first on the screen and then on TV, several of the works of his brother, author Irwin Shaw (whose own bibliography included *The Young Lions; Two Weeks in Another Town; Rich Man, Poor Man; Evening in Byzantium;* and others).

"Like virtually all of my colleagues in TV writing," David Shaw recalled for this book 50 odd years later, "I was on the set or in the control room during rehearsals and blocking—tweaking the script, as it were, if I or the director, generally Del Mann, felt it needed it, right up to taping [kinescoping]." Remembering one of those "oops" occasions from live TV, he said, "There was a script of mine that Del Mann was directing for *Philco*. The drama was *The Recluse*, back in 1953 with Dane Clark, and it was meant to be told backward, or in lengthy flashback. Somehow acts two and three got swapped. In act three, Dane was engaged in a bar fight, which got out of hand, and a shot glass thrown at him hit him on the nose and shattered. There was a good amount of blood. Fade ultimately to commercial, and then up on the next act, which was out of order, and there was Dane—six months or so earlier—still bleeding profusely with a big bandage on his nose."

In addition to writing in the genre of what came to be known as kitchen dramas on *Philco*, Shaw wrote musicals for television (for one, the song-and-dance adaptation on the *Kaiser Aluminum Hour* in 1957 for producer David Susskind of *A Man's Game*, from writing colleague Robert Alan Aurthur's 1952 baseball tale on *Philco Television Playhouse*). The new production starred Nanette Fabray and dancer (later TV director) Gene Nelson, plus Paul Ford, Bibi Osterwald, and Fred Gwynne, with Delbert Mann directing. And he was one of the writers of Broadway's *Redhead*, for director Bob Fosse and his wife, Gwen Verdon, and *Tovarich*, for Vivien Leigh.

Actress Judy Holliday made her TV acting debut in David Shaw's original 1954 farce *The Huntress* on *Goodyear*, and his friend Eva Marie Saint was in his *The Little Wife* on *Actors Studio* (that playlet would be restaged several times through the years on various anthology dramas) and *0 for 37* on *Philco* in 1953 as well as *Our Town* on *Producers' Showcase*. On *Playhouse 90* in 1958, Paul Newman (as a disillusioned halfback, living in the shadow of a long-past gridiron glory) and Joanne Woodward (as the wealthy girl he marries) costarred in the football tale *The 80-Yard Run*. "He is frustrated by his inability to support her, and, helpless, watches their relationship deteriorate," as the *New York Times* critic wrote. "A convenient reconciliation provided the anticipated pleasant ending. . . . The script became superior when it illuminated the conflicting values of the husband and wife." *Los Angeles Times* critic Cecil Smith observed, "The play is from one of the finest short stories I ever read, Irwin Shaw's *The 80-Yard Run*. It was adapted by David Shaw, the author's brother, and is directed by Franklin Schaffner, one of the giants of this racket."

Several other Shaw scripts for *Playhouse 90* stood out. One, *The Tunnel*, "a forceful historical drama," as the *New York Times* TV critic called it, was a Civil War story about how Union troops burrowed more than 500 feet and blew up a Confederate position in front of Petersburg, Virginia. Delbert Mann directed, and Richard Boone, a brutish, cynical colonel, and Rip Torn, an idealistic, genteel lieutenant, played the protagonists. Another, an adaptation of Fitzgerald's *The Great Gatsby*, was one of the better-realized versions of the illusive tale. Robert Ryan had the lead. A third, a hot potato, was called *Alas, Babylon,* an apocalyptic horror tale taken from Pat Frank's morality novel dealing with a Florida community in the wake of a Soviet nuclear attack that has wiped out most of the Western world. For political reasons—like not wanting to antagonize the Soviet Union during this Eisenhower era—the government was said to have pressured CBS not to air the show. It was postponed for several months from its initially scheduled airing, before finally being staged in early April 1960. Starring were Dana Andrews, Kim Hunter, Don Murray, Rita Moreno, and Everett Sloane. After *Alas, Babylon,* there would be just three more *Playhouse 90* dramas.

In later years, Shaw went on to write (and, as the show's story editor for a while, rewrite) a number of episodes of *The Defenders* in the early 1960s, and his last work for TV after four decades was involvement as writer and story editor for the 1988 series *The Mississippi*, which starred Ralph Waite (post *Waltons*). Between them, the peripatetic Mr. S. wrote the screenplay for the film comedy *If It's Tuesday, This Must Be Belgium*.

Another notable name golden age writer, Loring Mandel, wrote two *Playhouse 90* shows. One, *Project Immortality*, would star a very difficult

Lee J. Cobb. Mandel recalls, "I had given an outline of this show to John Houseman, who was interested, but then he left for Hollywood, and Hubbell Robinson, to whom the outline fell, didn't want to do it. Director Fielder Cook told me he'd try to get Kraft to bankroll it, but then *Kraft Theatre* went off the air. So it made its way back to Robinson, who kicked it around a bit before giving me the go-ahead." It was described in Jack Gould's review in the *New York Times* as "a play whose theme had both meaning and pertinency in the present era of scientific wizardry . . . the story of a dying genius whose pattern of thought processes is recorded in hopes that, after his death, his brain may still be employed to resolve problems associated with national defense."

Chicago-born Mandel began his career in broadcasting writing variety television locally between 1950 and 1952, before going into the army during Korea. After his discharge, some of his Chicago friends, Dave Garroway, Mike Wallace, and CBS news producer Perry Wolff, urged him to come to the Big Apple, where he wrote several segments of Wolff's Sunday afternoon educational show *Adventure,* made in conjunction with the American Museum of Natural History. "In April of 1954, I wrote a couple of dramas on spec, and Mike Wallace sent me to his agent, Ted Ashley, who sent the scripts to *Studio One.* They bought one of them—it ended up airing in late 1957 as *Shakedown Cruise* with Richard Kiley and Lee Marvin—and the day afterward, *Studio One* called me with my next assignment. To me that was really when my TV writing career began." Franklin Schaffner directed that script and many others of Mandel's. "I worked a lot with Frank, a fantastic man and a terrific director. After *Shakedown,* he asked me to do the 1955 TV adaptation of *The Caine Mutiny Court-Martial,* but Paul Gregory, who had produced the stage version with his production partner, Charles Laughton, and somehow held the TV rights, insisted on doing the adaptation himself." (TV history tells us that Herman Wouk, who had written the book and play, was given the writing credit for the show that aired on *Ford Star Jubilee.*)

For *Kaiser Aluminum Hour* in summer 1956, Mandel wrote *Army Game,* which was directed by Schaffner and starred Paul Newman as a malingering draftee who fakes mental illness to obtain a medical discharge. Mandel's *Studio One* drama *The Rice Sprout,* adapted from a novel by Eileen Chang dealing with Asian peasants in a small Chinese village, became a point of much controversy. It was not because, like in the 1930s film of Pearl Buck's *The Good Earth* and the 1940s one of Buck's *Dragon Seed,* it was cast with white actors, but because virtually all the performers had been blacklisted, and director Sidney Lumet insisted on using them. Mandel wrote about this much later in a lengthy piece for the publication *Television Quarterly.* He titled it "Live

TV Goes Awry, and What the Writer Learned from a *Studio One* Disaster":
"It was rigorously anti-communist, which proved to be ironic. The director
Herb Brodkin hired for this show was Sidney Lumet, a preeminent television
director rapidly approaching the beginning of an exceptional film career. And
Sidney, to whom we should all be grateful, cast the show from actors almost
exclusively from the blacklist. Some had not worked in TV for years and had
seen their careers, once glowing with promise, fallen to nothing."

Particularly agonizing, Mandel recalled, was actress Olive Deering's
ambivalence. "I have no doubt that [her] anger brought an intensity to her
performance that exceeded her considerable professionalism and talent.
But it was far more than that; her eyes—or at least the fully opened one
[there was a considerable problem with the Oriental-type makeup, causing
a problem with her eyes]—were aflame with rage and the rest of the cast, as
the drama progressed, grew more apprehensive. She was racing, leapfrog-
ging her lines. Her fury surpassed my peculiar as-translated dialogue and
the dramatic structure itself; sections from acts were transposed into other
acts, the play staggered along as I watched in horror in the sponsor's private
screening room. It was more like a runaway truck than a television play."

Probably the most remembered of Mandel's dramas was the beautiful *Do Not Go Gentle into That Good Night*, a poignant play about a senior
citizen's refusal to accept institutionalization. It aired on *CBS Playhouse* in
October 1967. "Fredric March and his wife, Florence Eldridge, were to have
starred, but AFTRA had called a strike just before we were to have gone into
rehearsal," Mandel said to this author, "and after several weeks of delay,
we finally were all set to go, Freddy suffered a stroke in his hotel room the
night before, and Flo was felled with a minor heart attack beside him. We
found them on the floor. Freddy's good friend Melvyn Douglas was pressed
into the role—somewhat reluctantly—along with Shirley Booth. Mel was not
happy about doing the part; he didn't feel that he did the same type of role
that Freddy did."

Regardless, Jack Gould of the *New York Times* reported the next day that
"Melvyn Douglas' superb performance as the elderly man who realizes that
meaningful activity and individuality are the best therapy for the retired
lifted the 90 minutes to a level of genuine theatrical stature." Gould also felt
that "in many respects, Mr. Mandel's work was a vivid editorial lament for
the disappearance of the multigenerational household and the dismissal of
its aged members to institutionalized waiting rooms to die." Mandel won
the Emmy for his writing. Incidentally, the program, directed by George
Schaefer, was presented, for the first time, without a middle commercial, by
agreement with the network.

In addition to writing for *Lux Video Theatre, Armstrong Circle Theatre, The DuPont Show of the Week,* and a number of others, still another Mandel script for *Playhouse 90*—and for director Schaffner—was a 1959 drama called *The Raider,* set in the world of big business. Paul Douglas, Rod Taylor, and Frank Lovejoy were featured.

He also wrote several dramas for public television. Mandel penned as well the first segment of CBS's 1974–1975 series of dramas about Benjamin Franklin and Carl Sandburg's *Lincoln* (all six episodes in 1974), with Hal Holbrook in the title role, along with Sada Thompson as Mary Todd. There also were a number of made-for-TV movies written by Mandel in the late 1970s and early 1980s. His most recent work, for which he earned an Emmy nomination, was the 2001 HBO drama *Conspiracy,* a historical drama recreating one of the most infamous gatherings of the twentieth century, when 15 top members of the Third Reich met outside Berlin, on January 20, 1942, to set in motion the Final Solution to the Jewish Question. Kenneth Branagh starred; Frank Pierson directed. Herb Brodkin recalled,

> When I came over to *Playhouse 90* as producer in the fall of 1958, I commissioned Ernie Kinoy to write a script, and he came up with one about a wealthy and retired toy manufacturer seeking to gain acceptance in a small New England community, but soon ends up with their hostility as an outsider. The drama was called *Shadows Tremble,* and I was lucky to get Edward G. Robinson for the lead—and then surrounded him with cast made up entirely of Broadway performers, bringing them all out to Hollywood, where the show was being done.

But of course, when *Playhouse 90* faded to black on the night of September 19, 1961 (following a summer of repeats), the TV screen still flickered with weekly dramas overlapping into the 1960s.

Regarding *Playhouse 90,* Ron Simon feels,

> Even from the beginning, they were creating and integrating bits of action, bits of business into the program—on tape and film, so everything was not being done live. There'd be several minutes here and there, then eventually more and more got recorded on videotape. It should also be known that *Playhouse 90* generally did three dramas a month. One of them was done on film back in New York.
>
> It was Frankenheimer who would go in for special visuals, close-ups, and he would prerecord some segments. Then, eventually, there were some dramas that were all prerecorded, and they seemed live because they were all on videotape.

During the period of *Playhouse 90*, there also was *The DuPont Show of the Month* (CBS, premiering September 18, 1957). It was produced by David Susskind, who staged a variety of dramas ranging from Mark Twain's *The Prince and the Pauper*, Thornton Wilder's *The Bridge of San Luis Rey*, and Terrence Rattigan's *The Winslow Boy*, to Shakespeare's *Hamlet*, William Saroyan's *The Human Comedy*, Dickens's *Oliver Twist*, even *Aladdin*, a lavish, original, 90-minute musical that would be Cole Porter's last work. Sal Mineo starred alongside Anna Maria Alberghetti, Basil Rathbone, Howard Morris, and Geoffrey Holder as the Genie. S. J. Perelman wrote the book. The show, unfortunately, was, as the *New York Times* wrote the next day, "sustained disaster . . . a portentious ordeal." Regardless, here would be 32 much-admired productions over four seasons. The final curtain fell on *Show of the Month* on March 21, 1961, with Julie Harris starring in a production of Horton Foote's original *The Night of the Storm*.

Jack Gould wrote in the *New York Times* the next day, "Another chapter in the disheartening story of drama on network television drew to a close last night; the *DuPont Show of the Month*, which once experienced some of the medium's glorious hours, gave its last performance. . . . Sadly, yet perhaps significantly, the farewell presentation constituted a brave hope that was not to be realized. At long last, David Susskind persuaded the sponsor to allow him to do an original drama rather than an adaptation of a revival." Gould concluded, "Five years ago, even ten years ago, network television managed to have a great deal of good drama along with the inevitable percentage of mishaps. But now TV is more prosperous economically and reaches over many more stations. It has grown terribly big. Yet the sense of theatre is slipping away and sponsors are going on to other things. Somebody has mislaid the magic."

Not to be confused with his first series, a CBS musical variety show that failed to catch on during the 1950–1952 seasons, and similarly titled, *The Frank Sinatra Show*, that aired on Fridays at 9:00 P.M. on ABC between October 1957 and the following June, was a mixed bag—and equally unsuccessful. A 30-minute show, it featured original dramas, some starring Sinatra ("A Gun at His Back," for one, with Pat Crowley; "The Brownstone Incident," for another, with Cloris Leachman), and musical programs, plus a couple of live half hours from the El Capitan Theatre in Hollywood. Sinatra, of course, hosted.

Westinghouse Desilu Playhouse (CBS, 1958–1961) was the anthology series that followed Desi Arnaz and Lucille Ball's landmark *I Love Lucy*. Hosted initially by Desi, it replaced *Studio One*, which left the air after a decade, and included not only original dramas, but also periodic Lucy-Desi adventures along with Vivian Vance and William Frawley. The material ranged from light to serious and boasted stories by Rod Serling, Ernest Kinoy, Adrian Spies, Aaron Spelling, Sheldon Reynolds, and other noted TV drama writers of the era. Ed Wynn starred in the biographical *The Man in the Funny Suit*, along with his son Keenan and a host of other TV comics, and won an Emmy nomination in the category outstanding single performance by a lead actor. (Wynn lost to Maurice Evans for *Macbeth* on *Hallmark Hall of Fame*.) Also nominated was Ralph Nelson, who wrote the drama for Wynn (Nelson also directed it). A *Desilu Playhouse* highlight would be the two-part pilot to *The Untouchables*, with Robert Stack in the role of Eliot Ness, which Van Johnson had turned down.

Shirley Temple's Storybook/Shirley Temple Theatre (1958–1963, NBC/ABC) returned to the limelight the onetime child star—arguably the most famous in movie history—as a lovely adult to host with grace and narrate an anthology drama show, adapting children's favorite stories and fairy tales and occasionally starring in some. A great many name actors appeared through the weeks and months: Charlton Heston and Claire Bloom in *Beauty and the Beast; Babes in Toyland* with Jonathan Winters; *Mother Goose* with Elsa Lanchester, along with Shirley herself and her three young children; and *The Legend of Sleepy Hollow* with Jules Munshin and Shirley and narrated by Boris Karloff. Director Paul Bogart, who also was one of the series's producers, called the shots on the Washington Irving tale, and in an interview with the author, he remembered how gracious and ladylike Shirley Temple was on the series: "She was the consummate professional. No ego, no foot stomping. Always deferential to the fellow actors and the crew." Bogart shared how Temple prepared for the camera: "My mother always prepared me with just two words: 'Sparkle, Shirley.'"

"Just after doing *Sleepy Hollow*, live in Hollywood for the East Coast and repeated three hours later on the miracle of tape for the West, Shirley, Jules, and I went to dinner at the Beverly Hills Hotel, where she whispered, 'I just hope none of the papers say Miss Temple was adequate,' which is just what one of the critics wrote." (This was Shirley Temple's TV acting debut on the show she hosted.) And what of Karloff? "I asked if he would watch the taped replay with us. After I explained how this was possible—remember, tape was brand new at this point—he politely said, 'Thank you, no. That's rather like a dog returning to its own vomit.' I loved him."

Breck Sunday Showcase (NBC, 1959–1960) was a David Susskind–produced series that presented specials along with dramas directed by John Frankenheimer, Delbert Mann (the two-part *What Makes Sammy Run?*, adapted by Budd Schulberg from his 1940 novel), Paul Bogart (a production of Oscar Wilde's *The Picture of Dorian Gray*), Alex March, George Schaefer,

William A. Graham, and others. Teresa Wright won an Emmy nomination for *The Margaret Bourke-White Story*. This series shared a rotating time slot with the historical *Our American Heritage*.

The DuPont Show with June Allyson (CBS, 1959–1961), a half-hour weekly filmed anthology series, was out of the very prolific Four Star Productions, of which Allyson's husband, Dick Powell, was one of the cofounders and had nearly two dozen shows on TV at the time. In the premiere of the series (also known as, simply, *The June Allyson Show*), with Allyson and Ann Harding, was *Those We Love*, a contemporized version of the Ruth and Naomi story of the Bible. Allyson hosted and occasionally acted in the series and made her first dramatic TV appearance with husband Dick Powell in *A Summer's Ending*. Harpo Marx made a rare dramatic appearance playing a deaf mute in *Silent Panic*. Allyson also costarred with old MGM colleague Van Johnson in *The Woman Who*, midway in the second and last season.

Rod Serling's classic *The Twilight Zone* (CBS, 1959–1965, a Friday night staple at 10:00) has been covered often, and anything else written about the influential program would seem redundant. Most of the entries were written, of course, by Serling, but there were other writers, Charles Beaumont, Richard Matheson, E. Jack Neuman, and George Clayton Johnson among them. After the original show left the air in the mid-1960s, there would be a 1984 theatrical *Twilight Zone* feature combining several of the best remembered stories from the original series and 10 years later a one-shot made-for-TV movie, à la the Hitchcock one, with a pair of Serling stories that were discovered by his widow, Carol (who remains keeper of the Rod Serling flame). Two decades after the original, the fascination was still there, and Serling's image was morphed into host duties, along with Charles Aidman, in a new *Twilight Zone* series in 1985–1986, then first-run syndication in 1987–1988, featuring Robin Ward as narrator, and a dozen or so years later, a *Twilight Zone* return on UPN beginning in 2002, with actor Forest Whitaker as host.

The Twilight Zone opening logo had an interesting history. The show's producers, seeking a distinctive look, contracted with UPA, the legendary animation studio that was responsible for the *Gerald McBoing-Boing* and *Mr. Magoo* cartoons dating back to the start of the 1950s. (UPA, created by Canadian animator Steven Bosustow, who was the executive producer for its entire history, had brought in a bunch of guys who happened to be musicians with Spike Jones's City Slickers.) Designer Joseph Messerli (not a City Slicker) was responsible for *The Twilight Zone*'s twinkling galaxy and the slightly off center titles over which Rod Serling recorded his familiar, mood-setting narration. And there was the familiar foreboding theme by Bernard Herrmann. Messerli remembers:

> While working at the UPA animation studio in Burbank in 1958, I was assigned to create the [Twilight Zone] logo—three lines of white hand lettering to work with twinkling stars over a painted background of a cave and environs. No established font, just one-stroke calligraphy. I crafted the logo and the stars . . . all airbrush dots, no depiction of any galaxy, just a pleasing array. Camera movements, music, narration—all magically brought together on film.
>
> Sam Clayberger did the layout and background. Rudy Larriva directed and animated. Rudy had done lots of Porky Pig cartoons in the early 1940s, then as an animator for *Song of the South* and *Melody Time* for Disney, and then much of the Magoos for UPA.

According to Herrmann, Messerli later moved across Burbank to NBC and "did a lot of title stuff, including the color drawings for the opening credits on *Bonanza*."

The Chevy Mystery Show (NBC, 1960), hosted initially by Walter Slezak, then Vincent Price, was the summer replacement for *The Dinah Shore Chevy Show* on Sunday nights. Even Dinah attempted to shoehorn an occasional drama into her *Chevy Show*. In 1961, she made her dramatic TV debut in a version of Noel Coward's *Brief Encounter* opposite Ralph Bellamy (it was reset in 1908 Boston from the mid-1940s of the famous movie). Weekly plays emphasized mystery and suspense on *The Chevy Mystery Show*. In one of the more notable entries, a shambling Lieutenant Columbo, a cunning LAPD cop, made his first television appearance, played here by character actor Bert Freed, in an original drama called *Enough Rope* by Richard Levinson and William Link. Their tale initially had been published as a short story for Alfred Hitchcock's mystery magazine. Levinson and Link first collaborated while in junior high school in Philadelphia and continued their partnership at the University of Pennsylvania.

Some years later, after military service, they reunited and sold two original dramas to a Canadian series, *General Motors Presents*, in 1958. They then sold a military drama, *Chain of Command*, to *Desilu Playhouse*, and its critical reception led to other assignments, including scripts for series like *Johnny Ringo* and *Black Saddle*. The two signed on with Four Star Productions, writing for *Richard Diamond, Private Eye*; *Michael Shayne*; and *The June Allyson Show*. The partners got caught up in a writers' strike in Hollywood, so they turned to Broadway and resurrected their Columbo character in a play, *Prescription: Murder*, later to be turned into a top-notch TV movie and the entire Columbo franchise that would generate nice paychecks over the next 40 odd years. Back in TV, they wrote hour-long episodes for *The Alfred Hitchcock Hour* as well as for *Dr. Kildare*, *The Rogues*, and *The Fugitive*. They created *Mannix*, which ran for 8 seasons on CBS, and later *Murder, She Wrote*, which ran for 12.

CHAPTER 10

Post *Playhouse 90*

I n their foreword to this author's third compilation of *Movies Made for Television*, Richard Levinson and William Link wrote,

> With the demise of *Playhouse 90*, it appeared that the audience was abandoning the anthology form; the half-hour and hour series had become the bread-and-butter staple of the medium. The conventional wisdom for the time dictated that "continuing characters" and a "family" of regulars would capture viewers in spite of banal scripts and assembly-line production values. Serious drama or even high quality regular entertainment was all but extinct.

But not quite.

The Barbara Stanwyck Show (NBC, 1960–1961) had the legendary movie actress front and center every week as hostess and star in this anthology of original 30-minute teleplays, a number of which were pilots to series that never materialized. As one of the show's gimmicks, viewers were asked to write to the network offering their opinions. The series ran at 10:00 on Monday nights. Stanwyck, who starred in all but a handful of the dramas, won the Emmy as outstanding lead actress in a series that television season, but it would be her next TV venture that would make her an icon on the tube: *The Big Valley*.

Thriller (NBC, 1960–1962) was developed by Hubbell Robinson, who was a top executive at CBS for many years—under Paley, he was, after Frank Stanton, the leading programming guy and championed everything on the so-called Tiffany network from *I Love Lucy* and *Gunsmoke* to *Playhouse 90* before moving to the competition. "Culturally [Hubbell's] interests were levels above many of his colleagues," Paley was quoted as saying. "His special flair was for high-quality programming."

Robinson, one of the giants from the early days of television, was with CBS from 1947 to 1956 as the network's executive vice president, and later was senior vice president of television programs. He had been a newspaper reporter and drama critic in the late 1920s and later became a radio producer for advertising agencies. He was with Foote, Cone, & Belding Advertising when CBS hired him away shortly after World War II, and he remained with the network for the next decade. He then left to form his own production company but returned to CBS in 1962 in a senior programming capacity.

In his autobiography *As It Happened*, William Paley referred to Hubbell Robinson as "the all-around man in our programming department." Robinson was the executive who oversaw the development of now classic shows through the 1950s. Then, after clashing with James Aubrey, then CBS president, he moved over in a senior capacity to ABC-TV.

In the last years of his life (he died in 1974), Robinson was a contributing critic to *Films in Review* when this author, having become a writer and then TV editor at that magazine, enjoyed a number of conversations with him about television. In one of those conversations, Robinson told this author,

One of my first producing jobs was director John Frankenheimer's staging in 1959 on *Ford Startime* of Henry James's *The Turn of the Screw*, from an adaptation by James Costigan. This was a big event because it marked the TV debut of Ingrid Bergman. And then there was Alec Guinness in his American TV debut in a drama called *The Wicked Schemes of Jebal Deeks*, that Franklin Schaffner directed, and Jimmy Stewart in *Cindy's Fella*, directed by Gower Champion. That was a Western musical variation on the Cinderella story.

I also was executive producer of *Climax!* and then *Playhouse 90* when we did all of those beautifully written and directed shows that TV historians like to talk about. Ralph Nelson with Rod Serling's *Requiem for a Heavyweight*; Arthur Penn with William Gibson's *The Miracle Worker* and Serling's *The Dark Side of Earth*; John Frankenheimer with Serling's *The Comedian* with Mickey Rooney and *A Town Has Turned to Dust* with Rod Steiger, and with Cornell Woolrich's *Rendezvous in Black* with Karloff; George Roy Hill with Abby Mann's *Judgment at Nuremberg*; Franklin Schaffner with *The 80-Yard Run* with Paul Newman and Joanne Woodward; Delbert Mann with David Karp's *The Plot to Kill Stalin*; Frankenheimer again with Hemingway's *For Whom the Bell Tolls*. Put them all together and you get the crème de la crème. TV drama at its very best.

It wasn't all without headaches, though, and I had my wranglings with the CBS brass. On *Requiem*, for one, Ed Wynn, that wonderful veteran comic actor, was brought aboard, at the instigation of his long-estranged son Keenan, who decided he wanted to work with his dad. The elder Wynn was cast in the dramatic role of Army, corner man for the washed up heavyweight, the role Jack Palance played so memorably. But Wynn had difficulty with his lines during rehearsal, and we reluctantly had to consider firing him. Keenan stepped up and told us he'd coach Ed with his lines and prompt him when we went on live—and he was just great and got an Emmy nomination for his performance. Ed Wynn went on after that in a number of dramatic television roles.

With *Nuremberg* we faced another problem, that of censorship. Turns out that one of the sponsors of the show was the American Gas Company, and they objected to our using the term *gas ovens* in this story about the Holocaust. They pressured CBS. Writer Abby Mann was irate. So was George Roy Hill, the director. And Herb Brodkin, the producer of the series. And so was I, and I let the brass know it in no uncertain terms.

As Mann recalled much later, when *Judgment* made it to Broadway,

One of the sponsors, American Gas Inc., had sent a memo demanding that we delete any mention of gas. They didn't want to be held responsible for what happened in the Holocaust under any circumstances. Herb Brodkin and George Hill refused. So when the climactic moment came in the production when Judge Haywood as played by Claude Rains says to Paul Lukas, the German judge, "I understand the pressures that you faced. No man can say how he would have faced those pressures himself unless he had actually been tested. But how can you expect me to forgive sending millions of people to gas ovens?" American Gas took matters into their own hands and had an executive at CBS pump out the words *gas ovens* so that Claude Rains mouthed the words, but no sound came out.

Hubbell Robinson vividly remembered,

It made all the papers the next day, and quite a few editorials followed, denouncing this act of censorship. It still hurts that *Judgment,* which was one of the great original dramas on the series was overlooked completely at the Emmys that season.

Later I became executive producer of Karloff's *Thriller* anthology. Then the cop series *87th Precinct* in 1961 and Burt Reynolds's detective series *Hawk.* In 1966, I got a second shot at working with Ingrid Bergman. On *ABC Stage 67* that I was doing, she starred for me in her memorable one-woman *The Human Voice.* Just this wondrous actress on the phone for a whole hour.

At NBC, where he was lured, Robinson enticed Fletcher Markle to help create what they referred to as "the *Studio One* of mystery and suspense"—although they reportedly were not sure of which they wanted to emphasize. The *Thriller* concept was to bring the writings of Edgar Allan Poe, Cornell Woolrich, the more contemporary Robert Bloch, Richard Matheson, and others into this anthology series and to get legendary Boris Karloff into the mix, as host and occasional star. (Karloff, years earlier, had hosted a filmed anthology series, *The Boris Karloff Mystery Theatre*, which ran for 13 episodes in 1949. Alex Segal produced and directed.)

Arthur Hiller directed the *Thriller* pilot (*The Twisted Image*, starring Karloff with George Grizzard, Leslie Nielsen, and Constance Ford) as well as the first couple of episodes. Other directors in the series included former movie stars Ray Milland, Ida Lupino, and Paul Henreid. Robinson, as executive producer, and Markle, as producer, apparently had a falling out, and Markle left the show after the first handful of episodes, to be replaced by Maxwell Shane, who remained for the rest of the 67 episodes in the hour-long, two-season series that was filmed at Revue Studios in Hollywood. One of the more notable productions was a second-season adaptation of Poe's *The Premature Burial*, in which perfectly cast Karloff costarred with Patricia Medina. (Ironically, this would be the only Poe tale in the entire *Thriller* series.) Another was a wry black comedy called *Masquerade*, in which Elizabeth Montgomery and Tom Poston are a couple of mismatched honeymooners who are menaced in a rundown hotel by John Carradine and a clan of vampires.

The Dick Powell Show (NBC, 1961–1963) continued the drama anthology format on film. Powell, as producer, host, and sometimes star, recruited a number of big-name stars to appear in his potent weekly drama series. The first of its 60 episodes, a caper film called *Who Killed Julie Greer?*, written by Frank Gilroy and directed by Robert Ellis Miller, boasted a lineup of Lloyd Bridges, Mickey Rooney, Ronald Reagan, Edgar Bergen, Jack Carson, Nick Adams, and many more, with Powell himself playing a detective named Amos Burke—the character later would spin off to its own series (portrayed at that point by Gene Barry). During each of its two seasons, *The Dick Powell Show* won an Emmy nomination as outstanding drama program, but lost both times to *The Defenders*. Among the highlights of the *Powell Show* were Milton Berle's dramatic Emmy-nominated turn in director Ralph Nelson's gambling movie *Doyle against the House*, Mickey Rooney's in director Arthur Hiller's *Somebody's Waiting*, and Peter Falk's winning one in *The Price of Tomatoes*. He plays a Greek truck driver whose tomato delivery schedule is interrupted when he picks up a pregnant hitchhiker (portrayed by Inger Stevens). David Friedkin directed the story by Richard Alan Simmons.

Director Sam Fuller did a drama, *330 Independence S.W.,* with William Bendix; Sam Peckinpah directed Rosemary Clooney and Lee Marvin in *The Losers;* and Buzz Kulik directed Powell in his last acting role, *The Court-Martial of Captain Wycliff.* Shortly after the drama series started its second season, Powell, who had established himself as a major TV producer, died of cancer, and the remaining shows—renamed after his death *The Dick Powell Theatre*—were guest hosted by Frank Sinatra, Ronald Reagan, June Allyson (Powell's widow), James Stewart, Jack Lemmon, Gregory Peck, John Wayne, and other A-list friends.

Theatre '62 (NBC, 1961–1962), produced by Fred Coe, offered classy, once-a-month, one-hour adaptations of film mogul David O. Selznick movies. These were vest-pocket versions à la *Lux Video Theatre* and *Twentieth Century-Fox Hour* of the previous decade. Paul Bogart directed *Spellbound* with Maureen O'Hara and Hugh O'Brian. Others included *The Spiral Staircase* with Elizabeth Montgomery; *Intermezzo* with Ingrid Thulin and Jean-Pierre Aumont; *Notorious* with Joseph Cotten; *The Paradine Case* with Viveca Lindfors, Richard Basehart, and Boris Karloff; *The Farmer's Daughter* with Lee Remick; and *Rebecca* with James Mason. The series alternated with *The DuPont Show of the Week* on Sunday nights.

Great Ghost Tales (NBC, 1961) had the distinction of being the last regularly scheduled TV series, an occult anthology, to be broadcast live from New York. It was hosted by Frank Gallop, who, ironically, also had hosted one of the first *(Lights Out!)* a decade earlier. Of the premiere, an adaptation of Edgar Allan Poe's *William Wilson* with Robert Duvall, the *New York Times* wrote, "*Great Ghost Tales,* a dash of live television at a time when the medium is more moribund than usual, demonstrated that quality need not be confined to ninety-minute network splurges." The series featured dramatizations of ghost stories and other tales of the supernatural, many of which were adapted from the writings of famous authors like W. W. Jacobs (*The Monkey's Paw*), Conrad Aiken (*Mr. Arcularis*), and so on. Actors appearing on the series included a young Richard Thomas, Lee Grant, Lois Nettleton, Mildred Dunnock, Kevin McCarthy, and Arthur Hill.

Bob Hope Presents the Chrysler Theatre (NBC, premiering October 4, 1963) was among the last memorable network anthology drama series in the golden age tradition. Hope hosted the hour-long filmed and/or taped series for the first three weeks of each month and then did one of his traditional comedy specials on the fourth. In addition to a number of originals by assorted top writers was, in the first season, a Sydney Pollack–directed drama called *Two Is the Number,* for which Shelley Winters won the Emmy as outstanding actress in a drama. Rod Serling also was Emmy honored for his adaptation of John O'Hara's *It's Mental Work,* and there was a powerful production of Alexander Solzhenitsyn's *One Day in the Life of Ivan Denisovich,* directed by Daniel Petrie and starring Jason Robards and Albert Paulsen (Emmy winner as outstanding supporting actor), with music by Johnny (later John) Williams—who, in fact, was the series's music director.

The premiere *Chrysler Theatre* offering was Rod Serling's *A Killing at Sundial* with Melvyn Douglas and Angie Dickinson. Besides Serling, Hope presented television plays by Budd Schulberg, Carson McCullers, William Inge, and a critically acclaimed Edward Anhalt drama, *Memorandum for a Spy,* that aired in two parts on consecutive weeks. Henry James's novel *A Time to Love* was adapted to Hope's show, with Claire Bloom and Maximilian Schell costarring. And Sam Peckinpah directed (against type, it seems) a lighthearted playlet called *The Lady Is My Wife* with Jean Simmons.

Ron Simon of the Museum of Television and Radio recalled, in an interview with this author, that

> On the *Chrysler Theatre,* Bob Hope did some interesting things. Again, it was sort of relating to the past—bringing in names, a star being sort of the signature—like Robert Montgomery, Loretta Young, and Irene Dunne and Jane Wyman, and, yes, Ronald Reagan—so it was sort of star based, and centered on the star, and again, there were a wild swing of genres. They weren't doing live, of course.
>
> *CBS Playhouse* also sort of ran irregularly in the late 1960s. Even in 1967–1968, NBC had a show called *Experiment in Television*—it wasn't prime time—and ABC had its *Stage '67,* which had some dramas [especially Truman Capote's wonderful *A Christmas Memory,* which he narrated, and starring Geraldine Page, both winning Emmys] but also had some music [like Stephen Sondheim's original, now classic *Evening Primrose* with Anthony Perkins, written for television by James Goldman and directed by Paul Bogart].

Airing periodically between 1966 and 1970, *CBS Playhouse* was a valiant attempt to recapture the glory and prestige of *Playhouse 90.* The idea was to present original dramas by new playwrights, under executive producer Barbara Schultz, who commissioned 13 plays. The first to air was not a new drama, but David Susskind's acclaimed production of Tennessee Williams's *The Glass Menagerie* with Shirley Booth and Hal Holbrook. After that, there were 90-minute versions of new works by Tad Mosel, Loring Mandel, Ellen Violett (one of TV's few female writers of drama), and Earl Hamner Jr., whose *Appalachian Autumn* in late 1969 was the precursor to his *Waltons.* A lengthy, appreciative piece in the *New York Times* indicated that other writers officially at work for *CBS Playhouse* included Reginald Rose, Ernest Kinoy, Adrian Spies, Peter Schaffer, and Roger O. Hirson. However, corporate changes at the network, then operating under a revolving door policy, ended this last great CBS drama experiment at just 11 original entries, plus Tennessee Williams.

An early, live on-set television production. Eddie Albert and Grace Brandt in Albert's *The Love Nest* on NBC, 1936. This was television's first original drama, written by Eddie Albert. Courtesy of Photofest.

On the set of the *Producers' Showcase* Old Vic production of *Romeo and Juliet*, with a sword fight between John Neville and Paul Rogers, 1957. Courtesy of Photofest.

"Me on my first TV job," Paul Bogart says, as floor manager and cue-card guy on *Broadway Open House* (1950).

Director Paul Bogart (left) with frequent colleague, veteran NBC art director Sy Tomashoff. Courtesy of Paul Bogart Collection.

Paul Bogart, standing center between talent agents Ira Steiner and Mort Gottlieb. Seated are Alan Bunce (left), who played Albert in the 1950s live comedy series *Ethel and Albert*; Peg Lynch, the genius who wrote every episode and played Ethel; and NBC executive Tom Loeb. Courtesy of Paul Bogart Collection.

Sidney Poitier on *Philco Television Playhouse* in 1952 with director Delbert Mann.

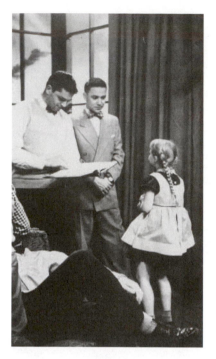

Paul Bogart rehearsing *One Man's Family* (1952) with show director Eddie Kahn and young Madeline Bolgard. Courtesy of Paul Bogart Collection.

Paul Bogart, by 1953 a full-fledged director of the *Revlon Mirror Theatre*.

Maurice Evens rehearsing *Macbeth* on *Hallmark Hall of Fame* in 1953. Courtesy of JC Archives.

Writer Paddy Chayefsky and director Delbert Mann discussing a scene in *Marty* on the *Goodyear Playhouse* in 1953. Courtesy of Photofest.

Hume Cronyn and Jessica Tandy in NBC's *The Marriage* in 1954. Courtesy of Paul Bogart Collection.

Paul Newman, Eva Marie Saint, and Frank Sinatra rehearsing *Our Town* on *Producers Showcase* in 1955. Courtesy of Photofest.

Nelson Eddy starring in *The Desert Song*, an NBC color spectacular in 1955. Courtesy JC Archives.

On the set of the series *Justice* in 1955—Paul Bogart (standing second left), star William Prince (to his left), and the crew, along with producer Gordon Duff (front row, dark suit). Courtesy of Paul Bogart Collection.

Delbert Mann (standing right) at a run-through of *The Answer* on *Play-wrights '56* with Paul Douglas (seated), Conrad Nagel, and Nina Foch.

Cloris Leachman in a 1955 pub-licity shot for *The General Electric Theatre* with a photo of the show's host, Ronald Reagan. Courtesy of Photofest.

Eva Marie Saint and husband, director Jeffrey Hayden. Courtesy of Photofest.

Mickey Rooney as Pinocchio and Walter Slezak as Gepetto in the 1957 musical. Courtesy of Photofest.

The cast of *The Comedian* on *Playhouse 90* wrapping up a rehearsal: Edmond O'Brien, Kim Hunter, Mickey Rooney, Mel Torme, and Constance Ford. Courtesy of Photofest.

Joanne Woodward and Paul Newman in David Shaw's *The 80 Yard Run* on *Playhouse 90*. Courtesy of Photofest.

Shirley Temple and Jules Munshin on the set of *The Legend of Sleepy Hollow* (1958).

John Frankenheimer directing Isobel Elsom and Ingrid Bergman in *Turn of the Screw* in 1959 as blonde Alexandra Wager looks on. Courtesy of Photofest.

Edward G. Robinson rehearsing on the set of the 1959 "Loyalty" episode of *Dick Powell's Zane Grey Theatre*.

Robert Culp and Shirley Temple rehearsing *The House of Seven Gables* on *The Shirley Temple Theatre* in late 1960. Partially hidden next to Culp is Agnes Moorehead. Courtesy of Photofest.

Paul Bogart (center) with Maureen Hurley and Maurice Evans on the *United States Steel Hour* in 1962. Courtesy of Paul Bogart Collection.

Actor Arthur Hill and director Paul Bogart on the set of *Dear Friends* on *CBS Playhouse* (1967). Courtesy of Paul Bogart Collection.

Director George Schaefer (front) rehearsing *Do Not Go Gentle Into That Good Night* with Lois Smith, Warren Stevens, Melvyn Douglas, and Shirley Booth (1967).

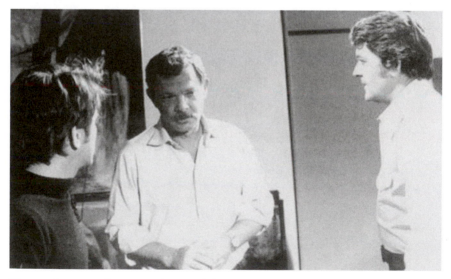

Director Lamont Johnson on the set of *That Certain Summer* (1972) with Martin Sheen (left) and Hal Holbrook (right).

Daniel Petrie directing 1977's *Eleanor and Franklin*. Courtesy of Photofest.

Japan's legendary Toshiro Mifune reviews a plot point in 1980's *Shogun* with director Jerry London (left). Courtesy of Photofest.

Paul Newman (crouching in foreground) with his cast of *The Shadow Box*—rear, from left: Ben Masters, John Considine, Melinda Dillon, and James Broderick; center, from left: Christopher Plummer, Joanne Woodward, Valerie Harper, and Sylvia Sidney; front, next to Newman: Curtiss Marlowe. Courtesy of Photofest.

Paul Newman directing *The Shadow Box* (1980). Courtesy of Photofest.

Tommy Lee Jones directing *The Good Old Boys* (1995), which he wrote and in which he also starred. Courtesy of Photofest.

Jerry London directs Maureen McCormick and Gregg Kean in *Get to the Heart: The Barbara Mandrell Story* (1997). Courtesy of Photofest.

Director Joseph Sargent (center) on the set of the drama *A Lesson before Dying* (1999) with Cicely Tyson and Don Cheadle. Courtesy of Photofest. Credit: Bob Greene/HBO.

Director Mick Jackson and Jack Lemmon on the set of *Tuesdays with Morrie* in 1999. Courtesy of Photofest.

Director Martha Coolidge (right) with Halle Berry on the set of *Introducing Dorothy Dandridge* (1999). Courtesy of Photofest. Credit: Sydney Baldwin/HBO.

On the set of 2005's *Warm Springs* with (from left) Kenneth Branagh, David Paymer, and director Joseph Sargent. Credit: Bob Greene/HBO.

John Frankenheimer framing a scene. Courtesy of Photofest.

CHAPTER 11

New Nighttime Dawns

I n my second book on movies made for television, Levinson and Link observed,

> Rescue came from an unexpected source, and for practical rather than esthetic reasons. Prompted by the need for product to replace the diminishing reserves of theatrical feature films, two industry behemoths, NBC and Universal Studios, came up with a new way to package the anthology concept. They began by dispensing with the dirty word "anthology" altogether. Instead, these films would be shrewdly promoted as a first look at newly-minted pictures. Viewers would be unaware that they were meeting their old friend, the anthology, in a new guise.
>
> An occasional work of quality managed to slip through, but it was usually an accident; the networks had no interest in a return to the Golden Age. [Soon] there were more and more departures, more risks taken as talented people, liberated from the constraints of series television, began to sense the possibilities of the Made-for-TV form.

Thus the medium turned to a different (but in many ways the same, only filmed) genre: movies made for television (MMFT).

The fall 1964 series under the umbrella title *Project 120*, an association between NBC and Universal Pictures, ushered in the genre familiarly known as the movie of the week. Some have argued that episodes of *The Wonderful World of Disney* constituted the first TV movies, although they ran only an hour each. Being self-contained, two-hour dramatic features, the network movies (a couple of decades later to be joined by those made for pay cable) would dominate the television landscape for the next 40 years. They were, in fact, an extension of what has come to be regarded as TV anthology drama, though in a slightly altered form.

NBC commissioned a handful of them over the next few years, and then CBS and ABC got in on the action (ABC began with a series of 90-minute films in 1967), and the genre became established. Many of the initial ABC movies were produced by Screen Gems and subsequently by Thomas/ Spelling Productions. Thomas, of course, was Danny, onetime stand-up comic turned hugely popular early TV star. Spelling was Aaron, onetime B movie actor who decided early on that that was not for him, and he turned to TV script writing and then would go on to become a mega producer with hundreds of TV credits to his (and his powerhouse company's) name. Thomas and Spelling went their separate ways (Thomas successfully part-nered with movie gangster/tough guy Sheldon Leonard, who became a keen TV producer and director) after a couple of years and a couple of hit series, but the 90-minute weekly ABC movie remained eminently viable and years later dominated television with *The Winds of War, War and Remembrance,* and other expansive and popular movies and miniseries.

MMFT would be generally stand-alone dramas ranging from 90 minutes to two (sometimes three) hours—self-contained because, unlike regular series, there were no recurring themes or characters. Like the dramas— serious and lighthearted—in the golden age, there were dozens of gems amid the dross, with probably the same basic ratio among the more than 5,600 films and miniseries through the end of 2006 as theatrical films.

The television movie covered just about everything from *A* to *Z:* from *A.D.* (a lavish $30 million, 12-hour epic, including commercials, from 1985, filmed in Tunisia with 400 speaking parts and the traditional Cecil B. DeMillean cast of thousands) to *Zuma Beach,* which had Suzanne Somers as a fading rock star donning a bikini in this 1978 surf-and-sand, back-to-the-beach romp, to change the direction of her faltering career.

A number of the name directors and writers from TV's golden age of drama contributed their talents through the years to the MMFT genre: direc-tors like Paul Bogart, George Schaefer, Sidney Lumet, Arthur Penn, Fielder Cook, Delbert Mann, and John Frankenheimer, and writers such as Loring Mandel, Reginald Rose, Abby Mann, and Rod Serling. They were joined by the likes of George Cukor, Franco Zeffirelli, Don Siegel, Peter Bogdanovich, Robert Wise, and even Mike Nichols and Woody Allen, who established their reputations through the years on the big screen, as well as relative newbies like John Carpenter, Joseph Sargent, and Dan Curtis.

But back to the so-called beginnings.

The first made-for-TV movie as we have come to know them was director Don Siegel's take on Hemingway's *The Killers*—quite altered from the 1946 Robert Siodmak version that starred Burt Lancaster (his film debut) and Ava Gardner. This new production featured Lee Marvin, John Cassavetes, and Angie Dickinson, and, in his last film acting role, Ronald Reagan, playing a vicious mob boss. NBC programmers reportedly became edgy when screening *The Killers* and decided that it was too violent for television (although times would certainly change). The network decided to pass on this one, and director David Lowell Rich's *See How They Run*, adapted by Michael Blankfort from his own 1946 novel *The Widow Makers*, instead officially became the premiere Project 120 offering.

This was followed several weeks later by Don Siegel's *The Hanged Man*, an update of Robert Montgomery's 1947 *Ride the Pink Horse*, which he had directed and in which he starred. (Siegel's *The Killers*, incidentally, was released theatrically and later found its way to television.) There was just one TV movie during the next season, *Scalplock*, a Western starring Dale Robertson, which served as a pilot for his series *The Iron Horse*.

It was during the 1966–1967 season that the made-for-TV movie really took hold. Most, though, were TV equivalents of the theatrical B movie or programmer at the beginning, with a passel of name actors from the big screen: Robert Taylor, Henry Fonda, Van Johnson, Robert Wagner, Walter Pidgeon, Anne Baxter, Lana Turner, Edward G. Robinson, and Richard Widmark.

The initial TV movies that aired on NBC were pedestrian thrillers and a Western or two. Among these were a white-knuckle disaster thriller *The Doomsday Flight*, written by Rod Serling; Henry Fonda's first TV movie, *Stranger on the Run*, which came from a story by golden age veteran Reginald Rose; and a couple of remakes of earlier theatrical features including James Stewart's superior hoss opera *Winchester '73* (but somewhat more mediocre without Stewart). And there was *Fame Is the Name of the Game*, which in the late 1940s had been made as an Alan Ladd movie called *Chicago Deadline*, based on a Tiffany Thayer novel, *One Woman*. It subsequently would evolve into a popular NBC series, *The Name of the Game*.

Writers/producers Levinson and Link noted, "Our own involvement with television movies was pure happenstance—we were under contract to Universal just as the so-called long form was gathering momentum. Our Broadway play *Prescription: Murder* became one of the early World Premieres [as these early TV movies were known]. Gradually, we began to feel that television could be more than a brief pit stop en route to theatrical features. Creative control was not obtainable for writers in the motion picture industry; it had passed from the studio to the director and/or star actor. But in television, for a variety of economic reasons, the producer was in charge."

As on the big screen, certain TV movies stood out—in quality, in production values, in writing and directing, and in acting. They would fall into the classic category: dramas like *Brian's Song*, the real-life buddy sports story of football stars Gayle Sayre (played by Billy Dee Williams) and cancer-stricken Brian Piccolo (James Caan). Forget the ill-advised TV movie remake of 2001. Another first-rate drama was *My Sweet Charlie*, based on a short-lived off-Broadway interracial play, with Patty Duke and Al Freeman Jr. playing nicely off one another. There also were *The Execution of Private Slovik* with Martin Sheen; *Fear on Trial* with William Devane playing blacklisted broadcaster/journalist John Henry Faulk; *Friendly Fire* with Carol Burnett and Ned Beatty as the grieving parents whose son died in Vietnam; *That Certain Summer*, for the time, a daring drama about gays, with Sheen and Hal Holbrook; *A Case of Rape* with Richard Crenna; the all-star *Holocaust; An Early Frost*, one of the first TV films to address the AIDS epidemic; and of course, the exceptional *Autobiography of Miss Jane Pittman*, with Cicely Tyson in a tour de force as an ancient woman whose life went from the era of slavery to the civil rights movement. Also classic was writer Richard Matheson's man versus machine thriller *Duel*, directed by a young Universal contractee, Steven Spielberg, who was put on the map with this tale. (Spielberg, 25 at the time, had already made a name for himself as an up-and-comer with episodic series work for the studio.)

In his foreword to my initial compilation of *Movies Made for Television* in 1979, prolific producer Quinn Martin offered, "The TV movie has evolved in many ways, but most important it is presently filling a void in a genre not made today in theatrical films. That void is the small, intense personal drama." He concluded, "When I first moved into the Samuel Goldwyn Studios, my next door neighbor was the proprietor of the place. Goldwyn himself. I got to know him quite well, and one of the things he liked to state was that a good producer was, above all, a good story editor and a good film editor. Goldwyn was correct. If your script is right and the film is edited correctly, you are going to make a successful one, with one caveat. That, in my opinion, is the cast. In the final assembly someone has to be up there on the screen acting out that good script."

CHAPTER 12

Public Television Comes Into Play

etween 1959 and 1961, WNTA—at the time, a local New York station—out of the ashes of the long-gone DuMont Network, offered on the prestigious *Play of the Week* two-hour taped stagings of major theatrical works, plus some by new playwrights. Beginning this top-drawer anthology series was *Medea*, director José Quintero's production of Euripides (from the 1920 Robinson Jeffers adaptation), starring Dame Judith Anderson. Other works included Graham Greene's *The Power and the Glory* with James Donald and Peter Falk, Steinbeck's *Burning Bright*, Jean-Paul Sartre's *Crime of Passion*, Gertrude Berg and Jack Gilford in *The World of Sholom Aleichem*, and Chekhov's *The Cherry Orchard* with Helen Hayes and E. G. Marshall. Sidney Lumet directed a two-part, four-hour *The Iceman Cometh* with Jason Robards (he was still Jr. at the time) and Robert Redford in 1960 and followed this up a few weeks later with Fay and Michael Kanin's play *Rashomon* with Ricardo Montalban, Oscar Homolka, Carol Lawrence, and James Mitchell. And later, Zero Mostel starred in Beckett's *Waiting for Godot*. Hardly cultural wasteland fare, as Newton Minow visioned it, and sometimes heavy going for those living in the New York minute, here was a show for theatrical cognoscenti, and it was the antecedent of what PBS would offer fairly regularly through the years.

This was followed not too long afterward by *NET Playhouse* and *Theatre in America* on the fledgling PBS (beginning in 1966), that premiered with Tennessee Williams's *Ten Blocks on the Camino Real* with a cast that included a young Martin Sheen, Lotte Lenya, Janet Margolin, Carrie Nye, and Hurd Hatfield. This was the occasional series of hour-long and 90-minute dramas on which such New York actors as Dustin Hoffman and Jon Voight made initial impacts on the tube (in Ivan Turgenev's *The Journey of the Fifth Horse* and Christopher Fry's *A Sleep of Prisoners*, respectively) and before easing into big-screen stardom—notably together in *Midnight Cowboy*. These and several dozen others were produced by Jac Venza.

Venza's early television career was as set designer for such 1950s shows as *Wonderful Town* on CBS, the musical that starred Rosalind Russell. For PBS, he produced *The Star Wagon* with Hoffman in 1966 as well as Arthur Miller's adaptation of Ibsen's *An Enemy of the People*. Moving up to executive producer, Venza would be the behind-the-scenes face of American drama on PBS, together with David W. Davis and Lindsey Law, for the next four decades. Officially, he was director of cultural and arts programs at WNET in New York. "Over the 25 years," he said in a major magazine piece published in *Current* in 1997, "I would look back and say most of the people who excelled in the unit [his core producers] had dedicated their career to very specialized material." Of legendary arts director Kirk Browning, Venza said, "Kirk was unusual because when we first started public television, there really were almost no directors who had concentrated on arts programs. He and one other, Roger Englander, directed all the NBC operas and could musically direct as opposed to working from text." Browning—who had directed the premiere of *Amahl and the Night Visitors* on *Hallmark Hall of Fame* in 1951—has been active in television for more than 55 years, having directed the PBS adaptation of Broadway's *The Light in the Piazza* on the *Live from Lincoln Center* series in June 2006. And both of those Browning shows were live.

Venza recalled, "When WNET [National Educational Television, the precursor to PBS] was formed, I became the first head of drama. . . . Later I inherited dance and then I took on music. For a while, in the late seventies into the eighties we were carrying the only American drama on public television, and when Exxon (the corporate sponsor) pulled out in 1988, and *Great Performances* was cut from 52 to 26 weeks, the series could no longer accommodate it."

Hollywood Television Theatre (PBS, 1970–1978) had Norman Lloyd, longtime Hitchcock colleague, and later Dr. Daniel Auschlander, on *St. Elsewhere*, in the role of producer—and sometimes director—for this anthology series of original plays and established dramas, originating at KCET in Los Angeles. Venza oversaw this program that ran for eight seasons irregularly (last three under the title *Conflicts*). George C. Scott's expansive production of

The Andersonville Trial (May 17, 1970) with a stellar cast headed by Richard Basehart was one of the major offerings in this taped series. Another was Lillian Hellman's *Another Part of the Forest,* directed by Daniel Mann, with Dorothy McGuire and Barry Sullivan. Richard Chamberlain starred in Christopher Fry's *The Lady's Not for Burning,* and Julie Harris recreated her Tony-winning stage performance in James Prideaux's *The Last of Mrs. Lincoln,* with George Schaefer directing. In 1973, when Valerie Perrine starred in a version of Bruce Jay Friedman's play *Steambath,* TV history was made when she went topless on several occasions.

In the early 1980s, PBS's *American Playhouse* was being promoted (by PBS) as "television's only weekly drama anthology series, exploring the human experience within the American Experience." The esteemed, long-running series had its inaugural telecast, John Cheever's *The Shady Hill Kidnapping,* on January 12, 1982, with Cheever himself narrating. Produced through the years were works by assorted American literary giants, from Mark Twain to Nathanael West, Philip Roth, Eugene O'Neill, Arthur Kopit, Isaac Bashevis Singer, and Sam Shepard. There has been a rather eclectic combination of American history, literature, drama, and comedy, ranging from the 1692 Salem witch hunts to the 1948 Alger Hiss-Whittaker Chambers spy case, with a stellar cast in a drama called *Concealed Enemies* (Emmy winner as outstanding limited series in the 1983–1984 season), to Lee Remick's one-woman *Eleanor Roosevelt,* to the multipart *Oppenheimer,* the story of the father of the atom bomb, with Sam Waterston in the lead.

Dramas like Jean Shepard's *The Great American Fourth of July and Other Disasters,* featuring James Broderick (Matthew's actor dad) and Matt Dillon in 1982; Katherine Anne Porter's *Noon Wine,* with Fred Ward and Pat Hingle in 1985; *Under the Biltmore Clock,* adapted from F. Scott Fitzgerald's short story "Myra Meets This Family" (also 1985); TV restagings of the Pulitzer Prize play *The Gin Game* with Hume Cronyn and Jessica Tandy, and the Stephen Sondheim musical *Sunday in the Park with George,* featuring Mandy Patinkin and Bernadette Peters, all were part of *American Playhouse.* (*The Gin Game* would be restaged later on TV with Dick Van Dyke and Mary Tyler Moore.) The PBS series, under Venza, through the years offered works by Eugene O'Neill (both the 1988 presentation of *Long Day's Journey into Night* with Jack Lemmon and Kevin Spacey and the superlative one in three parts of *Strange Interlude* with Glenda Jackson and José Ferrer) as well as Arthur Miller, Tennessee Williams, Arthur Kopit and Thornton Wilder, adaptations of F. Scott Fitzgerald, Mark Twain, and Shirley Jackson, and the talents of filmmakers such as Barbara Kopple, Gordon Parks, Robert M. Young, Gregory Nava, and Bill Duke. Several *American Playhouse* features were released theatrically (most notably *Testament* with Jane Alexander and *El Norte*, about Mayan Indian peasants) before airing on television.

For a bit, Ted Turner tried to emulate *American Playhouse* in the 1990s with the occasional film series TNT *Screenworks*, in association with, among others, Steven Spielberg's Amblin Entertainment. Horton Foote's *The Habitation of Dragons*, David Mamet's *The Water Engine*, and Arthur Miller's Depression era drama *The American Clock* were just some of the presentations, featuring a mixture of Hollywood and New York actors.

American Playhouse continued airing periodically through the late 1990s. Among other notable series executive produced by Jac Venza were *American Masters* and *Hollywood Television Theatre* as well as the historical miniseries *The Adams Chronicles* and *Tales from the Hollywood Hills*.

In 1999, a Peabody Award went to Venza, with the citation, "For more than four decades, Jac Venza has been a driving force in the presentation of cultural and arts programming on television, whose growing list of accomplishments includes *Dance in America, Theater in America, Great Performances,* and *American Masters,* of which he is one."

Masterpiece Theatre (PBS, premiering January 10, 1971) for four decades has remained the distinguished showcase for meticulously staged and generally sumptuous (primarily) British drama for American audiences, memorably hosted for many years by Alistair Cooke. The initial presentation was the 12-part drama *The First Churchills,* about Winston's family. During the early years, such literary classics as Thackery's *Vanity Fair,* James Fenimore Cooper's *The Last of the Mohicans,* Thomas Hughes's *Tom Brown's School Days,* and Wilkie Collins's *The Moonstone* were staged, along with several of the landmarks of dramatic television (British and American), including *Upstairs, Downstairs*—two splendid 1974 miniseries of 13 episodes each— and, several years later, *Brideshead Revisited* and *Jewel in the Crown.* The lavish multipart *Forsyte Saga* predated *Masterpiece Theatre* as we know it, being produced in 1967. PBS's other showcase British import through the years has been *Mystery!* with its classic opening credits by illustrator Edward Gorey and its hosting initially by Vincent Price and then Dame Diana Rigg.

Loring Mandel points out, at least for him, "Writing for PBS in the 1970s was easier than writing for the networks. There were fewer executives one had to satisfy at PBS, and there was a greater regard for talent. By then (as opposed to the 1950s), the networks had so stratified the development process that it took forever to shepherd a script through to either a green light or a pass. And there were many more taboos at the networks. In the 1950s, if the script editor, the producer, and the advertising agency rep said yes, the script was a go. That changed around 1959, when the creative heads of the programming at the networks were pushed out by the bean counters. Network TV lost its edge." For NET (the precursor to PBS), Mandel wrote *The Coming Asunder of Jimmy Bright*, which aired in 1971, and *Particular Men* the following year. Ken Kercheval starred in the former, Stacy Keach in the latter. And in 1977, along with Ernest Kinoy, Naomi Foner, Roger O. Hirson, and others, he wrote some of the eight-part PBS miniseries *The Best of Families*, dealing with three fictional New York City families—one wealthy (the Wheelers), one middle class (the Baldwins), and a clan of poor Irish immigrants (the Raffertys)—in the final two decades of nineteenth-century America.

CHAPTER 13

360 Degrees After 120

I t took a couple of years, but NBC's Project 120 found company in what came to be known popularly—and just about generically—as the movie of the week.

Quinn Martin, the prolific producer whose many hit TV series included *The Untouchables, The Fugitive, The Invaders, Dan August, Cannon,* and *The Streets of San Francisco,* as well as a great many television movies, wrote in the late 1970s in his foreword to my book, "There are two reasons for television making the more intense personal drama. One is economic; the other is the technical restriction of the TV screen. There is a saying that the art form changes as the technology changes. When we can get a six-foot screen with the working inside for the price of a regular color television set, you will see big external movies made for the home." And Herbert B. Leonard, producer of fondly remembered shows such as *Route 66* and *Naked City* as well as the TV movie version of *Friendly Persuasion,* among others, admitted to me, "Good dramas are people dramas. Because of the size of the screen, we had to keep thing intimate. Lots of close-ups, until the screens get big to let us do lots of action in medium and long shots." But even Mr. Martin and Mr. Leonard could not foresee a 92-inch plasma screen, it seems.

By the 1966–1967 season, ABC had joined the movies made for television (MMFT) game, and a season or two later, so did CBS with *Hawaii Five-O,* which also would go on to hitdom as a long-running (12-season) series. The venerable Levinson-Link team (seemingly their names would forever be hyphenated) would introduce Peter Falk as Columbo in *Prescription: Murder* from one of their plays and also bring forth the espionage tale *Istanbul*

Express; the Raymond Burr Ironside character would make its bow in a pair of TV movies, and Jack Webb would resurrect his Joe Friday persona in a new *Dragnet.* In fact, most of the early TV movies were made as prospective pilots from which the networks could judge viewer reaction and then create series.

During the 1969–1970 season, ABC began airing a weekly series of 90-minute TV movies, produced mainly by Paramount, through the network's association with it or by Thomas/Spelling Productions or Screen Gems. Somewhat above the run-of-the-mill TV movies of the 1960s was Rod Serling's *Night Gallery* (a pilot to his series, of course), which offered a trilogy of tales that he wrote and which were directed by, among others, newcomer Steven Spielberg. Also above average several weeks later (in 1969) was an adult drama, *Silent Night, Lonely Night,* adapted from Robert Anderson's play. It starred Lloyd Bridges and Shirley Jones. But for each *Silent Night, Lonely Night,* there seemed to be a *Gidget Grows Up,* which aired just two weeks later.

And just a fortnight after the *Gidget* movie came one of the early MMFT highlights, again with the Levinson-Link thumbprints. This was the superior *My Sweet Charlie,* which the pair adapted from David Westheimer's novel and Off-Broadway play. Patty Duke and Al Freeman Jr., as a pregnant white Southern girl and a black lawyer from New York, both on the run, happen to meet in a boarded-up house on the Texas coast and develop a close friendship for their mutual survival. This, like *Silent Night, Lonely Night,* was pure live golden age drama at its pinnacle—now in the guise of a made-for-TV movie.

Then more dross, and then a bit of gold—an adaptation of *David Copperfield,* with—except for the lead—the cream of the British acting establishment: Michael Redgrave, Ralph Richardson, Emlyn Williams, Richard Attenborough, Edith Evans, Wendy Hiller, and Laurence Olivier in a top-drawer, Emmy-nominated cameo as Mr. Creakle. The old golden age pro Delbert Mann directed this one: the fifth film version of the Dickens classic and the first in nearly 35 years. But being a British production, it could be pigeonholed as an anomaly of the time.

In September 1970, CBS created its own production outfit for TV movies, Cinema Center 100, with another old pro, onetime movie star Glenn Ford, making his television acting debut in a drama called *The Brotherhood of the Bell.* Some weeks later, for Aaron Spelling Productions on ABC, Edward G. Robinson starred in the thriller *The Old Man Who Cried Wolf,* and after that, Fred Astaire costarred in his only Western, a lighthearted one, to be sure: *The Over-the-Hill Gang Rides Again.* And Bing Crosby, in his only television movie, acted against type as a deceptively kind small-town doctor in *Dr. Cook's Garden*, who sees to it that the bad people in his community die before their time and the good live longer—just like the flowers in his garden. It was an adaptation of a short-lived 1967 Broadway play by Ira Levin. In later years, Bing's on-screen buddy Bob Hope also would make one, and only one, TV movie: *A Masterpiece of Murder*. These were notable primarily as showcases for fading movie stars working in a new genre (for them).

The second Peter Falk/Columbo movie, *Ransom for a Dead Man*, premiered in spring 1971, followed by his long-running series in which he played the wily rumpled police lieutenant on and off for the next three decades—probably longer than anyone else in television in the same character. A week later came *Vanished*, from Fletcher Knebel's 1968 thriller about the mysterious disappearance of a presidential adviser, with Richard Widmark in his TV acting debut. This was the first long-form original movie on television (at three hours and 10 minutes, plus commercials) and paved the way for subsequent filmed miniseries. And director Delbert Mann returned with another in the elegant British-made series of literary classics, *Jane Eyre*, which costarred George C. Scott and Susannah York.

The Homecoming—A Christmas Story, by Earl Hamner Jr., would serve as the pilot to the beloved Waltons series that aired on CBS from 1972 to 1981 and then moved on to a handful of MMFT reunions.

Several TV movies in the fall of 1971 could, nearly 20 years earlier, have passed for minimalistic golden age dramas: *In Broad Daylight*, with Richard Boone as a blind actor who, discovering that his wife (Stella Stevens) is cheating on him with his best friend, plots an elaborate double murder; *Suddenly Single*, a bittersweet tale of a newly divorced man (played by Hal Holbrook) trying to find a place for himself in the world of swinging singles; and *Goodbye Raggedy Ann*, with Holbrook, again, as a Hollywood writer determined to talk a young, down-on-her-luck actress out of suicide. She's played by Mia Farrow, in her TV movie debut.

Holbrook also starred with Martin Sheen in one of television's first gay-themed movies, the well-received *That Certain Summer* in 1972. It was written by Levinson and Link and directed by Lamont Johnson, actor turned prolific director, who won the Directors Guild of America (DGA) Award for his work on the film. *Death Takes a Holiday*, an updated remake of the 1934 movie that starred Fredric March, reunited in secondary roles Melvyn Douglas and Myrna Loy for the first time since the 1940s. And Barbara Eden and Larry Hagman, *I Dream of Jeannie* costars in the late 1960s, were reunited in a mediocre chiller, *A Howling in the Woods*, adapted from Velda Johnson's 1968 mystery novel.

Not long after this one came Steven Spielberg's cult man-versus-machine classic *Duel*, starring Dennis Weaver as a traveling salesman pitted against a 10-ton tanker truck on a lonely stretch of highway. Richard Matheson wrote the teleplay from his own story published earlier in *Playboy*. Spielberg was put on the map with this landmark movie, and he left television for more than a decade. And just two weeks after *Duel* came the equally acclaimed *Brian's Song*, adapted from the book *I Am Third* by Gale Sayers. This was a finely told and acted, four-hanky drama about Chicago Bears running back Brian Piccolo (played by James Caan), his lasting rivalry and friendship with fellow gridiron player Sayers (Billy Dee Williams), and his losing battle with cancer.

Producer Quinn Martin's police drama *The Streets of San Francisco* first aired as a TV movie in 1972 before going on to a successful series run, and Dan Curtis's occult film *The Night Stalker* and Jerry Thorpe's offbeat Western *Kung Fu*, which kicked off the martial arts craze, premiered as well. Curtis's would air with TV veteran Darren McGavin as *Kolchak*—not to be confused with *Kojak* (with Telly Savalas) or *Kodiak* (Clint Walker), the last named debuting on ABC the very night that McGavin's show did on CBS.

One of the better TV dramas, *A War of Children*, an Emmy Award winner as outstanding program of the 1972–1973 TV season, depicted two middle-class Belfast families—one Protestant, one Catholic—during the troubles of the time and how children in the two communities were affected. Written by James Costigan and directed by George Schaefer, it had an all British and Irish cast.

Another was Truman Capote's *The Glass House*, a grim jailhouse drama starring Alan Alda and Vic Morrow, which Capote wrote with Wyatt Cooper and which was filmed entirely in the Utah State Prison.

It was big TV movie news early in 1973 when Richard Burton and Elizabeth Taylor costarred in an unusual two-part British-made film, *Divorce His/Divorce Hers*—actually two stories running concurrently and airing on consecutive nights—delving into the dissolution of an 18-year marriage through the eyes of both parties. And spurred on by the success of *The Godfather* on the big screen was *Honor Thy Father*, based on Gay Talese's mobster novel about life inside the mafia and the collapse of a real-life crime family. Italian movie veteran Raf Vallone starred as Joe "Bananas" Bonanno, and Joseph Bologna played his son Salvatore "Bill" Bonanno.

Distinctively bald, lollipop-sucking Theo Kojak, as portrayed by Telly Savalas, came to television in spring 1973 in a first-rate three-hour movie titled *The Marcus-Nelson Murders*, written by Abby Mann and directed by prolific Joseph Sargent (both winning Emmys for their work). Suggested by journalist Selwyn Rabb's *Justice in the Back Room*, it was based on the sensational 1963 murders of Manhattan career girls Janice Wylie and Emily Hoffert, resulting in the case that ultimately led to the Supreme Court's Miranda decision three years later. Longtime character actor and basically a movie bad guy, Savalas skyrocketed to stardom as Kojak and headlined the 1973–1978 series, which ended up typecasting him.

Joseph Sargent broke into television as a character actor on such shows as *The Lone Ranger, State Trooper, Peter Gunn, Gunsmoke,* and Dick Powell's *Zane Grey Theatre.* He moved on to directing episodes of *Lassie, Bonanza, Star Trek, The Invaders,* and *The Man from U.N.C.L.E.,* among others, and then increasingly better MMFT, beginning with *The Sunshine Patriot* in 1968 and more than 50 others over the next four decades. In addition to *The Marcus-Nelson Murders,* he won Emmys for his direction of *Love Is Never Silent* (on *Hallmark Hall of Fame*) and *Caroline?* (also for *Hallmark*) and received nominations for several others; the DGA gave him their top award for *Marcus-Nelson,* the medical drama *Something the Lord Made,* and his ode to early FDR, *Warm Springs.* (Sargent also did an occasional feature film, like the action thriller *The Taking of Pelham One Two Three* and Gregory Peck's *MacArthur.*) One critic noted that "as a rule, if you see 'Directed by Joseph Sargent,' do not change the channel." Others tend to agree based on the wide variety of subjects that bear those four words, from *Tribes,* about a rebellious hippie drafted during Vietnam; to Sally Field's first serious dramatic role in *Maybe I'll Come Home in the Spring;* to the cancer tearjerker *Sunshine;* to *Amber Waves,* a paean to farm life in the mid-twentieth century; to the superb *Miss Rose White, Miss Evers' Boys,* and *Bojangles;* and even Dostoevsky's *Crime and Punishment,* which was hardly mainstream TV fare. His most recent TV movie, a new version of the classic from 1977, *Sybil,* had been scheduled for airing during the 2006–2007 television season.

In the weeks following the Kojak movie were TV adaptations of John Steinbeck's *The Red Pony* with Henry Fonda and Mark Twain's *Tom Sawyer.* There was also a work with the Serling name—not Rod, but his author brother Robert. It was a drama from his 1967 novel *The President's Plane Is Missing,* about a fictional incident shoving an incompetent vice president (played by Buddy Ebsen) into the Oval Office when Air Force One and its main occupant vanish. Ernest Kinoy and Mark Carliner wrote the teleplay.

The first genuine miniseries on network television, in November 1973, would be *The Blue Knight,* adapted from ex-cop turned successful writer Joseph Wambaugh's novel about a veteran cop on the Los Angeles Police Department on his last few days before retirement. William Holden made his dramatic acting debut on TV as Bumper Morgan and won an Emmy for his performance. This police story aired initially in one-hour segments on four consecutive nights. Later, George Kennedy would take over the Bumper Morgan role in *The Blue Knight* series, which lasted less than a season.

Billy Wilder's *Double Indemnity* was remade as a TV movie in late 1973. Adapted by Steven Bochco and directed by Jack Smight, it starred Richard Crenna, Samantha Eggar, and Lee J. Cobb in the original roles of Fred MacMurray, Barbara Stanwyck, and Edward G. Robinson. (There also had been a staging of that notable noir film on *Lux Video Theatre* in late 1954. Laraine Day was the femme fatale duping Frank Lovejoy, with Ray Collins as the latter's colleague and mentor. Buzz Kulik directed.)

Gene Wilder, Bob Newhart, Ellen Burstyn, and a top-drawer cast starred in a delightful 1974 adult comedy, *Thursday's Game,* that dealt with the marital and business problems of a couple of middle-aged men who continue their night out with the boys even after the breakup of their weekly poker game. It was another reminder of an earlier time on the *Philco/Goodyear Playhouse.* Though in the 1960s, Wilder acted on *Armstrong Circle Theatre, The DuPont Show of the Week,* and *The Defenders,* and in CBS's 1966 production of *Death of a Salesman,* he never did much television. Of course, Newhart would be an icon through his several hit sitcoms over the years.

Two controversial TV movies were aired in 1974. The first was William Bradford Huie's antiwar book *The Execution of Private Slovik,* starring Martin Sheen, about the only American GI since the Civil War to be shot—by firing squad—for desertion. The script was by Richard Levinson and William Link. (Sinatra once had planned to film the story but abandoned it because the producers refused to allow blacklisted Albert Maltz's screenplay.) The other was *Born Innocent,* which gained notoriety for its graphic broom-handle rape of a young teenage girl in a tough detention home. (Linda Blair played the 14-year-old; Kim Hunter played her mom.)

Another exceptional TV movie of the time was a 90-minute adaptation by playwright Lanford Wilson of Tennessee Williams's farm worker story *The Migrants,* with Cloris Leachman, Sissy Spacek, and Ron Howard. It was nominated as outstanding drama of the 1973–1974 season. And Dick Van Dyke gave a powerful dramatic performance as a closet alcoholic in *The Morning After,* adapted by Richard Matheson from Jack B. Weiner's novel.

A musical version of Dickens's *Great Expectations* aired in 1974—without the songs (at least in the one shown in the United States)—starring Michael York as Pip, Sarah Miles as Estella, and James Mason as Magwitch. Also airing were a new production by writer Carol Sobieski of the French film classic *Diabolique,* titled *Reflections of Murder,* with Tuesday Weld, Joan Hackett, and Sam Waterston, as well as TV versions of director John Ford's *Three Godfathers*, retitled *The Godchild*; John Huston's *The Red Badge of Courage*; Elia Kazan's *A Tree Grows in Brooklyn*; Rouben Mamoulian's *The Mark of Zorro*; and both *Turn of the Screw* and *Dracula*. The last two were directed by Dan Curtis.

Producer (and later director) Dan Curtis in 1973 offered a two-part tape-to-film adaptation of Oscar Wilde's *Picture of Dorian Gray* and a first-rate *Frankenstein*. Curtis's varied, five-decade TV career included the 1960s sports show *Challenge Golf* featuring Gary Player and Arnold Palmer. He continued through 2005 with two made-for-TV movies, *Saving Milly* (dealing with television journalist Mort Kondrake's struggle with his wife's fatal illness) and *Our Fathers* (about Boston's Cardinal Bernard Law and the Roman Catholic Church's sex abuse scandals of the 1990s).

In 1963, Curtis started *The CBS Match Play Golf Classic*, which ran for a decade and received an Emmy for achievement in sports.

The creator of *The Night Stalker* and *Dark Shadows*, Dan Curtis, as producer and/or director, long was a cult figure thanks to his *Trilogy of Terror* and his Warner Bros.–style gangster movies such as *Melvin Purvis, G-Man*, and *The Kansas City Massacre* (both starring cigar-chomping, tommy-gun-wielding Dale Robertson as Purvis). Then he showed a nostalgic side with two semi-autobiographical movies about growing up in Bridgeport, Connecticut: *When Every Day Was the Fourth of July* and *The Long Days of Summer*, both with Dean Jones. On these, Charles Aidman was the off-screen narrator as the Curtis persona. In the 1980s, Curtis produced and directed the monumental miniseries *The Winds of War* and *War and Remembrance*, based on the novels by Herman Wouk. Both, as it was pointed out in reviews, were cast with actors rather too old for their roles. "This was because Bob Mitchum, who was needed as star because he was such a commanding figure," Curtis later said, "was too old to be a simple naval commander, so our casting people had to get (almost) senior citizens like Polly Bergen and other rather too old for their character actors to fill out the main cast. By the time we did *War and Remembrance*, Bob was 71—and not even an admiral! His character would have been long retired by the U.S. Navy in real life. And Ralph Bellamy at 85 playing FDR, who died when he was only 63. Bellamy was there because, in addition to being a venerable and wonderful actor, he had made the persona of FDR as his own back in the 1950s on Broadway in *Sunrise at Campobello* and in the later movie."

Curtis, who died in 2006, is still remembered for his snappy comment when picking up the Emmy for the very expensive *War and Remembrance*: "I'd like to thank ABC for ponying up the dough to pay for this."

MMFT highlights during 1975 included the very stylish *Love Among the Ruins*, uniting Katharine Hepburn and Laurence Olivier, under TV-debuting George Cukor's direction; *The Legend of Lizzie Borden* with Elizabeth Montgomery; *Death Be Not Proud*, a dramatization of John Gunther's memoir about the life and death of his teenage son in 1947; *Queen of the Stardust Ballroom* with Maureen Stapleton and Charles Durning (later, it became a short-lived Broadway musical); *Huckleberry Finn* with young Ron Howard, and *Starsky and Hutch*, which led to the hit series. George C. Scott portrayed celebrity attorney Louis Nizer and William Devane folksy radio and television personality John Henry Faulk, who fell victim to the blacklist in *Fear on Trial*. Sissy Spacek enacted a pampered heiress who becomes a revolutionary in *Katherine*, a film written and directed by Jeremy Paul Kagan paralleling the Patty Hearst case of the time. Paul Shenar played—quite credibly—Orson Welles in *The Night That Panicked America*, recreating the famous 1938 radio broadcast, the *Mercury Theater* adaptation of H. G. Wells's *War of the Worlds*, directed by Joseph Sargent. A couple of decades later, actor Liev Schreiber portrayed Welles in *RKO 281*, an intriguing speculative MMFT dealing with the filming of *Citizen Kane*.

Eleanor and Franklin (1976), producer David Susskind's top-drawer presentation of the study of the Roosevelts from early youth to FDR's death in 1945, told through the recollections of the widowed Eleanor, and the sequel the following year, *Eleanor and Franklin: The White House Years*, won multiple awards (each received an Emmy as outstanding special). Both, adapted by James Costigan from the biographical book by Joseph P. Lash, starred Jane Alexander and Edward Herrmann and were directed by Daniel Petrie.

The wide range of TV movies in 1976 included *The Macahans*, a Western based on the 1960s Cinerama film *How the West Was Won* (and the forerunner to the occasional series under the sweeping movie's title); *Collision Course*, about the titanic clash between President Harry Truman (E. G. Marshall) and General Douglas MacArthur (Henry Fonda) over the conduct of the Korean War, drawn from fact and fleshed out with dramatic speculation by golden age writers Ernest Kinoy and David Shaw; *Louis Armstrong—Chicago Style* with Ben Vereen as Satchmo in the early to mid-1930s; *James Dean*, the first of two TV movies (the other several decades later) about the famed young actor, both with the same title; *Farewell to Manzanar*, dealing with the internment of Japanese Americans during World War II, based on the memoirs by one of those, as a young girl, in the camps; and *Charlie's Angels*, which went on to become the cult Aaron Spelling series. *The Boy in the Plastic Bubble* (1976) proved that there was life after sweat hog Vinnie Barbarino for the 22-year-old John Travolta, and *Helter Skelter*, based on the book by Vincent

Bugliosi with Curt Gentry, dramatized the explosive story of Charles Manson and was one of the biggest MMFT productions to its time, with 115 speaking parts.

Sybil was another notable television production of 1976. An acclaimed two-part, four-hour production (Emmy Award winner as outstanding special), in which Sally Field won an Emmy as best actress for playing a young woman so disturbed by childhood experiences that she develops 16 distinct personalities. Emmys also went to Stewart Stern for his teleplay and to the score by Leonard Rosenman and Alan and Marilyn Bergman. (*Sybil* would be remade for TV 30 years later.) The erstwhile Flying Nun really proved her dramatic talents with this role and another a number of years later in the starring part in *A Woman of Independent Means,* in which she ages 50 years.

The overwhelming success in 1976 of the 12-hour miniseries adaptation of Irwin Shaw's 1970 best seller *Rich Man, Poor Man,* with a star-laden cast headed by Peter Strauss, Nick Nolte, and Susan Blakely (each one Emmy nominated), assured the immediate future of the Novel for Television, an NBC umbrella for an ambitious series of films of popular contemporary literary works. Included would be Taylor Caldwell's *Captains and the Kings* in late 1976, then Anton Myrer's *Once an Eagle,* Norman Bogner's *Seventh Avenue,* Robert Ludlum's *The Rhinemann Exchange,* Harold Robbins's *79 Park Avenue, Aspen* (a combination of books by Bert Hirschfeld and Bart Spicer), Sara Davidson's *Loose Change,* Arthur Hailey's *Wheels,* and others.

Event programming such as *QB VII,* an absorbing adaptation miniseries based on Leon Uris's best seller about two successful men, an American writer and a Polish doctor, whose careers led to a confrontation in a London courtroom over a long past incident in a Nazi prison camp, boasted a stellar list of performers and garnered 13 Emmy nominations. It was one of the first TV movies dealing, even peripherally, with the Holocaust. More directly was another major television drama a few years later, *Holocaust,* which featured, among others, a young Meryl Streep in the cast. (A year or so earlier, she had starred with Michael Moriarty in writer Ernest Kinoy's hockey-themed drama *The Deadliest Season,* which, like *Holocaust,* was produced by Herbert Brodkin.)

CHAPTER 14

Family Portrait

Roots, Alex Haley's famed saga of American slavery (tracing the roots of his own family through two centuries), airing about a year before *Holocaust*, became the most watched dramatic television event to its time—memorable viewing that spanned the last week of January 1977. The 12-hour production, adapted by William Blinn from Haley's novel, had a massive cast, four directors, and four writers (Kinoy and Blinn among them). *Roots*, blending fact and fiction, changed the style of the TV miniseries, airing on consecutive nights rather than, like *Rich Man, Poor Man* before it, in weekly installments, and garnered the biggest audience in entertainment programming history to that time—eclipsed only by the finale of *M*A*S*H* six years later.

Ernest Kinoy has observed that there were no black writers involved with the initial *Roots*, and only one black director, Gilbert Moses. "Why there were no black writers on that project which so represented the black experience in those relatively early days of the civil rights movement has puzzled me through the years . . . this story about an extended black family." This echoed somewhat another of Kinoy's conundrums about an earlier time in television, when, in 2002, he mused to a writer from London's *Guardian*, "You'd come into *Studio One*, or *Kraft*, or *Philco*, and you'd tell them this long story about this marvelous Italian family. And they would say it's too Jewish, because they knew very well that it wasn't Italian, but it was a Jewish family. Paddy Chayefsky did it a number of times. *The Catered Affair* is about an Irish family. *Marty*, the Italian butcher. It was because a number of the Jewish writers would come in with the material and the networks would say it's too Jewish. The rest of America won't understand."

At the Emmy ceremonies, *Roots*, with a record 37 nominations, was named outstanding dramatic series of the 1976–1977 season. David Greene, who directed the first of eight parts, told me at the time, "*Roots* ranked with me with some of the work I'd done for television years ago on *Hallmark*—and such Shakespeare as *Othello* in 1953, *Macbeth* in 1955, *Twelfth Night* in 1957 for CBC in Canada. This was dramatic television at its best, and viewers, we were to find, responded en masse." (Almost half the country, 100 million viewers, saw the final episode. This figure claims one of the highest Nielsen ratings ever recorded, according to industry numbers—even three decades later.) Greene called this material "heavy stuff. It defied television conventions about black-oriented programming, which ABC executives feared might well be a ratings disaster. David [Wolper, the executive producer] and Stan [Margulies, the producer] and Alex [Haley, the author] blended fiction and fact in a soap opera package that included black heroes and white villains—practically unheard of in television. And by playing out the drama on consecutive nights for a whole week, *Roots* appeared on the edge of revolutionizing television." It did. It was a true cultural phenomenon.

Britisher David Greene was prolific in his work on American television, as both producer and director, going back to dramas on *Hallmark Hall of Fame* in the early 1950s and on *Suspicion, Playhouse 90, Shirley Temple's Storybook, The Twilight Zone, Espionage*, dozens of made-for-TV movies through 1998, and several segments of *Rich Man, Poor Man*. His TV movie work ranged from the exceptional *Friendly Fire* (Carol Burnett and Ned Beatty heartbreakingly played grieving parents who learn the truth about the death of their son during the Vietnam War), the 1988 *Inherit the Wind* (with Emmy-winning Jason Robards and Kirk Douglas), the 1991 *What Ever Happened to Baby Jane?* (with sisters Vanessa and Lynn Redgrave), and *Night of the Hunter* to biopics on Betty Ford (played by Gena Rowlands in an Emmy-winning performance) and Liberace.

OF BIBLICAL PROPORTIONS

As much of a phenomenon as *Roots*, and as *The Autobiography of Miss Jane Pittman* a couple of years earlier, with Cicely Tyson in a tour de force performance as a very elderly black woman who lived from Reconstruction to the civil rights movement, was the very reverent *Jesus of Nazareth* (1977), a biblical miniseries from noted Italian director Franco Zeffirelli. This particular production, with a stellar cast headed by British actor Robert Powell, remains the biblical drama on television against which all others are judged. The Bible always has been a wonderful source for drama—particularly on television, where it really did not have to compete with Cecil B. DeMille (although some latter-day producers had the misjudgment of trying).

The first significant biblical production, of course, was the Gian-Carlo Menotti TV opera *Amahl and the Night Visitor*. It was the premiere presentation on *Hallmark Hall of Fame* in 1951 and was restaged by the NBC Opera Company more than a half dozen times through the years. During the 1950s and 1960s, there would be an occasional foray into the Bible—original dramas ranging from *The Stone* with Tony Curtis as David and John Baragrey as King Saul on the *General Electric Theatre* in early 1959 to *Those We Love*, a modern day take on the story of Ruth and Naomi starring June Allyson (the premiere presentation on her *DuPont Show with June Allyson*, also in 1959) and Ann Harding, to *Give Us Barabbas* (produced in color on Easter Sunday, 1961) with James Daly (actors Tyne and Tim's dad) and Kim Hunter, written by Henry Denker for *Hallmark*. For a few weeks in 1966, ABC tried out *Great Bible Adventures*; then, in the late 1970s, NBC commissioned the folks behind *Classics Illustrated* for a weekly series, *Greatest Heroes of the Bible*. There were nine stories during the first season, with noted TV actors in beards and robes playing biblical notables and patriarchs, beginning with the story of David and Goliath (Roger Kern and Ted Cassidy). Another batch of biblical tales filtered through the *Classics Illustrated* format ran intermittently between 1979 and 1981.

In addition, there were periodic TV movies such as *The Story of Jacob and Joseph*, directed in 1974 by Michael Cacoyannis from a teleplay by Ernest Kinoy, with Alan Bates narrating and Keith Michell and Tony LoBianco starring, along with Colleen Dewhurst. This actually was a two-part movie—the tale of Jacob and Esau in the first, and Joseph and his brethren in the second. Another, also from producer Mildred Freed Alberg and writer Kinoy and starring Keith Michell, was *The Story of David* (in two parts with two directors) in 1976. Burt Lancaster, notably, starred in *Moses—The Lawgiver* in a six-part CBS miniseries in 1975 that concurrently was shown theatrically pared down to a bit over two hours.

A multinational cast headed by American actor Chris Sarandon dramatized in 1980 the events from the Last Supper through the arrest and trial of Jesus to the Crucifixion. The drama, *The Day Christ Died*, by screenwriters James Lee Barrett and Edward Anhalt, mixed biblical fact with fiction. Another all-star, basically British cast, in addition to Ava Gardner, John Houseman, Richard Kiley, and Susan Sarandon, peopled a biblical miniseries called *A.D.* the same year. Cowritten by Anthony Burgess (also of *Jesus of Nazareth* and

Moses—The Lawgiver) and set just after the death of Jesus, it chronicled the lives of Christ's disciples and events in Rome during the reigns of the emperors Tiberius, Caligula, Claudius, and Nero. And in *Masada*, adapted from Ernest Gann's 1971 book *The Antagonists*, Peter O'Toole made his American TV acting debut as the Roman general leading the epic first-century siege of the legendary mountain fortress where more than 900 Jewish Zealots made a heroic stand against 5,000 Roman soldiers. Peter Strauss, who skyrocketed to TV stardom in *Rich Man, Poor Man*, played the fiery leader of the freedom-fighting Zealots.

In the 1990s, Ted Turner's TNT presented a series of biblical dramas filmed in Morocco in association with Lux Vide, an Italian television conglomerate. Produced by Gerald Rafshoon, who had been high up in the Carter administration before becoming a filmmaker, these extravagantly retold stories began with *Abraham* (Richard Harris, along with Maximilian Schell) in 1994, followed by *Jacob* (Matthew Modine), *Joseph* (Paul Mercurio, along with Ben Kingsley), *Moses* (Kingsley), *Samson and Delilah* (Eric Thal and Elizabeth Hurley), *David* (Nathaniel Parker, along with Jonathan Pryce), and *Solomon* (Ben Cross, with Anouk Aimée as Bathsheba). Another in this series was *Jesus* (Jeremy Sisto, with Jacqueline Bisset as Mary), which escaped to CBS in 2000. Several others in the same series of films based on the Bible continue to air on Italian television, a handful of them with Anthony Quinn's son Danny as Jesus. Another biblical drama, *Solomon and Sheba*, turned up in competition with the TNT series on Showtime in 1995, with Jimmy Smits and Halle Berry in the title roles. *Mary, Mother of Jesus* was a reverent retelling of the biblical story produced in 1999 by Eunice Kennedy Shriver and son Bobby (and filmed in, of all places, Budapest) in their first venture into films for the Shriver Family Film Company. Swedish actress Pernilla August was beatific as Mary, and Welsh-born Christian Bale (who is approximately the same age as she) played Jesus. Shriver cousin Christopher Lawford (son of Peter Lawford and Pat Kennedy) turned up as Reuben, one of the disciples.

Ways of approaching religious topics on TV in kind of nonsecular terms go back to the early days of the medium—in CBS's *Lamp unto My Feet* (beginning in 1948 and going well into the late 1970s) and *Look Up and Live*, NBC's *The Eternal Light* (coming over from 1940s radio circa 1952 from the Jewish Theological Seminary during a combined 40-odd-year run) and *Frontiers of Faith*, and ABC's *Directions*. Name directors, writers, and actors (early John Frankenheimer, Roger O. Hirson, Theodore Bikel, Gene Wilder, James Dean, Alan Arkin) provided vignettes that told inspirational stories, generally in the wasteland of Sunday programming.

The syndicated *Insight*'s way, from the Paulists, was through an imaginative route: little morality plays with A-list actors working for peanuts. One of these was an Adam and Eve tale called *This Side of Eden*—what happened to them after being run out of the garden—with heavily bearded Walter Matthau (in Jed Clampett overalls), pouty Carol Burnett as a Bob Mackie–dressed first lady, and Ed Asner, natty in a robin's egg blue suit and bowler, as God. Another was comedy parable *Just Before Eve,* featuring Martin Sheen (in cutoff jeans and a sweatshirt emblazoned with a huge "#1" on the chest) as a disconsolate Adam—actually, he is totally bored—and Flip Wilson as a hip, boppin' angel who urges him to look at the big picture, providing Adam first with a warm puppy for companionship, then a surrogate colleague to plays checkers with him, and then a curvy Eve.

There were comedies, including one teaming up Bob Newhart (as God, disguised as a mild-mannered clerk stamping papers in Limbo) and Jack Klugman (as a brash, recently departed theatrical agent), and more serious subjects like the Northern Ireland problem of the time. There was a drama called *Arnstein's Miracle,* with Howard Da Silva as an aging violinist who wants to back out of a Thanksgiving benefit that will raise money for hospitalized children. His cynical reasoning: "What you give away for nothing is worth nothing." But what he really fears is growing old and losing his talent.

Insight produced more than 250 taped and filmed episodes (serious dramas and lighthearted parables) that ran in syndication, generally on Sunday mornings, but sometimes slotted as prime time specials, and was executive produced by Father Ellwood Kleiser during its entire 23-year run. Many of television's top writers, directors and stars, flocked to the show, generally at no salary or at union scale—which was reportedly donated to charity—and it won many Emmy Awards through the years. Martin Sheen, Jack Albertson, and Patty Duke (then Astin) were frequent *Insight*-ers, acting in scripts by such name writers as Michael Crichton, Howard Fast, John Meredith Lucas, Carol Sobieski, Edmund North, and William Peter Blatty.

CHAPTER 15

The Mini and the West

The first of the really big miniseries was *Centennial*, James Michener's historical fiction covering two centuries of the American West, with a cast headed by 86 name players. The saga ran 26 plus hours (with commercials), airing rather erratically over a four-month period on NBC in late 1978 and early 1979 in two- and three-hour segments. Eventually, HBO got rerun rights and aired the show in order over a 12-night schedule—pared down because there were no commercials. The epic, drawn from Michener's 1,100-page saga, spanned the decades from the late eighteenth century—beginning when a French-Canadian fur trapper and a frontiersman (Robert Conrad and Richard Chamberlain) strike up a friendship—and ending in the mid-1970s with the founding of the fictional town of Centennial, Colorado, by their present-day descendants. The miniseries, the most expensive film made for television to that time, with a $25 million budget, cost four times as much as *Roots*. The various segments, each with a distinctive chapter title, like a novel, were decided by producer John Wilder, who adapted Michener's work to be self-contained—even though there were a number of continuing characters—and shown independently of the others, if necessary. Despite the scope of the miniseries, it received only two Emmy nominations—for the editing of one segment and the art direction of another.

If *Centennial*, and another mini also with Richard Chamberlain, *Dream West* (1986), adapted by Evan Hunter from the historical novel by David Nevin about John Charles Freemont, can be classified as Westerns, television approached, at times through the years, the subject of Native Americans, primarily in a 1990s series of films overseen by Jane Fonda for then husband

Ted Turner's TNT and in a more recent Steven Spielberg–produced miniseries called *Into the West*. Cast primarily with Native American actors, the TNT series began with *Geronimo* and was followed months later by *The Broken Chain* (about the Iroquois League of Six Nations), *Tecumseh—The Last Warrior, Lakota Woman—Siege at Wounded Knee* (the story of real-life Mary Crow Dog), and *Crazy Horse*. This group of films, based on factual episodes in the history of this country's indigenous peoples, utilized the services of virtually every Native American actor in the Screen Actors Guild as well as those from Canada so that the producers had to augment the cast with whites in Indian makeup. *Into the West* dealt with a family of pioneers over several generations and the Native Americans whose paths they crossed and into which tribes they intermarried. PBS offered up adaptations of several of Tony Hillerman's novels (17 or so of them to that time) about contemporary Navajo police solving crimes on the reservation: *Skinwalkers* (2002), *Coyote Waits* (2003), and *A Thief of Time* (2004). Robert Redford was the executive producer. And back in 1982, Raquel Welch made her television movie debut as a Native American woman in *The Legend of Walks Far Woman*.

Among the prominent Westerns on TV, Larry McMurtry's eloquent though quite gritty *Lonesome Dove*, an epic 1989 miniseries, is the gold standard, with memorable performances by Robert Duvall and Tommy Lee Jones. (This was followed by a sequel that McMurtry disowned and a series, as well as an official McMurtry sequel, *The Streets of Laredo*, with James Garner in Tommy Lee Jones's role, and later, *Buffalo Girls*.) The works of McMurtry and prodigious Western writer Louis L'Amour kept the Old West alive in television movies. L'Amour's catalogue was championed by either Sam Elliott or Tom Selleck, or both stalwarts: *The Sacketts* (1979), *The Shadow Riders* (1982), *Down the Long Hills* (1986), *The Quick and the Dead* (1987), *Conagher* (1991), *Crossfire Trail* (2001), and others. In 2007, there was *Bury My Heart at Wounded Knee*, an adaptation of Dee Alexander Brown's 1971 nonfiction book chronicling how the Native Americans were being displaced by the troops of William Tecumseh Sherman as the country moved west. Interestingly, a modern-day (at the time, possible) presidential candidate, actor Fred Dalton Thompson, played an earlier U.S. president, Ulysses S. Grant.

Historical fiction writer John Jakes's novels, beginning with his Founding Fathers trilogy *The Bastard*, *The Rebels*, and *The Seekers*, airing in national syndication on the ersatz Operation Prime Time network, put an entertaining perspective on America's past. It continued with ABC's three-star-laden Civil War miniseries, Jakes's expansive *North & South; North & South, Book II*; and belatedly, *Heaven & Hell—North & South, Part III*. Similarly, there have been two miniseries about George Washington; the unmatched PBS mini called *The Adams Chronicles*; and assorted TV movies dealing with Lincoln, Teddy Roosevelt, Eleanor and Franklin Roosevelt, and the Kennedy dynasty (Martin Sheen had the opportunity to play both Jack and Bobby through the years as well as, of course, the fictional president Jeb Bartlett for seven seasons on *The West Wing*). There have been, in fact, more than two dozen made-for-TV offerings about the Kennedys, whether Joe Jr., Jack, Bobby, Ted, Jackie, or John Jr., as well as Ted Jr. and, dare it be said, Arnold Schwarzenegger, a Kennedy by marriage (although here in his bodybuilding days).

CHAPTER 16

Medical Attention

Through the decades, aside from the relatively frequent women in peril and disease of the week dramas—as they became rather disparagingly referred to, especially when producers and writers ran out of common diseases and began introducing relatively exotic, even esoteric maladies—and the dramatizations of 22 Danielle Steel potboilers and more than a dozen Mary Higgins Clark mysteries, there was a great deal of serious fare dealing with medical topics, particularly when the AIDS epidemic came along in the early 1980s. The first major movie made for television (MMFT) to deal with the subject was the emotional *An Early Frost* in 1985 (family members of a successful attorney, played by Aidan Quinn, cope with the news that he is gay and dying). Gena Rowlands and Ben Gazzara starred as his heartsick parents, she accepting and he rejecting their son. The film won four Emmys and a Peabody Award. The next year, Showtime presented a faithful TV staging of the Off-Broadway AIDS play *As Is*, with Robert Carradine (who had appeared in a West Coast version of it) and Jonathan Hadaray (who had been in the New York cast).

In 1991, Julie Andrews and Ann-Margret played disparate mothers, strangers who learn that their grown sons are gay lovers and that one is dying of AIDS, in the original (as opposed to a restaging for television of a theatrical production) TV movie *Our Sons*. Two years later came a somewhat unwieldy adaptation of Randy Shilts's landmark book *And the Band Played On*, with a stellar cast ranging from Matthew Modine, Alan Alda, and Richard Gere to Angelica Huston, Lily Tomlin, and Steve Martin, and some of the familiar players passing relatively unrecognizable. In addition to film biographies on Liberace (two of them) and Rock Hudson in the 1990s, there also was a much-admired one-hour AIDS drama *In the Gloaming*, directed by Christopher Reeve, starring Glenn Close. And in the new millennium, an eloquent two-part, six-hour HBO version was presented of Tony Kushner's much-honored Broadway hit(s) *Angels in America*, directed by Mike Nichols and starring Al Pacino (in a bravura performance as Roy Cohn), Meryl Streep (in several roles, including Ethel Rosenberg and an aged male rabbi), Jeffrey Wright, Emma Thompson, Mary Louise Parker, and an excellent cast. The film won 11 Emmys. Nichols earlier had directed Thompson in the television adaptation of *Wit*, another play dealing with pending death.

Pseudobiographical dramas about pop and sports figures came into prominence with MMFT. During television drama's golden age, there were a handful of dramas about entertainment figures like 1920s and 1930s crooner Gene Austin (played by George Grizzard on a 1957 *Goodyear Playhouse*) and actress/chanteuse Helen Morgan (portrayed by Polly Bergen on *Playhouse 90* the same year). And on *Bob Hope Presents the Chrysler Theatre*, there was a TV production of Hope's feature film *The Seven Little Foys*, with Eddie Foy playing his own father, and another on singer Lee Wiley, played by Piper Laurie.

Elvis (1979), the first, and still considered the best, of all the movies about the King, with Kurt Russell (who, as a child actor, had appeared with Elvis in a couple of the latter's films), was directed by John Carpenter, who had already established himself as a cult horror filmmaker with the big-screen *Assault on Precinct 13* and *Halloween*. Through the subsequent years, there would be filmed television biographies—known popularly as biopics—on dozens of personalities, from Abbott and Costello to Lucy and Desi to Jackie Gleason, from Elizabeth Taylor to Shirley Temple and Dorothy Dandridge. And Mel Gibson's production company even did a biopic on his favorite screen characters, The Three Stooges.

TV movie highlights of 1979 included *Guyana Tragedy: The Story of Jim Jones*. Then relatively unknown Powers Boothe's dynamic performance as the charismatic self-styled preacher who led the settlers of Jonestown, Guyana, to mass suicide in late 1978 won him the Emmy Award as outstanding actor. His appearance at the Emmy ceremony as the sole performer to show up (an actors' strike caused an almost total boycott of the Emmy presentations that year) brought him some headline-making publicity, although he admitted in his acceptance speech that he might be committing professional suicide by being there. Although he was not cast again for a couple of years, his career survived, and he played such diverse TV characters as Philip Marlowe in the British-made series that aired on HBO in

1983, American spy John Walker Jr. in *A Family of Spies*, and most recently, corrupt Cyrus Tolliver in the HBO series *Deadwood*. And he was Alexander Haig in Oliver Stone's theatrical Nixon movie.

A 1979 miniseries was made of James Jones's *From Here to Eternity*, with William Devane and Natalie Wood in the roles played on the big screen more than two decades earlier by Burt Lancaster and Deborah Kerr. A year later, it reemerged soap opera style as a more or less weekly series taking up where the book and film left off (with the Pearl Harbor bombing) but was moved by NBC all over its nighttime schedule—with Barbara Hershey moving into Wood's role—until viewers apparently gave up trying to find it and lost interest. Jones's first and most successful novel was offered to TV viewers the same year as the first production of a Barbara Cartland bodice ripper *The Flame Is Love*, which, regrettably, combined stilted acting with sappy dialogue. (American television later offered four more productions of Cartland novels.)

More toward the greatness level was director Fielder Cook's adaptation by Leonora Thuna and Maya Angelou of the latter's eloquent *I Know Why the Caged Bird Sings*. Paul Benjamin, Diahann Carroll, and Ruby Dee starred. Equally powerful was *Roots: The Next Generations*, the sequel in seven parts to Alex Haley's earlier miniseries, bringing the family saga to the 1970s. James Earl Jones portrayed Haley, and Marlon Brando made an extremely rare TV acting performance—just his third and last—as racist George Lincoln Rockwell (winning an Emmy). Haley had interviewed Rockwell for a 1960s *Playboy* article. A version of Howard Fast's 1944 novel *Freedom Road* starred Muhammad Ali playing a slave who was to become a U.S. senator after Reconstruction but proved conclusively that Ali was better in the ring than in the acting arena.

Backstairs at the White House was a lovingly filmed four-part, nine-hour version of the 1961 book by Lillian Rogers Parks, the crippled seamstress-maid who, along with her mother, served for 52 years as a White House domestic during eight presidential administrations. It was a mixture of pop history of the twentieth century and the private lives of the various first families (as portrayed by an all-star cast) as seen through the eyes of the various maids and butlers. Leslie Uggams played Parks and Olivia Cole her mother.

Richard Levinson and William Link, as both executive producers and writers, crafted an elaborate mystery in 1979, *Murder by Natural Causes*, which would have been perfect fodder for the long-gone *Thriller* that Boris Karloff hosted. It involved a famous mentalist; his unfaithful wife, who is trying literally to scare him to death; the best friend of the family; and the wife's ham actor lover—not only an intriguing who (or whether) dunit, but also a literate, adult dramatic puzzle with an endless series of twists. The creepy *Salem's Lot*, the first Stephen King novel to be adapted to television, drew a large, enthusiastic audience and became a cult classic overnight. Robert Duvall and Lee Remick starred in a biopic of Eisenhower (and his lover) during the war years in *Ike*; Bette Davis and Gena Rowlands did top-drawer turns in the leads of *Strangers: The Story of a Mother and Daughter*. The 1979 television adaptation of *The Corn Is Green* reunited star Katharine Hepburn and director George Cukor for the final time—their 10th collaboration on the big screen and in television—and there was the admirable miniseries *Blind Ambition*, based on the books by John Dean (played by the ubiquitous Martin Sheen) and his wife Maureen (Theresa Russell). At the other end of the spectrum were *Castaways on Gilligan's Island* and *Mysterious Island of Beautiful Women*.

CHAPTER 17

The Pay-TV Cable Factor

ate in 1979, Showtime dipped its toe into TV anthology drama, air-ing, on a series called *Broadway on Showtime*, taped productions of assorted stage ventures that were produced regionally and (this being pay-TV) shown without commercials. The inaugural production was the Off-Broadway revue *Tuscaloosa's Calling Me . . . But I'm Not Going*, which had won the Outer Critics Circle Award in 1975–1976. Next was a restaging of the Off-Broadway production of *The Passion of Dracula* with Christopher Bernau and *The Robber Bridegroom*, based on Eudora Welty's novella, with book and lyrics by Alfred Uhry and music by Robert Waldman. Succeeding shows that aired periodically well into the 1980s included Neil Simon's *The Odd Couple*, directed by Burt Reynolds and taped at his dinner theater in Jupiter, Florida, with Charles Nelson Reilly and Darryl Hickman as Felix and Oscar; *The Country Girl*, teaming Dick Van Dyke and Faye Dunaway; *The Hasty Heart* with Gregory Harrison and Cheryl Ladd; *Pygmalion*, star-ring Peter O'Toole and Margot Kidder; *A Talent for Murder*, uniting Laurence Olivier and Angela Lansbury; and O'Neill's *Hughie* and *Long Day's Journey into Night*, with Jason Robards and Jack Lemmon, respectively, as well as the Jessica Lange/Tommy Lee Jones production of Tennessee Williams's *Cat on a Hot Tin Roof*. By 1985, there would be more than three dozen offerings.

At about the same time, Showtime's cable rival Home Box Office (HBO) kicked off a competing series, *Standing Room Only*, later retitled *HBO Theatre*. Its initial dramatic presentation was the Williamstown (Massachusetts) Theatre Festival production of *Sherlock Holmes*, a staging of two and one-half hours of William Gillette's 1899 play starring Frank Langella. John

Frankenheimer returned to television after a 20-odd-year foray into theatrical movies, directing for this occasional HBO series a new production of N. Richard Nash's *The Rainmaker* (October 1982). It starred Tommy Lee Jones and Tuesday Weld. *The Rainmaker* had begun as an hour-long drama written for the *Philco Television Playhouse* in August 1953, featuring Joan Potter and Darren McGavin; then it became a Broadway play the following year (McGavin again, opposite Geraldine Page), a feature movie the year after that with Burt Lancaster and Katharine Hepburn, and the Tom Jones/Harvey Schmidt musical *110 in the Shade* a decade later. All four original versions had been directed by Joseph Anthony. The Frankenheimer production brought the original play full circle, back to television. Other HBO entries between 1981 and 1983 included versions of *Wait Until Dark* with Katharine Ross and Stacy Keach, *Separate Tables* with Julie Christie and Alan Bates, Neil Simon's *Plaza Suite* with Lee Grant and Jerry Orbach, and the Lerner and Loewe musical *Camelot*, taped in performance at the Winter Garden in New York.

In 1982, HBO trumpeted the first original made-for-pay-TV film anthology with *Chandlertown*, its series of short stories by Raymond Chandler. It actually was a group of Philip Marlowe stories, produced by a British company in Los Angeles beginning in 1983, with American actor Powers Boothe as the famed private eye. Adaptations of works by Chandler (who had died in 1959) were by David Wickes, Jo Eisinger, Jesse Lasky Jr., and Pat Silver. A second Boothe/Marlowe series was produced by a Canadian company a couple seasons later.

Two new cable ventures emphasizing cultural programming also were inaugurated in this time period. CBS Cable was announced in 1981, an updated version of sorts of TV's earlier *Omnibus*, crossbred with PBS's general fare. Its announced aim was to develop original contemporary drama; major dance productions; American jazz, modern, and classical opera; and innovative information programming. It aired 12 hours a day, seven days a week, in three-hour program segments. Kraft Foods signed on as the first advertiser. Among the original dramas, basically, were British imports such as *Napoleon and Love*, a nine-part series on the soldier/emperor's private life and loves, featuring Ian Holm as Napoleon and Billie Whitelaw as his long-suffering Josephine. (It had premiered on Thames Television in the United Kingdom seven years earlier.) Another element was a series of weekly one-hour romantic dramas under the umbrella title *A Play for Love*. The first was *The Gift of Friendship*, written especially for (British) television by John Osborne and starring Alec Guinness.

The CBS venture was rather short-lived—perhaps because at the time, there were too few viewers who had access to cable. It went on the air

October 12, 1981, and ceased operations somewhat prematurely in late 1982, not long after announcing its second ambitious but abortive season.

At around the same time, a rival cable venture, The Entertainment Channel, launched in June 1982. It was an admirable joint collaboration between Rockefeller Center Cable and RCA Cable. One of the first programs was a musical production, with a score by Barry Manilow, of the long-running temperance play (dating back to 1832) *The Drunkard*. A version of it opened in Los Angeles in 1933 and ran for more than 30 years. The TV adaptation starred Tom Bosley. Other fare on The Entertainment Channel included serializations of classic novels and popular contemporary works, including a four-part TV production of Michael Sadleir's melodrama *Fanny by Gaslight*, a multipart staging of Dickens's *Great Expectations*, and Henry James's *The Wings of the Dove*. The Entertainment Channel also brought the Stephen Sondheim Broadway musical *Sweeney Todd, the Demon Barber of Fleet Street* to TV audiences in a staging with Angela Lansbury and George Hearn that won several Emmy Awards. In addition were the hoary old *Charley's Aunt* with Charles Grodin, George Furth's 1971 Broadway hit *Twigs* with Cloris Leachman, and Tom Jones and Harvey Schmidt's musical *I Do! I Do!* costarring Lee Remick and Hal Linden. Like CBS Cable, The Entertainment Channel faded to black too soon: in the spring of 1983. Both were noble experiments in bringing popular culture, especially anthology drama, to early cable television.

When pay-cable really became a factor in America's viewing habits, along came actress-turned-producer Shelley Duvall and her *Faerie Tale Theatre* on Showtime in the latter part of 1982. This was sort of *Shirley Temple's Storybook* wryly done for adults. Soliciting the help of her many Hollywood contacts, Duvall brought top name performers, writers, directors, and production designers working in assorted visual styles and artistic concepts to transform popular fairy tales to imaginative, live-on-tape fantasies. For a while, it was the in show for the showbiz A-list, and stars literally lined up to work with Duvall—from Vanessa Redgrave, Robin Williams, Mick Jagger, and Liza Minnelli to Eric Idle, Joan Collins, Art Carney, and Vincent Price. And there were directors ranging from Francis Ford Coppola and Roger Vadim to Tony Bill, Peter Medak, and Joan Micklin Silver. Each week, there would be a somewhat cheeky 45- to 50-minute take on a popular favorite: *Sleeping Beauty* with Christopher Reeve and Bernadette Peters, *Little Red Riding Hood* with Mary Steenburgen and then husband Malcolm McDowell, *Beauty and the Beast* with Susan Sarandon and Klaus Kinski, and *The Three Little Pigs* with Billy Crystal, Jeff Goldblum, and Valerie Perrine. The series, which ran through 1987, included 27 episodes, and Shelley herself appeared in such as *Rapunzel* with Gena Rowlands and *Rumpelstiltskin*. *Faerie Tale Theatre* won a number of TV honors: Emmys, Ace Awards (for cable television), and the George Foster Peabody Award.

Shelley Duvall inaugurated a second anthology series in 1985 titled *Tall Tales and Legends,* "family-oriented adaptations of traditional American legends about larger-than-life folk heroes," as her company Platypus Productions described it. The series kicked off with *Annie Oakley*, starring Jamie Lee Curtis alongside Brian Dennehy as Buffalo Bill. Directed by Michael Lindsay-Hogg, it had original music by rock star Ry Cooder. The next week, Elliott Gould stepped up to the plate in *Casey at the Bat*, impressing adoring girlfriend Carol Kane. Subsequent productions included *The Legend of Sleepy Hollow, Johnny Appleseed, John Henry,* and a number of others.

This pay-cable series by Duvall was followed in 1989 by a somewhat eclectic, darker one: *Nightmare Classics,* an anthology of notable mystery and horror tales such as Robert Louis Stevenson's *The Strange Case of Dr. Jekyll and Mr. Hyde* and Henry James's *The Turn of the Screw.*

CHAPTER 18

More Gems, Some Dross

Beulah Land, a florid three-part network melodrama in 1980, based on a pair of novels by Lonnie Coleman about the Old South and telling of a Southern belle (Lesley-Ann Warren) who becomes mistress of a magnificent plantation, dipped its well-pedicured toe into *Gone with the Wind* territory. Not too dissimilar, a few years later was the foreign-made *Louisiana*, based on a pair of French novels. Directed by Philippe DeBroca and starring Margot Kidder, who was married to DeBroca at the time, the film marked the first movie made for television (MMFT) to air on cable's Cinemax.

When Richard Chamberlain, known in this time period not only for his lengthy stint as Dr. Kildare on the popular 1961–1966 NBC series, but also as the so-called king of the miniseries for the many that he did, starred as English navigator John Blackthorne in the epic *Shogun* (1980), he solidified his fan base as a matinee idol. (For some reason, he—like another major TV star, Tom Selleck—never really made it in feature films.) Based on James Clavell's novel, *Shogun* was shown over a 12-night period, much of it spoken in Japanese without subtitles (and narrated by Orson Welles), another ambitious first for television. Adapted by Eric Bercovici, *Shogun* was directed by Jerry London, who, from the mid-1960s onward, also enjoyed a prodigious TV career. It introduced to American TV audiences the great Japanese actor Toshiro Mifune as the chief samurai warrior.

"Directing an epic miniseries is like going to war," London later noted. "The director is the general. He hires his captains and majors. He hires an army of actor and crew. You move from location to location. The enemy is time and money. The war is won if you stay healthy and your mini is watched by millions, with good reviews."

Among the delvings into literature, there was an interesting range in 1980. There was the ambitious but confusing and unsuccessful NBC attempt to translate *Brave New World*, the satirical 1931 Aldous Huxley novel of a society in a place called Savageland 600 years in the future, with a large, relatively unknown cast reciting space-aged gibberish. On the other hand, John Le Carré's espionage thriller *Tinker, Tailor, Soldier, Spy*, which brought Alec Guinness back to television, proved superior. There would be a sequel, *Smiley's People*, a few years later (although the middle one of Le Carré's George Smiley trilogy remains unfilmed).

Arthur Miller's original 1980 drama *Playing for Time* starred Vanessa Redgrave (her American TV acting debut) and Jane Alexander as real-life Fania Fenelon and her friend Alma Rose among the female prisoners at Auschwitz who are spared from death in return for performing music for their captors. Miller, Redgrave, Alexander, and the film itself all received Emmys. The Paul Newman TV adaptation of Michael Cristofer's Pulitzer Prize and Tony Award–winning 1977 play *Shadow Box* focused on three terminally ill patients and how they and their families face the challenge. Newman made his TV directing debut with this film coproduced by his daughter Susan and starring his wife, Joanne Woodward, and a name cast. Also in 1980, there was a new television production of *The Diary of Anne Frank*, featuring Melissa Gilbert, Maximilian Schell, and Joan Plowright. Boris Sagal directed it. Gilbert and her Half-Pint Productions previously had done TV dramas of *The Miracle Worker* and *Splendor in the Grass*.

John Steinbeck's expansive (as opposed to the condensed James Dean movie of the 1950s) *East of Eden* aired in early 1981 in a four-part, eight-hour miniseries, with Jane Seymour in the lead, as did the romantic drama *The Manions of America*, chronicling the lives of two nineteenth-century families—one Irish, the other English—and the American family dynasties they began. *Manions* was a collaboration between American soap opera grand dame Agnes Nixon, who created *All My Children* and *One Life to Live*, and British writer Rosemary Anne Sisson, who created *Upstairs, Downstairs*. Steinbeck's *Of Mice and Men* also received a vivid new production with Robert Blake and Randy Quaid, along with veteran actor Lew Ayres.

Also airing in 1981 was Marilyn French's popular feminist novel *The Women's Room*, with a large cast of actresses such as Lee Remick, Colleen Dewhurst, and Patty Duke. In addition, there was Jacqueline Susann's *Valley of the Dolls 1981*, a wonderfully trashy update of the author's famous original novel. And Garson Kanin's novel *Moviola* provided three movies airing on three consecutive nights—chapters from each providing eye candy and guilty pleasures in star-laden dramas of the making of *Gone with the Wind* (*The Scarlett O'Hara Wars*), the ill-fated Greta Garbo and John Gilbert love affair (*The Silent Lovers*), and a version of Marilyn Monroe's life (*This Year's Blonde*).

A second MMFT, *Marilyn: The Untold Story*, followed not long afterward, as did one on Sophia Loren (with La Loren playing both herself and her mother) and one on Jayne Mansfield (with Loni Anderson in the lead and Arnold Schwarzenegger—in his only TV acting to date—as Mickey Hargitay).

Scared Straight! Another Story was a critically applauded fictional 1981 TV movie inspired by the brutally frank 1979 documentary *Scared Straight*, dealing with a prison encounter group involving juveniles, that won both an Oscar and an Emmy. Another dealing with prison matters, *People vs. Jean Harris*, was a well-made film about the refined private school headmistress who was convicted of killing her unfaithful lover, Dr. Herman Tarnower, the eminent "Scarsdale Diet" author. The tape-to-film, starring Emmy-nominated Ellen Burstyn, was unique in its time in that it premiered within weeks of the trial that sent Harris to prison for two decades. Burstyn would turn up again very briefly in another film on the same subject in 2006 (but in a different role, one that lasted a mere 14 seconds, with just 38 spoken words, but earned her a controversial—at least among the press—Emmy nomination).

Cagney and Lacy, the most famous of television's female buddy combinations (if not *Kate and Allie*), came to the medium in 1981 as a film starring Loretta Swit and Tyne Daly. Created by two television Barbaras, Avedon and Corday, the movie and the subsequent hit series spanning the 1980s initially had Meg Foster playing opposite Daly, and then Sharon Gless, whose chemistry with Daly clicked. In the 1990s, Gless and Daly paired again to reprise their roles in four made-for-TV movies. Over the years of the series (1982–1988), each took turns winning the Emmy as best actress in a drama series.

A large, relatively unfamiliar cast headed *Kent State* (1981), a three-hour dramatization of the four days of events leading up to the historic tragedy at Kent State University in May 1970, during the confrontation between National Guardsmen and students staging antiwar demonstrations. It was based on three books, including James A. Michener's *Kent State: What Happened and Why?*, and earned an Emmy for director James Goldstone. Two other factual events that were dramatized that year in TV movies were the previously mentioned *Skokie* with Danny Kaye and *Crisis at Central High*, which starred Joanne Woodward as the real-life Elizabeth Huckaby, one of the teachers at Little Rock, Arkansas's, Central High School in 1957 when the court ordered integration.

Ingrid Bergman's memorable career came to a close with her portrayal of Golda Meir in *A Woman Called Golda* (1982), for which she earned a best actress Emmy. Daughter Pia Lindstrom picked up the award posthumously and offered a poignant thank you. A later Golda was portrayed by Gertrudis Kuntz in the TV movie about Anwar Sadat (played by Louis Gossett Jr.) and by Colleen Dewhurst in *Sword of Gideon*—which was based on the same book that Steven Spielberg was to use for his *Munich* in 2005.

Two competing movies on Prince Charles and Diana Spencer aired in 1982 in the media frenzy of their wedding; Tommy Lee Jones gave a searing, Emmy-winning performance as convicted killer Gary Gilmore in a controversial production of Norman Mailer's *The Executioner's Song*, which Mailer himself adapted from his Pulitzer Prize–winning nonfiction book; Clint Eastwood's then girlfriend Sondra Locke had the starring role in *Rosie: The Rosemary Clooney Story*; and Ann Jillian sashayed her way through the biopic *Mae West*.

Agatha Christie's *Witness for the Prosecution* was remade as a MMFT in 1982, with Ralph Richardson, Deborah Kerr, Beau Bridges, and Diana Rigg (in the roles played on the big screen by Charles Laughton, Elsa Lanchester, Tyrone Power, and Marlene Dietrich). More of Dame Agatha was also on view in *Murder Is Easy*, an adaptation of her 1939 *Easy to Kill* (part of a CBS franchise with producers David Wolper and Stan Margulies offering classy versions of Christie's Miss Marple and Hercule Poirot over the next few years).

World War III (1982) found the world on the brink of a nuclear holocaust following a confrontation between the United States and Russia when an insurgent military group from the Soviet Union lays siege to the Alaskan pipeline in retaliation for an American grain embargo, and president Rock Hudson and Soviet general secretary Brian Keith find themselves hard-pressed to head off the escalating conflict. Veteran TV director Boris Sagal (actress Katey Sagal's father) was killed in a helicopter accident during the first days of location filming.

There were new adaptations of literature's *Hunchback of Notre Dame* and *The Scarlet Pimpernel* and a sweeping miniseries of historian Bruce Catton's Civil War novel *The Blue and the Gray* with a top-notch cast, including Gregory Peck (in his TV acting debut) as Abraham Lincoln and Rip Torn as Ulysses S. Grant.

Another miniseries, *Marco Polo*, telling of the odyssey of the Italian explorer of legend, won the Emmy that year, and in *Inside the Third Reich*,

Rutger Hauer, the Dutch actor, made his American TV movie debut as Albert Speer, Hitler's personal architect, in this two-part, five-hour dramatization of Speer's 1970 autobiography.

A stellar alphabetically billed cast and six Emmy Award nominations distinguished the four-hour *Little Gloria . . . Happy at Last,* a dramatization of Barbara Goldsmith's 1980 best seller about the bitter 1934 child custody case involving 10-year-old Gloria Vanderbilt, America's famous "poor little rich girl."

Two of the big television events of 1983 were the sweeping multipart adaptation of Colleen McCullough's romantic novel *The Thorn Birds* and the quite controversial nuclear disaster–themed *The Day After* from an original teleplay by Edward Hume, directed by Nicholas Meyer. *The Thorn Birds* was a grade-A soap opera about a young Australian priest with Vatican ambitions who becomes entranced by a pretty woman, questions his own vows, fights off a wealthy matron who will do anything to have him, and through the years, despite his delving into forbidden love, moves into the highest circles of the church. Richard Chamberlain had the lead role, and at the time, it caused critical concern that as the older priest in the later portion, he was far too young, even with aging makeup. Ironically, when a sequel of sorts was crafted some years later (1996), the now much older Chamberlain was thought to be too old the play the young priest. And in the original, there was the portrayal verging on camp by Barbara Stanwyck (winning a best actress Emmy) as the love-starved socialite, willing to give her entire fortune to the church, who crawled across the floor to literally get her claws into Chamberlain and get him to bed her. Other Emmy Awards went to Jean Simmons and Richard Kiley in supporting roles for the hugely popular miniseries's secondary plotline.

In the somewhat unique, rather controversial *Special Bulletin,* a 1983 TV movie simulating an actual newscast, nuclear protestors threaten the destruction of Charleston, South Carolina, unless warheads stored there are deactivated. The program was taped rather than filmed, and so viewers would not be scared out of their wits—as in Orson Welles's memorable *War of the Worlds* radio show of the late 1930s—frequent audience alerts were superimposed at the bottom of the TV screen. *Special Bulletin* received an Emmy Award as outstanding drama special, as did writers/producers Marshall Herskovitz and Edward Zwick.

The widely viewed *The Day After* was a grim three-hour MMFT dramatizing a nuclear catastrophe causing the destruction of Lawrence, Kansas, home of America's missile arsenal that has become the focus of a superpower confrontation. It was a picture of rural life before, during, and after a nuclear blast, with a large cast headed by Jason Robards as a college pro-fessor. The film stirred up a firestorm of debate (was it Soviet propaganda, certain factions of ABC's stockholders wanted to know) and media attention and provided ammunition for antinuclear peace groups in the United States and Europe. Steinbeck's final novel, *The Winter of Our Discontent,* was also dramatized in 1983.

CHAPTER 19

Cable TV Offers Original Movies

The first original pay-cable movies, airing on Showtime in 1983, were *Falcon's Gold* and *Prisoners of the Lost Universe*, both unrelated B fantasy adventure tales in the mold of the Indiana Jones flicks (and prospective series pilots). HBO entered the game months later, first with a Canadian import called *The Terry Fox Story* (about a real-life Canadian runner, an amputee, who walked across his country for charity), and then with the homegrown *Between Friends*, teaming Elizabeth Taylor and Carol Burnett—as divorcée pals, one looking for diamonds, the other settling for just a man—and adapted from Shelley List's book *Nobody Makes Me Cry*.

Next for HBO was in 1984's three-part, British-made *The Far Pavilions*, faithfully adapted from M. M. Kaye's epic novel of nineteenth-century colonial India. And on cable, Bette Davis and James Stewart costarred for the only time in the drama *Right of Way*, based on Richard Lee's 1978 play about seniors who craft a suicide pact. It had been staged at the Guthrie Theatre in Minneapolis but never got to Broadway. Within two decades, cable television would dominate the made-for-TV scenes.

Harriette Arnow's 1954 novel *The Dollmaker*, about an illiterate Kentucky mountain woman—Jane Fonda, in her TV movie debut—who moves to Detroit with her husband and kids during World War II and tries to make extra money with her gift as a wood-carver, was adapted by Susan Cooper and Hume Cronyn into a three-hour production. It was directed by Daniel

Petrie and costarred Geraldine Page and Amanda Plummer. Fonda won the Emmy as best actress.

Something About Amelia, directed by Randa Haines, was a controversial, highly publicized 1984 drama about incest, spotlighted at the time as TV's "last taboo," with Ted Danson—as far from his *Cheers* character of Sam Malone as imaginable—playing the father accused by his teenage daughter of having molested her. The film won the Emmy as outstanding drama. Equally as controversial was *The Burning Bed,* which starred Farrah Fawcett as a battered wife charged with her husband's murder after setting his bed afire following years of beatings and humiliations.

Other significant 1984 TV movie productions included a new *Streetcar Named Desire* with Ann-Margret; *Terrible Joe Moran,* James Cagney's only TV acting; the historical miniseries about *George Washington,* starring Barry Bostwick and Patty Duke; and *The Ewok Adventure,* bringing George Lucas's *Star Wars* vision to television (a sequel aired the following year).

The famed Dustin Hoffman version of Arthur Miller's *Death of a Salesman* was among the television highlights of 1985, along with Lucille Ball's only dramatic acting in the medium, as a homeless woman in *Stone Pillow,* and in a fictionalized biopic, *The Hearst and Davies Affair,* starring Robert Mitchum as newspaper mogul William Randolph Hearst and Virginia Madsen as his paramour, movie star Marion Davies, as well as the first of more than two dozen Perry Mason movies reuniting Raymond Burr (until his death) and Barbara Hale (until her retirement).

James Michener's spirited tale of America's space race, called, understandably *Space; F.* Scott Fitzgerald's romantic *Tender Is the Night;* Faulkner's *The Long Hot Summer;* and an expansive mini dealing with Christopher Columbus and another one on Robert Kennedy with Brad Davis all were part of the TV programming landscape that year. There also was a multinight, star-laden adaptation of the Jeffrey Archer best seller *Kane & Abel,* about two tycoons who become obsessed by their attempts to destroy one another, and the epic 12-hour *A.D.,* which had 400 speaking parts and, according to press releases at the time, 18,000 extras.

Two TV movies about Mussolini aired that year—one with George C. Scott as Il Duce, the other with Bob Hoskins—in addition to a nostalgic get-together of Jackie Gleason and Art Carney in *Izzy and Moe,* a fictionalized look at the true adventures of a pair of 1920s ex-vaudevillians who went to work for the feds in New York as prohibition officers.

Alfred Hitchcock Presents was brought back to television in 1985, even though Hitch had been dead for five years. The anthology made-for-TV movie strung together four classic tales, recreated from the landmark show of three decades earlier, with introductions by a computer-colorized Hitch and voice-over narration by John Huston (who also acted in one of the quartet of tales). Later, these four stories turned up on the newly constituted Hitchcock series.

At the other end were such fare as an update of *Peyton Place*, a look at *I Dream of Jeanie—15 Years Later*, *Gidget's Summer Reunion*, and a biopic on John Lennon and Yoko Ono. There was a flurry of publicity on this one at the time since the actor named to play Lennon was a lesser-known British actor named Mark Chapman—ironically the name of the man who shot Lennon in front of the Dakota in New York. He bowed out and was replaced by the equally lesser-known Mark McCann.

Bob Hope made his only television movie, *A Masterpiece of Murder*, in 1986. It was his first starring film in over a dozen years, and he was teamed with veteran actor Don Ameche. In this flick about an art heist, Hope was a down-on-his-luck gumshoe, Ameche, a wealthy, retired master thief. Mary Tyler Moore starred opposite Robert Preston in a delightful cable movie called *Finnegan Begin Again*, directed by Joan Micklin Silver, one of the few women directors in TV movies of the day. Moore starred as a schoolteacher in her early forties who drifts into a relationship with an aging, married reporter now working the lonely hearts desk.

Barry Bostwick and Patty Duke returned as George and Martha Washington in the miniseries sequel to the earlier *George Washington*; Richard Chamberlain starred as John Charles Freemont in a robust three-part dramatization of author David Nevin's *Dream West*; Maximilian Schell had the starring role in the ultralavish *Peter the Great*; George C. Scott recreated his Oscar-winning portrayal of George S. Patton in a lengthy sequel, *The Last Days of Patton*, along with Eva Marie Saint (and directed by her golden age pal Delbert Mann); and there were sequels or prequels to earlier TV movies or series: *North & South, Book II*; *Dallas: The Early Years*; *Kung Fu: The Movie*; *Return of Mickey Spillane's Mike Hammer*; *Rage of Angels: The Story Continues*; and *Adam: His Song Continues*.

Ambitious *Amerika* was a controversial postapocalyptic drama in 1987 set 10 years after the Soviet takeover of the United States. It captured TV audiences for 14½ hours over a weeklong period to tell the story of an independent underground movement and its clash with the leaders of the occupying forces in a surreal new world of the 1990s. Both *At Mother's Request* and *Nutcracker: Money, Madness and Murder* were multipart docudramas telling the same sordid tale of manipulative, real-life Manhattan socialite Frances Schreuder, a twice-divorced mother of three who harangued her wealthy Utah-based parents for money to support her opulent lifestyle. When her father, Franklin Bradshaw, was found murdered in July 1978, suspicion pointed her way, but she craftily diverted the spotlight to her pliable son. The former, from a book by Jonathan Coleman, starred Stefanie Powers; the latter, from Shana Alexander's novel, featured Lee Remick. Equally melodramatic was the two-part adaptation of Dominick Dunne's *The Two Mrs. Grenvilles*, with Ann-Margret and, returning to the medium in her only TV movie, Claudette Colbert.

Two other so-called women's movies also premiered during 1987: *Poor Little Rich Girl*, with Farrah Fawcett in the lead, told the romanticized story of Woolworth heiress Barbara Hutton, and Candice Bergen starred in *Mayflower Madam*, a somewhat whitewashed drama inspired by the life of Sydney Biddle Barrows, the former debutante turned socialite-careerist, active in the best social circles, who became the proprietor of a high-class Manhattan escort service. (It was semilegitimate since Barrows herself was one of the producers.)

A sumptuous, somewhat idealized three-part, six-hour drama about one of history's great romances was 1987's *Napoleon and Josephine: A Love Story*. It boasted a polyglot international cast headed by Manhattanite Armand Assante and Britisher Jacqueline Bisset as the passionate French lovers, along with Anthony Perkins as the wily Tallyrand. The teleplay was by prolific writer James Lee. In addition, two popular theatrical films of the 1950s were remade for television, though hardly as well as the first time around: *Roman Holiday* and *Quo Vadis?*

Other above-average offerings that year were the inspiring true drama *Escape from Sobibor*, with Alan Arkin as its daring leader, and, on the sentimental side, Jason Robards and Eva Marie Saint, from the golden age of live television, costarred in *Norman Rockwell's Breaking Home Ties*—an adaptation of one of the artist's famous *Saturday Evening Post* covers of World War II. *Queenie*, based on publisher/novelist Michael Korda's 1985 best seller, was the thinly veiled story of actress Merle Oberon (who was discovered by and married to film mogul Alexander Korda, the author's late uncle), told as a two-part, five-hour movie with a stellar cast headed by Kirk Douglas.

On the other hand, a sequel to the big-screen *The Stepford Wives* and TV's earlier *Revenge of the Stepford Wives*, titled *The Stepford Children*, illustrated, sadly, how mediocre the made-for-TV genre sometimes can be.

James Arness donned his Marshal Matt Dillon buckskins, which he put in the trunk back in 1975 after two decades of television, in the first of several new *Gunsmoke* movies, *Return to Dodge*.

Such varied literary works adapted to television in 1988 included James Clavell's *Noble House* with Pierce Brosnan, Gore Vidal's *Lincoln* with Sam

Waterston and Mary Tyler Moore in Ernest Kinoy's teleplay, Harriet Doerr's *Stones for Ibarra* with Glenn Close (in an adaptation also by Kinoy), Mario Puzo's *The Fortunate Pilgrim* with Sophia Loren, Sidney Sheldon's potboiler *Windmills of the Gods*, and Howard Fast's *April Morning* with Tommy Lee Jones on the first day of the American Revolutionary War. Fast's historical fiction, adapted by James Lee Barrett, had an offbeat pedigree: although set basically on the Lexington commons, it was filmed in Quebec by director Delbert Mann and had Jones, with his distinctive Texas drawl, playing a British subject turned patriotic minuteman.

And there were TV productions of noted theatrical works: Herman Wouk's *The Caine Mutiny Court-Martial*, Robert Bolt's *A Man for All Seasons* with Charlton Heston and Vanessa Redgrave, and Lawrence and Lee's *Inherit the Wind* with Kirk Douglas and Jason Robards. Wouk and Bolt wrote their own teleplay adaptations. There were, as well, TV reimaginings of such big-screen classics as Howard Hawks's *Red River*, with James Arness in old buddy and mentor John Wayne's role, and Hitchcock's *Suspicion*, with Jane Curtin doing the Joan Fontaine part and Anthony Andrews in Cary Grant's.

The Bourne Identity, adapted by prolific Carol Sobieski from Robert Ludlum's 1980 spy thriller, was a well-made 1988 two-part made-for-TV movie and starred Richard Chamberlain as seasoned CIA agent Jason Bourne. That was nearly 15 years before it was turned into a theatrical feature with a substantially younger Matt Damon—an anomaly as the only TV movie to date that was remade for the big screen; traditionally, it has been the other way around.

Among the original TV works were *Hemingway*, a two-part, six-hour biopic with Stacy Keach as the legendary writer; *The Woman He Loved*, about the Prince of Wales and Wallis Simpson; *Onassis: The Richest Man in the World*; and several fact-based dramas: *Murder of Mary Phagan*, dramatizing the story of the still controversial 1913 Leo Frank case (he was wrongly accused of rape and murder and railroaded to the gallows in Georgia); *Baby M*, the emotional well-acted docudrama revolving around the landmark child custody case of the mid-1980s; and *The Attic: The Hiding of Anne Frank*, telling the famed World War II story from the perspective of Mies Giep, the Dutch woman who tried to protect the family. And then there was *Bring Me the Head of Dobie Gillis*, a long-coming reunion movie bringing together the original cast of the 1959–1963 series.

Day One, about the Manhattan Project that produced the atomic bomb in the 1940s, was among the dramas in 1989 that caused the critics to talk. An arresting three-hour film produced by Aaron Spelling and directed by Joseph Sargent, it was Emmy nominated as outstanding drama. The source for David Rintels's teleplay was Peter Wyden's 1984 book *Day One: Before Hiroshima and After.* A similar big-screen view of the same subject, *Fat Man and Little Boy,* with Paul Newman as Gen. Leslie Groves (played here by Brian Dennehy), was released several months after the premiere of the television movie.

Other serious subjects were approached in *Roe v. Wade* (it shared the outstanding drama Emmy with *Day One*), *Murderers among Us: The Simon Wiesenthal Story* (with Ben Kingsley in the title role), and *My Name Is Bill W,* true stories all adapted to challenging adult viewing. The really big dramas were the sprawling Western *Lonesome Dove* and the final five parts of the wartime fiction *War & Remembrance* (the first seven parts were at the end of 1988), by Larry McMurtry and Herman Wouk, respectively. Others from popular literature were new versions of Charles Dickens's *Great Expectations* (with Jean Simmons, who was Young Estella in the 1946 film, now playing Miss Haversham, along with Anthony Hopkins as Magwitch), Jules Verne's *Around the World in 80 Days* (Pierce Brosnan as Phileas Fogg at the head of the traditional all-star cast in cameos), and Mark Twain's *A Connecticut Yankee in King Arthur's Court,* refashioned by Pulitzer Prize–winning playwright Paul Zindel as a star vehicle for Keshia Knight Pulliam, remembered as the adorable youngest daughter on *The Cosby Show.*

Mentioning the Pulitzer Prize, there was also a TV movie that year called *Roxanne: The Prize Pulitzer,* a titillating docudrama based on Roxanne Pulitzer's scandal-plagued autobiography when she was married to the much older publishing heir. Equally as melodramatic was the production of Judith Krantz's page-turner *Till We Meet Again.* Superior to these were *The Women of Brewster Place,* from Gloria Naylor's 1983 novel about seven African American women who struggle to overcome the barriers of poverty, racism, and unfulfilled dreams, living the black experience in an inner-city tenement building on a walled-off street (Oprah Winfrey executive produced and starred), and *Age-Old Friends,* adapted by Bob Larbey from his short-lived 1987 play *A Month of Sundays.* Hume Cronyn and Vincent Gardenia both won Emmy Awards (as outstanding actor and supporting actor in a miniseries or special, respectively) for playing two pals who beat life with spirit and humor in a retirement home.

There were TV remakes in 1989 of Tennessee Williams's *Sweet Bird of Youth* with Elizabeth Taylor; George S. Kaufman and Edna Ferber's *Dinner at Eight* with Lauren Bacall; and the late 1940s Barbara Stanwyck flick *Sorry, Wrong Number.*

CHAPTER 20

The Nineties

One of the leading filmed dramas of 1990 was *Drug Wars: The Camarena Story*, Emmy winner as outstanding miniseries. It was a three-part, six-hour tale recounting the exploits of U.S. Drug Enforcement Administration agent "Kiki" Camarena, who, in 1985, was tortured for information and then killed in Mexico because his investigation threatened major drug lords. Three writers adapted Elizabeth Shannon's 1988 nonfiction book, and Britisher Brian Gibson directed. He previously had done *Murderers among Us: The Simon Wiesenthal Story* and subsequently directed *The Josephine Baker Story*.

Eva Marie Saint recalls getting a terrific, Emmy-winning part as vacuous Lil Altemus, "a well-bred woman who is so consumed by her world of privilege that she has lost touch with her own humanity" (as described in the network's publicity at the time), in 1990's *People Like Us*. It was a two-part adaptation of Dominick Dunne's 1988 novel dealing tangentially with the 1982 stalker death of his actress daughter Dominique (she had starred in the film *Poltergeist*, among others). "It was one of those parts that I found myself playing as a younger actor in what was called 'kitchen dramas' on *Philco* and *Goodyear* decades ago. Ben Gazzara played a fictional alter ego for Dunne." The director was Billy Hale; the writers were Mart Crowley and Kathleen E. Sheely.

In 1990, there was another top-drawer Kennedy family miniseries, *The Kennedys of Massachusetts*, from one of Doris Kearns Goodwin's books, along with *The Court Martial of Jackie Robinson*, dramatizing a little-known wartime incident in the life of the future baseball star. Among the literary works adapted to TV were Hemingway's *The Old Man and the Sea* with Anthony Quinn (the producer had the temerity to add characters and a subplot to the tale because, as he told interviewers while promoting the film, "Papa would probably have wanted it that way"); back-to-back Robert Louis Stevenson with *Treasure Island* and *Jekyll & Hyde* premiering, by coincidence, on consecutive nights on different networks; Tennessee Williams's *Orpheus Descending* with Vanessa Redgrave; and, in a throwback to the style created in the early days of television on *Omnibus, Women & Men: Stories of Seduction,* an anthology drama featuring three short films adapted from stories by Hemingway ("Hills Like White Elephants"), Dorothy Parker ("Dusk before Fireworks"), and Mary McCarthy ("The Man in the Brooks Brothers Shirt"), each by a different director.

There also was a period piece, *A Ghost in Monte Carlo,* from Barbara Cartland's florid period novel, and adaptations of books by Jackie Collins and Danielle Steel (the first of 20 novels that NBC used as a franchise of sorts over the next six years) and of Stephen King's horror tale *It,* the first of a dozen King novels from ABC over the succeeding years.

Christopher Reeve played Union detective Allan Pinkerton in *The Rose & the Jackal,* fanciful historical fiction set during the Civil War, and Charles Dance starred, with top-billed Burt Lancaster as his father, in playwright Arthur Kopit's nonmusical adaptation of *The Phantom of the Opera* (Kopit, around the same time, had a musical version of it touring the country as an alternative to Andrew Lloyd Webber's more famous one).

Aside from the notable biopic *The Josephine Baker Story* in 1991, for which Lynn Whitfield, in the starring role, won the Emmy (reportedly, Diana Ross earlier had optioned the story, planning to play Baker, but balked at doing Baker's memorable seminude banana dance), there were interesting dramas that included *Sarah, Plain & Tall,* adapted from Patricia MacLachlan's 1985 book, with Glenn Close and Christopher Walken (they made two sequels over the next few years: *Never Forget,* a Holocaust remembrance drama featuring Leonard Nimoy as real-life Mel Mermelstein, a survivor who confronted a holocaust denial organization's lies in court, and *Ironclads* for history buffs, Civil War fiction about the famed sea battle between the *Monitor* and the *Merrimack*). In addition, the sentimental and uplifting original *Mrs. Lambert Remembers Love* with Ellen Burstyn and Walter Matthau—and directed by Matthau's son Charlie—and *Darlings of the Gods,* based on the Garry O'Connor book about an incident just after the war in the lives of Laurence Olivier and Vivien Leigh, also premiered.

James Woods and John Lithgow, in 1991's *The Boys,* played lifelong friends and writing partners confronted with the realization that one of them is terminally ill in this sometimes funny, sometimes poignant drama written by William Link and modeled after his own professional partnership with Richard Levinson, who died of lung cancer in 1987. The title referred to the term given to them by their colleagues in television—especially Peter Falk, their Lieutenant Columbo.

Winning an Emmy as outstanding miniseries was *Separate but Equal,* an impressive drama with Sidney Poitier as Thurgood Marshall at the time of the Supreme Court's landmark *Brown v. Board of Education* in 1954. This film returned Poitier to television after 35 years in the role of a *young* Thurgood Marshall, then a New York attorney working with the National Association for the Advancement of Colored People Legal Defense Fund. Poitier, then 66, believably played the future chief justice of the U.S. Supreme Court at age 31. Portraying the opposing lawyer was aging Burt Lancaster in his acting swansong.

Beau Bridges won the Emmy as best actor for his portrayal in *Without Warning: The James Brady Story* of Ronald Reagan's press secretary, severely wounded in the Reagan assassination attempt, and in *One Man's War,* Anthony Hopkins added another real-life portrayal to his gallery as Joel Filartiga, a Paraguayan doctor who supported the clinic he ran by selling paintings in the United States and, with his wife, crusaded for human rights in the name of his son, who was tortured to death.

Vanessa and Lynn Redgrave played the Joan Crawford and Bette Davis roles in the TV remake of *What Ever Happened to Baby Jane?* that year, and Vanessa also headed a stellar cast that year in *Young Catherine* (not in the title role—that was played by Julia Ormond), an opulent $8 million costume drama about the eighteenth-century Prussian teenager chosen by Russian empress Elizabeth to marry her nephew and successor to the throne, Grand Duke Peter. Another historical epic, *A Season of Giants,* a splendidly appointed four-hour period drama directed by Jerry London, had a teenage Michelangelo crossing paths with Leonardo da Vinci and Raphael in the Renaissance Italy of Pope Julius II and the complex politics of the time.

And so it was in the early 1990s—from the noirish cable thriller *Cast a Deadly Spell* with rogue, wisecracking private eye H. Phillip Lovecraft in 1948 Los Angeles, hired to recover a stolen book of occult spells, to *Chernobyl—The Final Warning,* with Jon Voight in his television movie debut as Dr. Robert Gale, the American bone marrow transplant specialist who organized an international team of doctors to aid the victims of Chernobyl (adapted by Ernest Kinoy from Gale's published memoirs), to the popular *A Woman Named Jackie,* a miniseries based on C. David Heymann's best seller that starred Roma Downey as Jackie Kennedy and Stephen Collins as JFK.

The previous year's *Women & Men: Stories of Seduction* spawned a sequel, *Women & Men 2: Three Short Stories*. This anthology trio offered short dramas by Irwin Shaw ("Return to Kansas City"), Carson McCullers ("A Domestic Dilemma"), and Henry Miller ("Mara").

And because Arnold Schwarzenegger made his directing debut, worth mentioning is the romantic comedy *Christmas in Connecticut*, an updated remake of a bit of Yuletide fluff that Barbara Stanwyck made in the mid-1940s. The vagaries of filming found the shooting done in the fake snow-covered Grand Teton National Park, giving Christmasy Connecticut a mountain range. Schwarzenegger later also was to direct at least one episode of the horror anthology *Tales from the Crypt*.

In a first time ever move, the movies made for television (MMFT) scene opened in 1993 with three rather lightweight films about real-life Amy Fisher, the Long Island teenager who shot her much older lover's wife. These dramas—one per network—aired in a five-day period and starred, respectively, Canadian actress Noelle Parker, Alyssa Milano, and Drew Barrymore.

Director Michael Ritchie's satirical *The Positively True Adventures of the Alleged Texas Cheerleader-Murdering Mom*, a pay-cable movie in 1993, starring Holly Hunter in the Emmy Award–winning title role, was based on a true (not especially humorous) story that also was depicted some months earlier in another MMFT, *Willing to Kill: The Texas Cheerleader Story*. That one was directed by David Greene and starred Lesley Ann Warren. *John Carpenter's Body Bags* was an anthology drama combining three chilling stories, "The Gas Station" and "Hair," both of which he directed, and "Eye," directed by Tobe Hooper—sort of a *Night Gallery* for the 1990s.

A new adaptation of *Mary Shelley's Frankenstein* and *They*, adapted from Rudyard Kipling's turn-of-the-century short story, were two dramas out of British literature that aired in 1993, and so did Alex Haley's *Queen*, an three-part extension of sorts of his exceptional *Roots*, chronicling the origins and life of his paternal grandmother (played by Halle Berry), the daughter of a slave and a white Civil War colonel of Irish descent.

Arthur Miller's *The American Clock*, adapted from his 1980 drama based in part on Studs Terkel's *Hard Times*, was about the decline and fall of a wealthy New York family during the Depression. This, and an original baseball-themed story called *Cooperstown*, aired under a TNT umbrella title, Screenworks, produced in conjunction with Steven Spielberg's Amblin Entertainment. Larry Gelbart's witty adaptation of the best-selling 1992 book *Barbarians at the Gate* shared the outstanding movie/miniseries Emmy with *Stalin*, which starred Robert Duvall. Hume Cronyn and Jessica Tandy acted together for the last time in a tender rendition of Terry Kay's best seller *To Dance With the White Dog*.

Chantilly Lace (produced, directed, and cowritten by Linda Yellen) was an original, improvised production (the script was written after the cast developed its characters and spoke its words) featuring seven actresses as longtime friends with different lifestyles meeting three times in the course of a year. And in the course of this year, among the drama highlights was the aforementioned AIDS story, *And the Band Played On*, from Randy Shilts's passionate 1987 best seller chronicling the early years of the deadly epidemic.

The 1994 Hallmark Hall of Fame dramatization of Thomas Hardy's 1878 romantic novel *The Return of the Native* (it was the first ever filming) with an all-British cast headed by Catherine Zeta Jones as the bewitching Eustacia Vye was rather an offbeat venture for CBS that doubtless obtained only a miniscule audience. Another in the same vein, though on basic cable, was Joseph Conrad's 1902 novella *The Heart of Darkness*, set in the time of the original in the early twentieth century (and the source, of course, of Francis Ford Coppola's *Apocalypse Now*). John Frankenheimer returned to directing television drama full-time since leaving after *Playhouse 90* nearly 35 years earlier and won the first of three consecutive Emmys for *Against the Wall*, dealing with the 1971 Attica prison uprising.

The Old South's *Scarlett* aired as a four-part, eight-hour miniseries, a sequel after 55 years to what is often considered the most celebrated love story ever filmed. It was based on the greatly hyped 1991 best seller written by Alexandra Ripley, who was commissioned by Margaret Mitchell's family. The sweeping mini incorporated more than 200 speaking roles, 2,000 extras, and 53 locations in the United States and Great Britain. Another Civil War era tale, John Jakes's long-coming sequel *Heaven & Hell: North & South, Part III*, aired over several nights. And the woman who brought the world the original Scarlett O'Hara herself had a fictionalized biopic: *Burning Passion: The Margaret Mitchell Story*, with Shannen Doherty in the lead.

The Twilight Zone: Rod Serling's Lost Classics rekindled memories of the landmark series, combining two original Serling stories, discovered by his widow long after his death a decade earlier: the approximately half-hour "The Theater" (with a script by Richard Matheson) and the 90-minute "Where the Dead Are." In more or less the same strange-things-are-happening league was Stephen King's *The Stand*, an all-star four-part dramatization of his thriller about a showdown between good and evil that he adapted from his 1978 novel.

Parallel Lives, like the previous *Chantilly Lace*, was a partially improvised drama featuring a stellar cast and, like its predecessor, was produced, directed, and written by Linda Yellen. Diane Keaton made one of her infrequent acting appearances on television in *Amelia Earhart: The Final Flight*, a dramatization of Doris L. Rich's 1989 biography about the enigmatic adventuress who disappeared in 1937 while circumnavigating the globe, and eye-patched George C. Scott chewed the scenery in *The Whipping Boy*, a British-made Disney film based on Sid Fleishman's Newbery Award–winning children's novella of 1986.

The Burning Season, about the real-life activist and union organizer Chico Mendes, whose fight to protect his home and his people in a village in the Amazon rain forest from cattle ranchers and land speculators ended in his murder, brought Raul Julia a posthumous Emmy as best actor and another directing Emmy for John Frankenheimer.

World War II: When Lions Roared was a speculative two-part drama dealing with FDR (John Lithgow), Churchill (Bob Hoskins), and Stalin (Michael Caine) and how they individually and together planned their strategy against Nazi Germany. Joseph Sargent directed David W. Rintels's original teleplay that might well have been a production of the long ago *Playhouse 90*. And so might have been *Roswell*, a fact-based story of Jesse Marcel, an air force intelligence officer, and his attempt to learn the truth behind a flying saucer landing in the desert outside of Roswell, New Mexico, in the summer of 1947 and the supposed government cover-up through the decades.

There were the sublime: a TV remake of Marjorie Kinnan Rawlings's *The Yearling*, Truman Capote's autobiographical *One Christmas* (this would be star Katharine Hepburn's final acting role), and a new version of Woody Allen's *Don't Drink the Water*, directed by and starring the Woodman himself. And there were the ridiculous: *two* movies about Roseanne Barr Arnold and *two* about the Menendez brothers, who, as teenagers, were convicted of killing their parents in their Beverly Hills home.

The golden age of the television movie (in quantity if not quality) reached its peak in 1995, when at least 265 separate titles were released. Within a decade, the output had declined to a point where only CBS among the networks regularly made original movies, and even the cable stations cut way back. What led TV anthology drama to fade ultimately to black, as it were? George Schweitzer, president of CBS Marketing Group, speculated in an interview with the author that

for one thing, it was economics. It simply got to be too expensive to start a whole program from scratch every week, with new characters, talent, sets. For another, it was that viewers came to look forward to continuing relationships with the people [characters] that they invited into their living rooms. They became used to making connections and getting to know, rather intimately over time, Archie and Edith Bunker, Sheriff Andy Taylor and Opie, Frasier Crane and Lilith, Frasier's brother Niles and his never-seen better half, Maris. Even Tony and Carmella Soprano.

With the drama shows of the past, despite it being the so-called golden era, viewers would meet people in 25-minute dollops or 50-minute ones, and then they'd be gone forever, and another set of people had to be introduced. The entertainment market over the years has exploded, as we view it, and, from a marketing—and economic—standpoint.

Among the highlights of film dramas during 1995 was *The Tuskegee Airmen,* an acclaimed dramatic retelling of the story of the U.S. Army Air Corps's Fighting 69th, the World War II squadron of black combat fighter pilots who had to fight prejudice at home and the Axis in Europe. Jason Robards and Eva Marie Saint costarred (again) in the beautiful *My Antonia,* from Willa Cather's 1917 novel, directed by Joe Sargent, and in a well-received adaptation by Wendy Wasserstein of her 1988 Pulitzer Prize–winning play *The Heidi Chronicles,* directed by Paul Bogart. Both of these aired on basic cable.

There also were three sprawling multipart Westerns—both *Buffalo Girls* and *The Streets of Laredo* from Larry McMurtry novels and *Texas* from James Michener—and new productions of Frances Hodgson Burnett's *Little Lord Fauntleroy* (edited down from its premiere as a British miniseries), Dickens's *The Old Curiosity Shop,* Tennessee Williams's *A Streetcar Named Desire* (Jessica Lange and Alec Baldwin reprising their roles from the 1992 Broadway revival), and Henry James's *Turn of the Screw* (this time reworked under the title *The Haunting of Helen Walker*).

Kingfish: A Story of Huey Long, with an original teleplay by Paul Monash, gave John Goodman a bravura title role, as did *Serving in Silence: The Margarethe Cammermayer Story* (executive produced by Barbra Streisand, among others, with an Emmy-winning original teleplay by Alison Cross) for Glenn Close, as a much decorated air force officer who was found out to be gay and was drummed out of the military, and *Indictment: The McMartin Trial,* written by Abby and Myra Mann, for James Woods. All three were fact-based dramas.

On the lighter side, there was a Disney TV remake of *Freaky Friday* as well as an adaptation of the 1960 Broadway musical *Bye Bye Birdie.*

In 1996 came riding in *Riders of the Purple Sage,* a Western saga adapted from Zane Grey's oft-filmed classic, a parable of individual freedom in which a frontier woman struggling to hold on to her ranch must turn for help to a mysterious drifter when the people she has trusted betray her. Husband and wife actors Ed Harris and Amy Madigan starred and executively produced. This led a minirevival (if three can be considered a revival) of the Western. Later, there was Larry McMurtry's *Dead Man's Walk*, a colorful two-part prequel to his *Lonesome Dove*, wrapping up his Western trilogy, which also included the subsequent *The Streets of Laredo*. David Arquette and Jonny Lee Miller had the parts made famous in the 1989 miniseries by Robert Duvall and Tommy Lee Jones. And then came a spoof of the Westerns called *The Cherokee Kid* with actor/comedian Sinbad.

Jane Austen's *Pride and Prejudice* got a TV redo, as did Kipling's *Captains Courageous*, plus a sumptuous version of Jonathan Swift's *Gulliver's Travels* (Simon Moore won an Emmy for his adaptation, and the drama won for outstanding miniseries). From more contemporary literature, there was a major new version of Truman Capote's *In Cold Blood* and Peter Benchley's fish story *The Beast* as well as Dominick Dunne's *A Season in Purgatory*, a fictionalized version executive produced by Aaron Spelling of the then unsolved Skakel murder case in Connecticut involving the Kennedys.

Three very different biopics were produced in 1996. Gary Sinese gave an acclaimed performance in the title role of *Truman*, from David McCullough's biography of the president; Alan Rickman won an Emmy for playing the so-called Mad Monk of Russia in the lavish dramatization *Rasputin*; and Stephen Rea portrayed Bruno Hauptmann, who was executed in the Lindbergh baby kidnapping case of the early 1930s, in *Crime of the Century*, based on the 1965 book *The Airman and the Carpenter* by Ludovic Kennedy. (Hauptmann was played by Anthony Hopkins in another MMFT in the 1970s.)

With the controversial 1996 drama *Bastard out of Carolina*, actress Anjelica Huston made her directorial debut. An adaptation of Dorothy Allison's best-selling autobiographical novel set in the South Carolina of the early 1950s, it told of a young girl nicknamed "Bone" who lives with her pliant, trailer-park mom and suffers cruel emotional, physical, and sexual abuse at the hands of her stepfather. It was made initially for Ted Turner's TNT, but Turner was said to have found the whole thing distasteful, and the network declined to show it. Instead, the film aired on Showtime.

Anjelica Huston was one of at least two dozen female directors on the MMFT and television drama scene, the most prolific of whom has been Karen Arthur. Others include noted actresses like Diane Keaton, Goldie Hawn, Sally Field, Cher, Michele Lee, Joanna Kerns, Kathy Bates, Helen Shaver, and Salma Hayek. And there are Jane Anderson, Martha Coolidge, Lesli Linka Glatter, Agniezka Holland, Mary Lambert, Mimi Leder, Nancy

Malone, Melanie Mayron, Mira Nair, Linda Otto, Susan Seidelman, Joan Micklin Silver, Joan Tewksbury, and Betty Thomas.

It was Betty Thomas who directed the much-discussed *The Late Shift* in 1996, a fictionalized dramatization of the feud between Jay Leno and David Letterman over owning late-night television with their competing shows. And Sidney Poitier returned to the classroom for *To Sir with Love II*, a virtual remake of his earlier 1967 film, except that this time, the setting was an inner-city school in contemporary Chicago, rather than 1960s London. Peter Bogdanovich directed.

Frankenheimer again was honored with an Emmy for directing *Andersonville*, an original by David Rintels about the notorious Confederate prison during the Civil War.

On the lighter side were adaptations of two Neil Simon plays, *London Suite* and *Jake's Women*. And there was the anthology movie *If These Walls Could Talk*, a trio of stories of three women in three different decades, written by Nancy Savoca, about how the changing political landscape affects their life choices: Demi Moore in the 1950s, Sissy Spacek in the 1970s, and Anne Heche in the 1990s. Cher directed and costarred in the third. As Cher made her directing debut in this one, Goldie Hawn was making hers in an original drama called *Hope*, a coming-of-age tale about a young white girl in the 1960s South who lives with her paralyzed mother, fearful aunt, and duplicitous uncle.

Director Arthur Penn had this to say of his later work in the medium, years after he departed for theatrical movies:

> *Inside* was a wonderful story that I turned into a TV movie in 1996. When I was working on *Alice's Restaurant*, I had a producer named Hilly Elkins—he did *Golden Boy* as well—and he came to me with this Showtime script and I liked the cast he put together—just three people—so we went to South Africa to do this little film by a writer named Bima Stagg about the time in the wake of Apartheid in the 1980s. The Hallmark people bankrolled us. That and *The Portrait*, with Gregory Peck and Lauren Bacall and Greg's daughter Cecilia—based on Tina Howe's lovely Off-Broadway play called *Painting Churches*, somewhat in the mold of *On Golden Pond* —brought me back to television, and then I went in briefly as executive producer on *Law and Order*, before turning that job over to my son Matthew. And next, working with my friend Sidney Lumet on his New York–based cable series *100 Centre Street*. And here are Sidney and myself back to where we were during the golden era—plus 50 odd years!

Victor Hugo's *The Hunchback of Notre Dame*, here called simply *The Hunchback* and starring a rather unlikely Mandy Patinkin, was one of the literary classics gussied up for contemporary television in 1997. Another was Jack London's robust *Call of the Wild*, much of it told from the point of view of the husky Buck, as was London's novel, and many of the actors (nearly all Canadian) are seen only from the waist down. Jules Verne was given a double dose that year—two disparate versions of *20,000 Leagues under the Sea*. And Louisa May Alcott's newly discovered romantic drama *The Inheritance*, written when she was 17, was filmed as a TV movie. So was a new version of Dickens's *Oliver Twist*, with Richard Dreyfuss as Fagin. Works from the twentieth century included Faulkner's *Old Man* (it had been done before on *Playhouse 90*), Truman Capote's *A Christmas Memory* (it had been done before on *ABC Stage 67*), Carson McCullers's *Member of the Wedding* (adapted this time by David Rintels), Neil Simon's *The Sunshine Boys* (with Peter Falk and Woody Allen), Howard Fast's *The Crossing* (with Jeff Daniels as General George Washington), and Horton Foote's graceful family drama *Alone*. Reginald Rose's *12 Angry Men*, with a cast headed by Jack Lemmon and George C. Scott, received a new production, as did *The Defenders: Playback*, the first of a series of films based on Rose's series characters from the 1960s.

What would be the forerunner to the politically controversial *The Path to 9/11* nearly a decade later, *Path to Paradise: The Untold Story of the World Trade Center Bombing*, aired as a fictionalized dramatization that did not sit well with Arab Americans, who condemned it. On the other hand, there was the bright and shiny new film version of Rodgers and Hammerstein's *Cinderella*, which initially aired live with Julie Andrews during the golden age, as well as the inspiring *Miss Evers' Boys*, which won the Emmy as outstanding made-for-TV movie.

A new multipart production of Stephen King's *The Shining*, expanded from the Stanley Kubrick theatrical of 1980, premiered, as did the dark, quite true to the Brothers Grimm version of *Snow White: A Tale of Terror*, featuring Sigourney Weaver as the wicked stepmother. And there was an unexpected project that brought *Homer's Odyssey* to television (Andrei Konchalovsky won the Emmy for directing it). Spectacular in scope and running in two parts on NBC, it starred Armand Assante in the lead and Bernadette Peters as Circe, plus an array of special effects.

Reminding one of the days when the early *Hallmark Hall of Fame* regularly would feature heady classic dramatic works, there would be *Dostoevsky's Crime and Punishment*, directed by Joseph Sargent, and *The Tempest* (Shakespeare set in the Mississippi bayous during the Civil War), *Hamlet* (relocated to twentieth-century America with a multiracial cast), and *King Lear* (reimagined as *The King of Texas*, set in the Old West of the nineteenth century)—all on network television and basic cable in prime time. Somewhat far afield from these imaginative—if not quite audience grabbing—productions in 1997 was *House of Frankenstein*, which uses the title but hardly the plot of the old 1940s movie and at one point gives the Creature a gun to protect himself from other monsters.

Mafia movies included Mario Puzo's *The Last Don* and an adaptation of Lynda La Plante's 1991 novel *Bella Mafia*, about mob wives (headed by Vanessa Redgrave). These would precede what would be the phenomenon of *The Sopranos* by about 18 months.

Two of Rod Serling's *Playhouse 90* scripts were reworked as TV movies in the late 1990s. *In the Presence of Mine Enemies*, a Holocaust drama that had been the last production on *Playhouse 90* in 1960, was newly filmed by director Joan Micklin Silver. Not long afterward came a new adaptation of Serling's mob violence Western *A Town Has Turned to Dust* in 1998.

Also in 1998 was the epic *From the Earth to the Moon*, an Emmy-winning, 12-part miniseries chronicling the history of NASA's Apollo Space Program from 1961 to 1972 and executive produced by Tom Hanks. Hanks narrated, wrote several of the episodes, directed at least one, and starred in another. His old pal Sally Field (Hanks's girlfriend in *Punchline* in 1988 and his mother in *Forrest Gump* six years later) also directed one of the episodes in the miniseries.

A number of hit movies from the past were remade for television: *Moby Dick*, with Patrick Stewart as Ahab; *David and Lisa*, presented by Oprah Winfrey, with Sidney Poitier in the role of the psychiatrist; *Rear Window*, refashioned for its paralyzed star Christopher Reeve; *The Ransom of Red Chief* (it had been a segment of the theatrical anthology *O. Henry's Full House* in 1952); and *The Taking of Pelham One Two Three*. And a hit popular TV show from the past, *Naked City*, received a 1990s reworking in a handful of cable films with Scott Glenn and Courtney B. Vance, here as cop partners who patrol the streets of the Big Apple undercover in a yellow cab—not quite the way their earlier counterparts, John McIntire and James Franciscus, did the job.

Poodle Springs, the last Philip Marlowe tale by Raymond Chandler, who died before completing it (detective novelist Robert B. Parker finished it), aired as a pay-cable movie. James Caan starred as sort of an over-the-hill Marlowe. Anjelina Jolie gave a quite astonishing (and quite nude) performance in the title role of *Gia*, about the rise and fall of hedonistic late 1970s supermodel Gia Carangi, who became a drug addict and died of AIDs at the age of 26. Like the biopic on *Gia*, there were those on Walter Winchell and Harry Houdini. Stanley Tucci starred in *Winchell* and Johnathon Schaech in *Houdini*.

Barbra Streisand executive produced a series of short dramas about the Holocaust under the title *Rescuers: Stories of Courage* (three stories per movie), and there was a cable-produced sequel to Armistead Maupin's *Tales of the City*, the original having premiered on PBS, which became edgy over the nudity and language involved and declined to proceed with further chapters. Other notable television dramas included a new version of Aldous Huxley's *Brave New World*; another of *The Day Lincoln Was Shot*, from Jim Bishop's 1955 best seller, which was staged earlier during the golden age; and a somber, nonmusical production of *The Tale of Sweeney Todd*, the last TV work of director John Schlesinger

The 1990s were closed out in the MMFT genre by a couple of costume dramas, *Cleopatra* and *Joan of Arc*. There also was a colorful biopic, *P. T. Barnum* (in the person of Beau Bridges this time), that was written by the estimable Lionel Chetwynd and directed by Aussie Simon Wincer, and another on Dashiell Hammett and Lillian Hellman in *Dash and Lilly*, directed by Kathy Bates and featuring Sam Shepard and Judy Davis. Jules Verne's *Journey to the Center of the Earth* and Washington Irving's *Legend of Sleepy Hollow* were filmed again, and Jason Miller's Pulitzer Prize– and Tony-winning play *That Championship Season* was contemporized for television, starring Paul Sorvino as the coach as well as the film's director. Veteran Stanley Donen made his TV directing debut in 1999 with a loving version of A. R. Gurney's popular two-person play *Love Letters*, opened up by Gurney for this television movie with a dozen or so other actors.

Two particularly engrossing dramas were *Introducing Dorothy Dandridge*, starring Halle Berry as the beautiful singer/actress whose life spiraled out of control, leading to suicide in the early 1960s, and *Tuesdays with Morrie*, based on Mitch Albom's best-selling nonfiction book about his weekly visits with his beloved college professor, who is dying. Jack Lemmon had his last acting role, winning an Emmy as Morrie Schwartz, who taught at Brandeis. Martha Coolidge directed the Dandridge movie, and Berry won the Emmy as best actress. Dustin Hoffman was one of the executive producers of the Holocaust story *The Devil's Arithmetic*, aimed at younger audiences, with Kirsten Dunst in the lead as a contemporary teen who finds herself time warped from the family Seder table at Passover to Nazi-held Warsaw of 1942—and there learns of her religious heritage. Hoffman made a rare return to television, appearing on camera to introduce the film, which was adapted by Robert J. Avrech from Jane Yolen's 1988 novel for young people. Avrech won an Emmy, as did director Donna Deitch.

By 2000, the output of television movies had dropped off precipitously. The year kicked off with a quite good remake of Owen Wister's *The Virginian* (Bill Pullman was producer, director, and laconic star) and proceeded over the next 12 months with new versions of popular big-screen hits such as *On the Beach, High Noon, The Spiral Staircase, The Miracle Worker* (third time on television, where it began its life), *David Copperfield, Jason and the Argonauts,* and *The Hound of the Baskervilles* as well as *Dune*—which was quite apart from David Lynch's original take on the Frank Herbert sci-fi book in the 1980s. And there were a slew of TV biopics on Muhammed Ali (two of them), Audrey Hepburn, Natalie Cole, Linda McCartney, John Lennon, the Beach Boys, The Three Stooges, Little Richard, Meat Loaf, David Cassidy, and Jackie O (again). Mary Tyler Moore and Valerie Harper reunited in *Mary and Rhoda,* bringing their landmark CBS characters together again on ABC two decades later in a somewhat pedestrian fashion.

Nuremberg proved a powerful drama in dealing with the Holocaust but is not to be confused, because of its similar subject matter, with Abby Mann's memorable though fictionalized *Judgment at Nuremberg.* The new one, a two-parter with Alec Baldwin in the lead, was adapted by David Rintels from Joseph E. Persico's 1994 book about the post–World War II war crimes trial. Also well crafted was *Sally Hemings: An American Scandal,* an original if soapy period drama by Tina Andrews about Thomas Jefferson's slave mistress.

An imaginative five-part, 10-hour, special-effects-laden trip through the looking glass, inspired by famous literary fairy tales and their characters in bizarre settings, *The 10th Kingdom,* an original by Simon Moore, received disappointing ratings and doomed the lengthy miniseries on the networks. *Don Quixote,* with John Lithgow as Cervantes's windmill-tilter, and *Arabian Nights,* another expensive spectacle, along with the aforementioned *Jason and the Argonauts* rounded out the costume dramas as the twentieth century waned. But then, there also were a couple of biblical tales—*Jesus* on CBS and *Esther* on the PAX mininetwork, both from the same producers as Turner's dramas from the Bible earlier in the decade.

Leonard Maltin wrote in his foreword to my 2005 multivolume MMFT compilation covering 40 years of the genre,

When made-for-TV movie became a reality in the 1960s, some people refused to take them seriously, regarding them as little more than elongated television episodes. By the 1970s, telefilms began to attract to talent, on both side of the camera, and attracted groundbreaking subject matter. Most TV movies were ephemeral, but some, like *Brian's Song* and *The Autobiography of Miss Jane Pittman*, managed to make a lasting impression.

In the heyday of network movies, scripts were geared to incorporate a series of mini-climaxes (for commercial interruptions) and filmmakers had to fight time and budget problems. By the time HBO commissioned Mike Nichols to bring Tony Kushner's *Angels in America* to the small screen, the budget was a reported $60 million, and there was nary a compromise in sight.

CHAPTER 21

What Else Is On?

During the last three decades of the twentieth century, with the made-for-TV movie being the prime source of television drama (aside from the weekly series with recurring characters), there remained some vestige of the anthology drama of yore.

Night Gallery (NBC, 1970–1973) was Rod Serling's well-remembered follow-up to his classic *The Twilight Zone*. It premiered after the success of a TV movie pilot containing several short, often supernatural tales (an anthology within an anthology, it turns out, with Serling hosting from an art gallery setting) the previous year that is remembered as a springboard for young director Steven Spielberg. Halfway through the series's run, NBC cut it back from 60 minutes weekly to 30, then abandoned it completely. (Serling, it should be remembered, had another short-lived series between *The Twilight Zone* and *Night Gallery*, a stark, moody Western called *The Loner*.)

Sebastian Cabot hosted an NBC program called *Ghost Story* (1972–1973) in the guise of the fictional Winston Essex, wealthy owner of the Mansfield House, and spinning supernatural tales every Friday from 9:00 to 10:00 P.M. Cabot departed after the first 13 weeks, and the title of the series changed to *Circle of Fear*.

Jason Robards and Stella Stevens starred in the premiere episode, *The Dead We Leave Behind*, and actors like Melvyn Douglas, Helen Hayes, Gena Rowlands, Patricia Neal, and Tab Hunter (actually twice the Tab: he had a dual role) did weekly turns. Particularly interesting was the pairing of real-life marrieds Rip Torn and Geraldine Page in a real shocker, *Touch of*

Madness. Torn himself hosted a similar show, *Ghost Stories,* in another totally different anthology in syndication in the late 1990s.

The British suspense anthology show *Roald Dahl's Tales of the Unexpected,* dramatizing Dahl short stories (including his *The Man from the South* and *The Lamb to the Slaughter*—both of which are associated with *Alfred Hitchcock Presents* from an earlier time), aired in the United States in syndication from 1979 to 1981 but ran for seven more years in the United Kingdom. Generally, there was one noted American name at the head of the all-British cast of José Ferrer, Julie Harris, Elaine Strich, Telly Savalas, and others. This anthology should not be confused with producer Quinn Martin's somewhat similar *Tales of the Unexpected,* narrated by William Conrad, that aired briefly on NBC in 1977.

The Hitchhiker (HBO, 1983–1988, 39 episodes; USA 1989–1990, 46 episodes) was a Canadian-made anthology series that specialized, like *Circle of Fear,* in supernatural tales. It was hosted by Nicholas Campbell (first season) and then Page Fletcher, as a hitchhiker thumbing his way across the lonely Canadian landscape and offering up creepy tales featuring such actors as Klaus Kinski, Kirstie Alley, David Dukes, Susan Blakely, Stephen Collins, Robert Vaughn, Edward Albert, Karen Black, and Jerry Orbach. The half-hour dramas were directed by the likes of Phillip Noyce, Roger Vadim, Eric Till, Ivan Nagy, Mai Zetterling, Mike Hodges, Timothy Bond, and David Wickes.

Tales from the Darkside was a popular horror/supernatural anthology that ran in syndication from 1984 to 1988 (90 episodes) and included some tales by Stephen King and sci-fi writer Harlan Ellison, many with O. Henry–style endings. Most had casts of lesser names.

Steven Spielberg's Amazing Stories was a major event for NBC during the 1985–1987 seasons. In the years following his memorable TV movie *Duel,* Spielberg had moved on to become a major American director and an industry force. In the mid-1980s, he was urged to use his clout to bring a new freshness to the old anthology drama concept. NBC, with unwavering confidence, signed him to produce 44 half-hour shows and promoted the project sight unseen, before a single scene was shot—thus his interesting anthology *Amazing Stories,* with a series of dramas, many of which he wrote, some of which, including the first one (*Ghost Train* with veteran actor Roberts Blossom), he directed. And his name was in the show's title, giving the whole enterprise an additional caché. He brought to the project as directors Clint Eastwood (in the only work he had done on TV since departing to become a huge movie star), Martin Scorsese, Peter Hyams, Bob Balaban, Burt Reynolds, Joan Darling, Timothy Hutton, Danny DeVito, Joe Dante, Mick Garris, Robert Zemeckis, and Tobe Hooper. Spielberg also directed a critically acclaimed one-hour World War II story, *The Mission,* and filmed it in sepia, with Kevin Costner and Kiefer Sutherland starring. One second-season episode, written and directed by Brad Bird, with the voices of Stan Freberg, Mercedes McCambridge, Annie Potts, and others, was a funny animated piece focusing on the life of a frisky pooch living in a suburban middle-class home. *Amazing Stories,* to the network's dismay, achieved only limited success but developed a large cult afterlife.

On *Ray Bradbury Theatre* (originally on HBO from 1985 to 1987, six episodes; USA Network, 1987–1992, 59 episodes), the prolific sci-fi author served as host for dramatizations of his own short stories in this Canadian-made series, with such diverse performers as William Shatner, Tyne Daly, Peter O'Toole, Jean Stapleton, Drew Barrymore, Alan Bates, Leslie Nielsen, and Robert Vaughn.

The creative PBS series *Tales from the Hollywood Hills* (six episodes during the 1987–1988 season) presented 50-minute filmed adaptations of notable short stories by writers who worked in Hollywood, for the most part in the 1930s: John O'Hara, Budd Schulberg, F. Scott Fitzgerald, P. G. Wodehouse, William Faulkner, and, from the 1950s, Gavin Lambert. Directors from veteran Paul Bogart to relatively new Leon Ichaso, a Cuban émigré, helmed the action with such stars as Michelle Pfeiffer, Darren McGavin, Donna Murphy, Christopher Lloyd, Rosemary Harris, and Lynn Redgrave acting in the assorted tales.

Of directing the first episode of *Tales from the Hollywood Hills,* John O'Hara's short story "Natica Jackson," which starred Pfeiffer, Paul Bogart recalls,

> Time constraints were omnipresent. Time governed all. As for "Natica Jackson" and *The Last Mile* [a short film from writer Terrence McNally for *Great Performances*], both were for PBS and had no commercial breaks. Once, on the air live, I cut an entire last scene of a drama because the script supervisor said we were running out of time. She had miscalculated and so we had five minutes for the credits. I'm afraid to think that the audience didn't notice that the play ended abruptly.

Bogart, when asked the question of how he worked in various television situations (drama, comedy, musicals), said, "The only difference in directing for a network versus PBS or cable was usually the material. I didn't change my ways." In his critique in the *New York Times,* TV columnist John O'Connor wrote,

> As directed by Mr. Bogart, *Natica Jackson* captures the almost dreamlike unreality of the Hollywood factories while revealing the very ordinary people

wandering through them. Meanwhile, very nearly offstage, there is kept in reserve a plot twist that will turn the fragile little story into a tragedy. The result is a beautifully conceived and executed television production.

Tales from the Crypt (HBO/Fox/syndication, 1989–1996) offered stories (93 hour-long episodes) with many themes, including horror, twists, black magic, sci-fi, and even an animated revisionist gore fest of the Three Little Pigs, all introduced by a sinister puppet named the Crypt Keeper. Often, like on Serling's *Night Gallery,* there were multiple short tales on a single program, each with a different director and cast. Among those calling the shots were Arnold Schwarzenegger, John Frankenheimer, Richard Donner, Robert Zemeckis, Michael J. Fox, Tom Hanks, Walter Hill, and Tobe Hooper—many working on the series as the in thing at the time. This often gruesome anthology series, described by some as a cross between *The Twilight Zone* and modern horror movies, was based on William Gaines's ghoulish and graphic EC Comics series of the 1950s and found a whole new audience not only in 1980s and 1990s TV, but also in a batch of Saturday morning cartoons and in several big-screen spin-offs.

Airing on Showtime between 1992 and 2002 was *Red Shoe Diaries,* Zalman King's erotic Canadian anthology series starring pre-*X-Files* David Duchovny as Jake Winters, the host. Generally, aside from Duchovny, there would be at least one known American actor amid a supporting cast of Canadians.

Fallen Angels, a 1993–1995 crime anthology series on Showtime, had among its stable of directors Peter Bogdanovich, Steven Soderbergh, Agnieszka Holland, Tom Hanks, Tom Cruise, and Kiefer Sutherland. The shows featured hard-boiled, neo-noir short stories by Raymond Chandler (with Danny Glower receiving an Emmy nomination as the first black Philip Marlowe in the 1938 "Red Wing"), Cornell Woolrich, Dashiell Hammett, and Mickey Spillane. *Angels* ran rather irregularly for 15 episodes.

Masters of Horror, a Canadian series also airing on Showtime during the 2005–2006 and 2006–2007 seasons, was created by Mick Garris, often associated with writer Stephen King. Assembled was a group of directors best known for dabbling in horror movies: John Carpenter, John Landis, Joe Dante, Tobe Hooper, Dario Argento, Larry Cohen, Stuart Gordon, and Garris himself, with stories by Ambrose Bierce, H. P. Lovecraft, Richard Christian Matheson, Clive Barker, and others. The anthology included 13 hour-long episodes each season, and those who relish the genre really relished.

Nightmares & Dreamscapes: From the Stories of Stephen King, a four-week TNT television event in 2006, spun eight mind-bending stories blurring the line between fantasy and reality in a *Twilight Zone* style, with themes ranging from time travel, alternate realities, and treasure hunting to living among the dead and the destruction of the world. Each self-contained tale had a different director, a different writer adapting a Stephen King short story, and a different cast. William Hurt starred in *Battleground* (a bad guy versus toy soldiers thriller played out sans dialogue); William H. Macy in two roles in *Umney's Last Case*; Kim Delaney in *You Know They've Got a Hell of a Band*; and Tom Berenger in *The Road Virus Heads North*, among others.

Also premiering during the 2006–2007 season was *Masters of Science Fiction*, an hour-long ABC anthology series based on some of the most highly regarded stories in the genre (by the likes of Harlan Ellison, John Kessel, Robert Heinlein, Howard Fast, Robert Sheckley, and Walter Mosely). This series, produced in Canada, was modeled somewhat after the British *Mystery!* but was hosted by noted physicist Stephen Hawking.

CHAPTER 22

Into the Millennium

Among the movie made for television (MMFT) highlights of 2001 was *Conspiracy*, a historical drama recreating one of the most infamous gatherings of the twentieth century, when 15 top members of the Third Reich met outside Berlin on January 20, 1942, to set in motion the Final Solution. Kenneth Branagh (Emmy winner as outstanding actor) portrayed Reinhard Heydrich, and Stanley Tucci portrayed Adolf Eichmann. It was executive produced and directed by Frank Pierson, then president of the Directors Guild of America, with a script by Loring Mandel, who remembers in an interview with this author,

> The idea of *Conspiracy* was brought to HBO by Frank Pierson and Peter Zinner in 1997, and when HBO took it on, they offered me the opportunity to write it. I did the preliminary research, wrote the first draft, after which HBO accepted it and brought on a paid full-time researcher to assist me. However, due to the complexity of programming it in tandem with another Holocaust script, HBO eventually canceled both projects around 1999. In 2000, however, after a shift in the HBO executive ranks, *Conspiracy* was reactivated to our great pleasure and satisfaction.

A not too dissimilar cable film involving the Nazis during World War II was *Varian's War*, a fact-based drama about American journalist Varian Fry (played by William Hurt), who risked his life by traveling to Marseilles in 1940 to rescue from the Nazis prominent European artists and writers. Decades later, before Oskar Schindler and Raoul Wallenberg, he was honored by the Israeli government for his wartime heroism. *Varian's War* was produced by Barbra Streisand and Edward Wessex, the UK's Prince Edward, and was written and directed by Lionel Chetwynd.

Another notable 2001 project was executive producers Steven Spielberg and Tom Hanks's sprawling miniseries *Band of Brothers,* from Stephen Ambrose's 1992 nonfiction war novel (with several episodes written by Hanks, who also directed and acted in one of the segments). It followed Easy Company of the U.S. Army Airborne Paratrooper division and their mission in World War II France during Operation Overlord through the war's end in Europe.

Other MMFTs were biopics on Judy Garland, with Judy Davis and Tammy Blanchard as older and younger Judy and each winning an Emmy for acting; Shirley Temple; James Dean; and Bill "Bojangles" Robinson. Mike Nichols made his TV directing debut with *Wit,* starring Emma Thompson as a terminally ill patient, adapted by the two of them from Margaret Edson's 1999 Pulitzer Prize–winning play. Nichols and the movie were both awarded Emmys. And there were TV versions of the Rodgers and Hammerstein musical *South Pacific,* with Glenn Close and Harry Connick Jr., as well as Agatha Christie's *Murder on the Orient Express* and Conan Doyle's Sherlock Holmes tale *The Sign of Four.* To illustrate how cable television had made inroads into the MMFT genre, nearly all of these—including director Billy Crystal's *61*,* about the 1961 race between New York Yankees rivals Mickey Mantle and Roger Maris to break Babe Ruth's long-standing home run record—were nonnetwork productions.

Steven Spielberg's Taken was an epic 2002 sci-fi miniseries—10 two-hour parts—spanning 50 years, beginning with the fabled landing of UFOs in Roswell, New Mexico, in the late 1940s. The story, by Leslie Bohem, interwove the lives of three generations of three families (some half alien) who were interconnected in one way or another with the event. Each part had a different director, but not Spielberg, whose role was simply executive producer and having his name in the show title.

The ambitious TV movie of *The Magnificent Ambersons,* from Booth Tarkington's 1917 novel, found itself, regrettably, as flawed a production as Orson Welles's of the early 1940s. Though it dealt with a family from America's Midwest at the turn of the last century, it was filmed in Dublin, Ireland, by Mexican director Alfonso Arau. Another drama about a dysfunctional family, a more contemporary one, was *We Were the Mulvaneys,* adapted by Joyce Eliason and Peter and Nancy Dalton Silverman from Joyce Carol Oates's 1995 best seller. In addition to Booth Tarkington, there was a contribution from a contemporary of his in *Mark Twain's Roughing It*—hardly ever filmed, Samuel Clemens was portrayed here by James Garner in bushy mustache and white suit.

The Rosa Parks Story was a 2002 drama exploring the life of the Montgomery, Alabama, seamstress whose act of civil disobedience on December 1, 1955, by refusing to give up her seat and move to the coloreds only section of a segregated city bus, made this a defining movement in the modern civil rights movement. Angela Bassett starred, and Julie Dash, one of the only African American women directors on television, called the shots.

Stephen King's Rose Red was, as has come to be expected, a disturbing fictional thriller, spun in two parts in 2002, while *The Matthew Shepard Story* was a disturbing real-life one about gay-bashers and their victim, the third TV movie revisiting the story of the college student from Laramie, Wyoming, who was bullied by his homophile contemporaries and literally hounded to death in October 1998, his body later found strapped to a barbed wire fence.

Among the interesting dramas that aired during 2003 were a new version of Tennessee Williams's 1950 novella *The Roman Spring of Mrs. Stone*, starring Helen Mirren and, in her final acting role, Anne Bancroft (in the parts played on the big screen in the 1960s by Vivien Leigh and Lotte Lenya), and Mike Nichols's epic filming of Broadway's *Angels in America*, which swept all the major television awards. The politically charged biopic on Ronald and Nancy Reagan was judged by Democrats to be politically incorrect, forcing CBS to push its two-part movie off the schedule and give it to its corporate pay-cable network, Showtime. There *The Reagans* was shown as a single film of about three hours and garnered a number of Emmy nominations for directing, for writing, and particularly for its stars, James Brolin and Judy Davis. It was interesting to see the fiercely liberal Barbra Streisand at the Emmy ceremonies cheerleading for her husband Brolin, who had the lead as the much-maligned (in politically liberal circles) conservative president. The same type of political furor was unleashed several years later on the eve of the premiere showing of *The Path to 9/11*.

In 2003, viewers also were offered new TV versions of the theatrical *Sounder*, adapted from William H. Armstrong's popular novel for young people, a Newbery Medal book in 1969, which initially was filmed in 1972; Meredith Willson's splashy *The Music Man*; Emily Brontë's *Wuthering Heights*, reimagined as a contemporary, musicalized production for the MTV generation; and *Children of Dune*, a sequel to Frank Herbert's original *Dune*.

The moving, fact-based cable drama *Something the Lord Made* (2004) chronicled the somewhat reluctant partnership between a headstrong white surgeon, Dr. Alfred Blalock, who pioneered open-heart surgery during the 1930s at the Johns Hopkins University, and a talented black janitor turned lab technician turned agile assistant. Their story, which changed the face of modern medicine, was an original by Peter Silverman and directed by Joseph Sargent. It won the Emmy as outstanding movie made for television. Geoffrey Rush was an Emmy winner as best actor for his title portrayal in *The Life and Death of Peter Sellers*, and Stephen Hopkins won as best director.

Author Mitch Albom adapted his 2003 best seller *The Five People You Meet in Heaven* into a three-hour contemporary fable, in which, in the afterlife on a way station on the road to heaven, a man (played by Jon Voight) who died in a bizarre accident meets several people from his former life who help him reexamine it before he finishes his eternal journey. Neil Simon rewrote his 1977 film *The Goodbye Girl* for a new generation, and there were new, made-for-cable versions of *Mary Shelley's Frankenstein* (two, in fact, on consecutive nights); H. Rider Haggard's adventure yarn *King Solomon's Mines;* James Goldman's stage and screen drama *The Lion in Winter,* teaming up Glenn Close and Patrick Stewart; and a TV production of the Broadway musical version of Dickens's *A Christmas Carol,* with Kelsey Grammer as Ebenezer Scrooge.

Tom Selleck (shaven headed and sans mustache) played General Dwight D. Eisenhower in *Ike: Countdown to D-Day,* and William H. Macy played a mute in *The Wool Cap,* which he and production partner director Steven Schachter adapted from Jackie Gleason's *Gigot. Traffic: The Miniseries* also ranks as one of the television highlights of 2004, an important three-part, six-hour drama intertwining the lives of assorted drug agents, dealers, smugglers, and underworld figures in the violent world of narcotics. And then there was *The Michael Jackson Story.*

Two earlier MMFTs also were filmed again in 2004: Stephen King's *Salem's Lot* on basic cable and Vincent Bugliosi's *Helter Skelter* (about the Charles Manson murders) on the cable network. Neither lived up to the original.

The richness of *Warm Springs,* dealing with FDR's initial affliction with polio through his reentry into politics in the early 1930s (an original script by Margaret Nagle, directed by Joseph Sargent), and Oprah Winfrey's production of *Their Eyes Were Watching God,* based on Zora Neale Hurston's 1937 Harlem Renaissance novel, provided just two of the dramatic MMFT highlights of 2005—the former on cable television, and the latter being one of the increasingly diminishing network MMFTs (as they came to be called familiarly).

In addition, there was the production, with a stellar cast (including Paul Newman and Joanne Woodward—Emmy nominees both—from the golden age 50 years earlier), of *Empire Falls,* adapted by Richard Russo from his 2002 Pulitzer Prize novel. Noted Australian director Fred Schepisi made his American TV directing debut on this, filmed in Maine and set in a fictional small town there. Another stellar cast peopled the highly regarded *Lackawanna Blues*, an expanded film version of actor/writer Ruben Santiago-Hudson's autobiographical one-man 2001 Obie-winning Off-Broadway play about his growing up in Lackawanna, New York, in the late 1950s and early 1960s. This marked the film debut of noted stage director George C. Wolfe. Santiago-Hudson wrote the teleplay and also played one of the characters—but not himself.

Anjelica Huston directed the inspirational Hallmark Hall of Fame production of *Riding the Bus with My Sister*, which starred Rosie O'Donnell as a mentally challenged woman and Andie MacDowell as her careerist sibling, based on Rachel Simon's autobiographical book of 2002. An original drama by Randy Feldman, *The Reading Room* brought James Earl Jones acclaim for his moving performance of a wealthy widower who, fulfilling his late wife's dying wish, establishes a library in a bad section of town.

The last great miniseries of the first half decade of the twenty-first century was *Into the West*, the executive producer of which was Steven Spielberg. Heavily promoted at the time as a "Six Week Television Event," the ambitious production, an adventurous exploration of the American wilderness (much like Michener's *Centennial* of the 1970s), the clash of two distinct cultures, and the building of a new civilization, was written by William Mastrosimone, Cyrus Nowrasteh, Craig Storper, and Kirk Ellis. Each of the two-hour segments had a different director.

Television drama in 2005 ran the gamut from *Reefer Madness: The Musical*, a tunefully surreal movie inspired by the notorious 1936 antimarijuana propaganda film that has become a cult low-budget movie classic, the campy stage musical of it produced in Los Angeles in 1999 and Off-Broadway in 2001, to *Faith of My Fathers*, an adaptation of John McCain's 1999 memoir, a deeply felt dramatization of the Arizona senator and Vietnam War hero at the beginning of his naval career through his five and a half years of captivity as a prisoner of war at the infamous Hanoi Hilton; from an effects-laden new version of Jules Verne's *Mysterious Island*, to *Four Minutes*, about Roger Bannister's running the four-minute mile back in 1952; *Human Trafficking*, about modern-day white slavery; and three ultrareverent movies about Pope John Paul II.

In 2006, Helen Mirren had the starring role (and won an Emmy for her performance) in *Elizabeth I*, a BBC offering. The same year, she also won an Oscar on the big screen in *The Queen*—this time playing Elizabeth II. The lushly produced TV film was given the Emmy as outstanding miniseries, with another going to Mirren's costar, Jeremy Irons as the Earl of Leicester, and another to director Tom Moore.

Then there were a number of films surrounding the horror of 9/11, notably *Flight 93*, dealing with the aircraft that was crashed into a field in Shanksville, Pennsylvania, when passengers attempted to take their plane back from terrorist hijackers, and *The Path to 9/11*, a controversial fictionalized drama that focused on the efforts to track Islamic terrorists in the wake of the 1993 World Trade Center attack to the fateful one eight and a half years later. Like the earlier TV movie *The Reagans*, this was a political hot potato because of the way producers put words into the mouths of senior government officials, spreading the blame around between the Clinton and the Bush administrations.

The MMFT genre, like the golden age topics of yore, covers the gamut of subjects—and quality—be it *It* or *They* or *Surviving Gilligan's Island: The Incredibly True Story of the Longest Three-Hour Tour in History*. According to MTR curator Ron Simon in an interview for this book,

> Of course, the basis of anthology drama in New York was theater. Then it moved to Hollywood talent. There was a whole sensibility in the 1950s that isn't there anymore. When Clooney was doing *Fail Safe*, I remember there were a number of technicians on that show who were from the 1950s period, and the whole ability of summoning up the team to do it is totally foreign to television today. The audience's appreciation, the sensibility of that is now gone.
>
> But the anthology dramas were certainly compelling, and when you watch the individual episodes—like *The Comedian* that I think was a landmark, with Mickey Rooney that Frankenheimer directed—just brilliant in its staging. The wonderful audacity—I just can't see the TV industry summoning up that energy again. [The name Frankenheimer, toward the end of his life, became a brand name in itself.] The interesting thing is that the TV drama and then the TV movie or even the regular movie seen for the first time on television was then the most prestigious event in the medium (*Gone with the Wind, The Wizard of Oz, The Godfather*).
>
> The television critics and the most knowledgeable viewer would always gravitate to those events—that they would deal with social substance. Live television did that, then the television movie, and that whole impetus is gone. Today the television movie seems so secondary with so little discussion. When you look at the category, it's now an HBO movie that they don't even promote that much. That whole series drama, and even the idea of movies on television—that was the main event for 30 years. Now even cable creates its own original series. The idea of creating appointment viewing with television movies is gone. Lifetime now has its own version of what a TV movie is like—it's very much formulaic. Although it keeps alive the anthology drama in its own weird way. But it's not part of the general culture.

> It's shocking how this prestigious format can sort of become almost invisible on television. And what people talk about when a group gets together is just not there anymore.

Live drama on television became a lost art in the early 1960s and was viewed as stunt telecasting when the networks occasionally staged it in the 1970s with several productions on NBC before selected audiences. Then, of course, there was the faux cinema vérité live version in 1997 of *ER* that obviously encouraged George Clooney to use his name clout for a live black-and-white production of *Fail Safe* (about the 1962 Cuban missile crisis) in April 2000. That was followed a year later by Julie Andrews and Christopher Plummer (they reunited 35 years after the movie version of *The Sound of Music*) starring in a TV adaptation of *On Golden Pond*, directed by the author, Ernest Thompson. Clooney's announced decision in 2006 to do a live *Network* still has not come to fruition. But in 2005–2006, there were the live presidential debates between candidates Jimmy Smits and Alan Alda on *The West Wing* and two episodes of the sitcom *Will and Grace*.

But it is often agreed that economics is what killed the beast (to paraphrase the famed closing line of *King Kong*). What has been the television movie for the last 40 odd years is what has happened to the TV anthology drama. What has happened to live television, aside from the majority of news programming and most of the sporting events, remains PBS's periodic *Live from Lincoln Center*, which is all music—though it is all live.

It all started with rabbit ears and a round, seven-inch screen and progressed into the era of plasma screens in a period of just seven decades.

Index

About the Author

ALVIN H. MARILL has spent his career in broadcasting, direct marketing, the recording industry, and publishing. He is the author of more than two-dozen books dealing with stage, screen, and television, including the encyclopedic *Movies Made for Television* and its several updates through 2004, long considered the definitive compilation of the genre. Among his other works are *More Theatre: Stage to Screen to Television, The Complete Films of Edward G. Robinson, Robert Mitchum on the Screen, Samuel Goldwyn Presents,* and career studies of Anthony Quinn, Sidney Poitier, Tyrone Power, The Three Stooges, and Tommy Lee Jones, as well as *The Ultimate John Wayne Trivia Book* and the screen music compendium *Keeping Score: Film Music 1988–1997.*